CRITICAL PERIODS OF HISTORY

Robert D. Cross and Paul K. Conkin, GENERAL EDITORS

American

THE ELECTION OF ANDREW JACKSON
by Robert V. Remini

RACE AND POLITICS *Bleeding Kansas and the Coming of the Civil War*
by James A. Rawley

LINCOLN AND THE FIRST SHOT
by Richard N. Current

IRISH-AMERICAN NATIONALISM, 1870-1890
by Thomas N. Brown

McKINLEY, BRYAN AND THE PEOPLE
by Paul W. Glad

DARKNESS AT THE DAWNING *Race and Reform in the Progressive South*
by Jack Temple Kirby

LABOR IN CRISIS *The Steel Strike of 1919*
by David Brody

TVA AND THE POWER FIGHT, 1933-1939
by Thomas K. McCraw

WAR AND SOCIETY *The United States, 1941-1945*
by Richard Polenberg

European

THE NAPOLEONIC REVOLUTION
by Robert B. Holtman

THE LONG FUSE *An Interpretation of the Origins of World War I*
by Laurence Lafore

WHY LENIN? WHY STALIN? *A Reappraisal of the Russian Revolution, 1900-1930*
by Theodore H. Von Laue

THE END OF GLORY *An Interpretation of the Origins of World War II*
by Laurence Lafore

WAR AND SOCIETY

THE UNITED STATES
1941–1945

Richard Polenberg

J.B. LIPPINCOTT COMPANY
PHILADELPHIA NEW YORK TORONTO

PAPERBOUND: ISBN-0-397-47224-2
CLOTH BOUND: ISBN-0-397-47225-0
LIBRARY OF CONGRESS CATALOG CARD NUMBER: 76-155879
PRINTED IN THE UNITED STATES OF AMERICA
INTERIOR DESIGN BY ROBERT C. DIGGES
COVER DESIGN BY MICHAEL LOURIDAS

7   9   8

For Marcia

Contents

Prologue

WORD OF THE JAPANESE ATTACK
on Pearl Harbor startled most Americans. For two years
public attention had centered on Europe rather than Asia.
The expanding American commitment to aid Great Britain,
and the sinking of American destroyers by German submarines
in the fall of 1941 had strengthened the expectation that war,
if it came, would come as it had in 1917. Consequently, people
at every level—from State Department officials in Washington
to factory workers in Detroit—expressed surprise at Japan's
sudden move. Yet within a short time, as the first wave of
disbelief passed, the coming of war took on an aura of inevitability. "The years between Munich and Pearl Harbor,"
said E. B. White, "were like the time you put in in a doctor's
waiting room, years of fumbling with old magazines and un-
confirmed suspicions, the ante years, the time of the moist
palm and the irresolution."

Those who had favored United States entry on the side of

the Allies saw Pearl Harbor as a godsend. The attack seemed likely to unify a divided nation and heal the scars of a long, bitter conflict over foreign policy. One Congressman, who had sponsored the Selective Service Act of 1940, said he regarded the prospect of war with sorrow but admitted to "a feeling of real relief, that at last we are a united people. . . . The atmosphere has cleared." Similarly, Secretary of War Henry L. Stimson remarked: "My first feeling was of relief that the indecision was over and that a crisis had come in a way which would unite all our people." The new harmony was symbolized by the desire of most isolationists to forget the past and stand by the President. Charles Lindbergh, a leading critic of interventionism, declared, "If I had been in Congress, I certainly would have voted for a declaration of war." The archisolationist Chicago *Tribune* changed the slogan on its masthead from "Save Our Republic" to "Our Country Right or Wrong."

National unity was not the only benefit some Americans hoped to derive from war. In the weeks after Pearl Harbor men concluded that there had been little of which to be proud in the years since 1918—years marked first by a gaudy, irresponsible affluence and then by the specter of jobless men walking the streets. Many Americans believed that their society had been characterized by selfishness and a loss of confidence, that they were "a people grown negative, tentative, minus-signed and soft." War promised to change all this. "The twenties are gone with self-indulgence. The thirties have disappeared with self-pity," wrote Jonathan Daniels: "The forties are here in which Americans stand on a continent as men." In this view, the necessities of war would purge Americans of greed, demonstrate the nation's resilience, and lend a more noble purpose to life.

While it was freely predicted that war would foster solidarity, a price would be exacted in the form of individual suffering, broken families, and a lower living standard. In 1942 a sociologist affirmed that war would produce an increase in mental illness, widespread destitution, a nomadic way of life, regimentation of behavior, and "sadistic, macabre" trends in the arts. Harry Hopkins, perhaps Roosevelt's closest advisor at the time, forecast that goods would be rationed, men told where to work, and universities turned into military training centers. ("I see no reason for wasting time on what today are nonessentials, such as Chaucer or Latin," Hopkins wrote: "A diploma can only be framed and hung on the wall. A shell that a boy or girl helps to make can kill a lot of Japs.") He believed that while the nation's standard of living would be as low as in the worst days of the depression, supplies would be more evenly distributed so that none would live in luxury and none in want.

Wide agreement existed that the experience of World War I would not simply be duplicated. Even at the close of 1941 it was apparent that the economic, political and military role of the United States would not be the same as in 1917: the war would be fought on more fronts and would last much longer, the military situation would be more perilous, the armed forces would require larger numbers of men, the cost would necessarily be greater and the economy controlled more rigidly. "I never took any stock in the idea that you could preserve the experience of the First World War and use it in the second one," recalled one official. This attitude led those who had taken part in the first mobilization to complain that their experience was disregarded. George Creel, who had directed the Committee on Public Information under Woodrow Wilson, failed to find a place in the war administration of Franklin Roosevelt. As Creel put it, "The young men to whom I talked, many of them looking as if they had just come from commencement exercises, were very courteous but seemed to have difficulty in differentiating between the 1917 conflict and the Punic Wars."

Then, too, the experience gained in fighting the depression was of limited use in waging war. While the New Dealers had acquired some expertise in regulating the economy, the problems they had faced in the 1930s differed from those raised by World War II. The goal in the 1940s was to find men for defense industries rather than to create jobs for idle men, to boost production rather than limit it, to hold down wages and prices rather than encourage inflation. If anything, the depression left a mood of uncertainty that hindered mobilization: businessmen were reluctant to enlarge plant capacity because they doubted that postwar markets would exist, farmers were afraid to produce surpluses that might someday drive down prices, and workers held the grim belief that jobs would again be scarce when peace was restored.

Just as the twenties had ended with the stock market crash in October 1929, so the thirties came to a close on December 7, 1941. "That which has been shall be no more," one observer commented, "All the rules we have learned and which guided our way . . . have been broken, but the new ones have not been agreed to or announced." World War II radically altered the character of American society and challenged its most durable values. The war redefined the relationship of government to the individual and of individuals to each other, and it posed questions about the relationship between civilians and the military, between liberty and security, and between special interests and national purpose which continue to perplex Americans. Pearl Harbor marked more than the passing of a decade; it signified the end of an old era and the beginning of a new.

FORGING A WAR ECONOMY

IN THE EIGHTEEN MONTHS after Pearl Harbor the Roosevelt administration developed economic policies to meet the hard necessities of war. Mobilization demanded a huge increase in production through conversion of civilian industries, expansion of existing plants, and construction of new facilities. Other problems that called for solution included acquisition of raw materials, production scheduling to avoid logjams, provision of adequate transportation, and recruitment of skilled workers for national defense. With government expenditures soaring and the economy operating at full tilt, ways had to be found to check inflation. This meant wage ceilings to limit what people could buy, price control and rationing to assure a fair distribution of goods, and bond drives as well as heavy taxes to soak up purchasing power. The structure that finally emerged preserved important features of capitalism but differed substantially from the prewar system of private enterprise.

Economic regulation, affecting as it did the fortunes of large and small businessmen, workers and employers, rural and urban dwellers, and different geographic regions, was linked with politics and social policy. The government attempted to strike a balance between voluntarism and compulsion, to determine how much competition was consistent with maximum output, and to decide whether aid to the underprivileged could be reconciled with the demands of stabilization. Because these decisions affected people's lives so directly they could not be divorced from political considerations but served as a breeding ground for conflict.

That political and social considerations affected mobilization was apparent as early as 1939. In that year the War Department proposed the creation of a War Resources Administration to act as the President's agent in regulating the economy. At the urging of Assistant Secretary of War Louis Johnson, Roosevelt appointed a War Resources Board composed mainly of businessmen and headed by Edward R. Stettinius of United States Steel. While many assumed that this group would evolve into the planning branch envisioned by the Army, the Board drew criticism from all sides. Liberals charged that it was an instrument to clamp conservative control on the economy, and isolationists asserted that it was a device to catapult the nation into war. Roosevelt was warned that "one of these financial camels might pass through the needle's eye of middle western public opinion, but hardly the whole herd."[1] Regretting his hasty decision to form the Board, the President turned around and slashed its funds, gave Cabinet members a green light to attack it, and announced that it would disband in short order. The Board filed a report in November 1939 which was not released for seven years.

The President spurned the War Resources Board because he believed that its plan for industrial mobilization drained too much power from his office. "I would simply be abdicating the presidency to some other person," he explained. Even worse, power would be handed over to businessmen, many of whom had fought the New Deal tooth and nail and desired "above everything else in the world that some person other than 'F.D.R.' were president." The Board did in fact recommend that "patriotic business leaders" supervise the economy and that some laws protecting workers be laid aside in wartime. There was some truth in Hugh Johnson's view that New Dealers—in Johnson's words "the present pack of semi-Communist wolves"—did not "intend to let Morgan and Dupont men run a war." Furthermore, stringent controls seemed unwarranted at a time when orders for munitions could still be absorbed by a pool of unemployed men and idle factories. "I do not believe that there is an awful lot of Government action that is needed at the present time," Roosevelt said in May 1940: "We have got surpluses in almost everything. The shelves are still pretty well stocked."[2] Finally, Roosevelt feared that his political opponents would construe preparations for war as a plot to intervene.

The agencies that Roosevelt eventually established in the years before Pearl Harbor—the National Defense Advisory Commission (May 1940), the Office of Production Management (January 1941), the Office of Price Administration and Civilian Supply (April 1941), and the Supply Priorities and Allocations Board (August 1941)—permitted him to protect executive prerogatives, satisfy the New Deal coalition and avoid political embarrassment. When he set up the NDAC, Roosevelt was asked, "Who is our boss?" He replied, "Well, I guess I am." Often when authority was delegated it was also divided; as late as December 1941 critics could charge that SPAB had seven "bosses" and "there is no final authority except the President to whose ear everybody has access."[3] Parcelling out authority to several people not only left final decisions to the President, but also enabled him to give a say in policy to diverse interest groups. The OPM, for example, had as co-directors union leader Sidney Hillman and industrialist William Knudsen. Ordinarily these agencies were created under existing law so that Congressional approval was not required.

Despite the caution with which he approached the matter, Roosevelt made some progress in placing the nation on a war footing. In mid-1940 Congress enabled the President to give precedence to the production of military supplies, and a year later authorized priorities for essential civilian goods as well. In 1941 the government helped finance plant expansion, curtailed the use of certain scarce materials, and began requiring conversion of civilian industries. None of this occurred speedily enough to suit advocates of all-out defense, who pointed to the snail's pace at which preparations moved and the wasteful rivalry between defense agencies whose jurisdiction was poorly defined. Nevertheless, from January to December 1941 munitions production increased by 225 percent. While the administration moved by slow degrees, and then only when it felt confident of public backing, each of the production agencies created in 1940 and 1941 in turn exerted more authority, and each imposed greater restrictions on the life of the nation. Given the political conflicts inherent in economic planning, this was no small achievement.

Many constraints that had hobbled Roosevelt dissolved once Congress declared war. Controls were no longer as politically inexpedient or the need to placate various interests quite as important. Congress granted sweeping powers to the President, who, with military problems first in his thoughts, was better disposed to delegate authority to subordinates. On January 16, 1942, responding to insistent demands that the administration assert a firmer grip on economic mobilization, Roosevelt created the War Production Board. The Board's task was to develop policies governing all aspects of production, and to "exercise general responsibility" over the nation's economy. The Second War Powers Act of March 1942 bolstered its authority by permitting the government to allocate materials or facilities in any manner it thought necessary for defense, and by making it possible to prosecute for noncompliance. Roosevelt had rejected a suggestion to call the new agency the War Production Administration on the grounds that the initials might evoke images of the New Deal relief program: "We had a WPA. . . . I don't think we want to confuse people with two WPAs."[4]

To head the agency Roosevelt chose Donald Nelson, who had taken a part in defense planning since 1940. Although Nelson's career had been made in business with Sears, Roebuck and Company, most New Dealers and Democratic leaders in Congress held him in high regard. The President recognized that he was selecting a man who at times acted indecisively—one associate later said that Nelson conducted WPB meetings as if he were moderating a debate and obliged to see that each side had equal time—yet most other candidates either were too closely identified with big business to be acceptable or else harbored political ambitions. Nelson had none of these drawbacks. As one official observed: "It was probably preferable to take him with his known limitations than to take a new man whose positive or negative qualities were unknown."[5]

Within a few months Nelson made decisions, or acquiesced in ones, that were to shape economic policy throughout the war. First, he did not oppose Roosevelt's appointment of "czars" to cope with difficult problems relating to petroleum, rubber and manpower. Although Bernard Baruch had warned Nelson that "you must be the boss and when you say anything . . . it just has to go," the creation of autonomous, coordinate agencies seriously diluted the War Production Board's authority. Nelson also agreed to allow military procurement to remain with the Army and Navy, partly because the services already had well established purchasing agencies which would be time-consuming to dismantle, and also because he believed that officers would be less vulnerable than civilians to the pressures involved in letting contracts. Finally, Nelson decided that he could best gain the cooperation of the business community by dangling incentives before it in the form of profits and tax write-offs. While he ultimately imposed sharp restrictions on industry, Nelson wanted wherever possible "to establish a set of rules under which the game could be played the way industry said it had to play it."[6]

The War Production Board faced stubborn obstacles in its first task—converting industry to military production. Throughout 1941 industrialists had resisted conversion because business was booming, profitable arrangements with customers would be disturbed, and competitors who did not change over might secure a larger part of the domestic market. In addition, memories of Congressional attacks on World War I munitions makers still were crisp enough to give war profiteering a bad name. Even after Pearl Harbor conversion carried certain disadvantages, for expensive tools would have to be jettisoned and workers retrained for new tasks. Moreover, business would lose a measure of freedom by placing itself at the disposal of one buyer, the government, whose requirements and specifications might change without notice. Above all, businessmen feared that they would be left holding the bag of inflated capacity when the war ended. According to Secretary of Commerce Jesse H. Jones: "They didn't want to invest a lot of their own funds in equipment to manufacture things they believed would not be in demand after the shooting ceased."[7]

Even though industry preferred to mark time, the War Production Board at first hesitated to apply much pressure to speed up conversion. To some extent, normal civilian requirements held up the change over. It was impossible, for instance, to convert the steel casting industry to tank armor production because steel was needed for railroad car castings. Then too, since the WPB did not place military contracts it often lacked necessary information about the availability of existing facilities. The businessmen recruited to staff WPB bureaus sometimes did not enforce limitations on civilian output strictly. The Board thought it important "to get men who can talk the language of an industry, who know its problems, who speak to its members in the terms they understand themselves, who know whether a given program or a given suggestion is a reasonable or unreasonable thing,"[8] and these appointees were understandably receptive to the pleas of manufacturers who wanted to squeeze all they could out of existing production lines. In any case, if conversion ran too rapidly ahead of military orders, unemployment and hardship could result; the Board wished to proceed with the least possible disruption of the economy.

The automobile industry was at the hard core of conversion difficulties: its assembly lines were needed to turn out tanks and planes, and it used a vast amount of vital material— nearly 80 percent of the nation's rubber, 18 percent of its steel, and 14 percent of its copper. Yet in 1941 nearly a million more cars rolled out of Detroit than in 1939. At its first meeting the War Production Board outlawed the manufacture of cars and light trucks after January 31, although it provided a ten-day extension in some cases; all heavier trucks were to be discontinued after the middle of March. Even so, some WPB officials complained that industry men who had been hired by the Detroit branch were torpedoing conversion by granting various extensions and exemptions. As late as April a WPB attorney concluded that the office employed "former automobile salesmen and sales managers" who had "a fixed attitude of admiration for the automotive industry and all its works" and who were jockeying for good jobs after the war. "No one in the Branch shows any inclination to 'act tough'," he lamented.[9]

Conversion finally shifted into high gear in the spring of 1942, when the War Production Board issued orders limiting nonessential production and forbidding the use of scarce materials. Then the Board severely restricted the use of iron and steel in consumer goods and banned further home construction. By the end of June 1942, 29 percent of the prewar production of consumer durable goods had been cut off. "It was like nothing else the nation had ever felt or witnessed,"

Nelson later wrote: "It was not so much industrial conversion as industrial revolution, with months and years condensed into days." Manufacturers switched from making shirts to mosquito netting, from model trains to bomb fuses, from metal weather-stripping to mortar shells, and from kitchen sinks to cartridge cases. One economist reported with some astonishment: "It is quite evident that once we have determined to get going on this thing, it is possible to get the manufacturers of refrigerators, hardware, plumbing, stoves and cash registers to make all kinds of munitions."[10]

Conversion of existing factories, however, was not nearly sufficient to fill the staggering needs of the armed forces; existing plants had to be enlarged and new ones built. Again, businessmen proved reluctant to move ahead too rapidly because of the risks involved and the WPB had to devise procedures to coax them along. In essence, the government promised to underwrite much of the cost of expansion, guaranteed that military contracts would be profitable, and shelved antimonopoly restrictions that hampered production. According to Henry L. Stimson: "If you are going to try to go to war, or to prepare for war, in a capitalist country, you have got to let business make money out of the process or business won't work."[11]

The government offered industry mouth-watering incentives to operate at full throttle. Under a plan first developed by Nelson in 1940 and used extensively early in the war, industry could amortize the cost of expansion over only five years, thereby deflating taxable income while inflating earning capacity. Even excess profits taxes were recoverable since if a business showed a loss after the war it could claim a refund. An economist later termed this arrangement "the biggest and most resilient cushion in the history of public finance."[12] Yet another invention to erase uncertainty was the cost-plus-a-fixed-fee contract, used extensively by the Army and Navy. Since it was difficult to estimate the cost of producing new military items that required frequent changes in design, the

government agreed to meet all the costs incurred by the manufacturer and pay in addition a fixed fee, or a guaranteed
profit. The government assumed all major risks. While this
set-up sometimes encouraged contractors to waste materials
and hoard labor, pressure to retain it was so strong that it
remained in force through most of the war. Corporate profits,
after taxes, climbed from $6.4 billion in 1940 to $10.8 billion in 1944.

Just as the government removed certain financial risks, so
it broke down barriers to business cooperation. The administration granted immunity from the anti-trust laws to firms
which engaged in pooling and other cooperative arrangements, provided that they first obtained approval by demonstrating a link between increased efficiency and war needs.
Ultimately, six hundred such plans were accepted. Furthermore, in March 1942 the President suspended all anti-trust
suits which might slow down essential production. There
were, of course, firms which could not adapt to war requirements, compete for lucrative contracts, or benefit from com-
bination, and were driven out of business. The most common
view in the War Production Board was that these casualties
could not be helped; one official doubted whether government
aid could "counteract the process of natural selection in the
business world."[13] Conversion and expansion moved inexorably
forward: as much new industrial plant was built in three
years of war as in the preceding fifteen years, and nearly
twice as much was manufactured in 1942 as in 1939.

Productive energies could be fully released only if some
method of allocating raw materials was found. Since there was
not enough copper, steel and aluminum to go around, the
War Production Board had to see that each contractor received a supply sufficient to fill his orders. In June 1942 the
Board took a first step: the Production Requirements Plan,
which had been used on a voluntary basis for several months,
became compulsory. Under this plan, each factory with a
government contract submitted a production schedule to the

WPB and received a quota of basic materials. But it soon became apparent that this sytem worked poorly. Procurement agencies often contracted for more than their suppliers could possibly produce with available materials, and businessmen frequently overstated their needs in order to get as much as possible. Priority ratings became little more than hunting licenses used to track down nonexistent supplies. "It was a pathetic spectacle to me," reported Secretary Stimson after one grueling conference with other users of vital material, "like four hungry dogs quarreling over a very inadequate bone."[14]

To break this bottleneck, Nelson called on a former New York investment banker, Ferdinand Eberstadt, who devised the Controlled Materials Plan in the fall of 1942. Rather than require thousands of individual firms to present their needs to the War Production Board, Eberstadt proposed that each of the claimant agencies—including the War and Navy Departments, Maritime Commission, Lend-Lease Administrator, and Office of Civilian Supply—present its requirements. The Board would then allot specific quantities of whatever copper, aluminum and steel was available to these agencies to be distributed among their prime contractors. These three metals were heavily used for producing ammunition, aircraft, heavy weapons, tanks and ships. Under the new system, purchasing agencies could not order more than manufacturers could produce with the existing supply of basic industrial materials.[15] The plan, adopted early in November, went into full operation in mid-1943 and continued to control the distribution of material for the duration of the war.

Some shortages, notably that of rubber, were not as easily remedied. By early 1942 Japan had blocked off 90 percent of America's crude rubber supply by seizing the Dutch East Indies and Malaya, and the amount on hand—some 500,000 tons—was hardly enough to meet projected needs. Every armored tank took a ton of rubber, and every battleship seventy-five tons. The most common form of synthetic rubber, Buna-S, was made by the polymerization of styrene and butadiene, but while technical obstacles largely had been overcome, production had not gotten off the ground. In the late 1920s Standard Oil (N.J.) had entered into an arrangement with the German chemical combine, I. G. Farbenindustrie, which restricted independent efforts in the field. Moreover, it had been widely assumed that crude rubber stockpiles were sufficient, or that new sources could be developed in South America if necessary. Finally, since Buna-S was expensive, there was no market for it as long as crude rubber could be imported. Late in 1940 Stettinius informed Roosevelt that the "uneconomic nature" of synthetic rubber meant that plants would not be built unless the government financed construction and assured a market for the product.[16] Consequently, in 1941 annual synthetic rubber capacity stood at a scant 40,000 tons.

Even after Pearl Harbor, when considerations of patent rights and profits no longer barred the way, conflict between interest groups hindered the creation of a synthetic rubber industry. Since butadiene could be derived from either petroleum or alcohol, the Buna-S program triggered a clash between oil companies and agricultural groups, each of which stood to gain from the use of its product. Petroleum found a spokesman in Harold Ickes who contended that the industry could supply as much butadiene as was required. Ickes also believed that the industry could provide the necessary expertise. In recruiting a staff for the petroleum agency he headed, Ickes admitted "we have necessarily drawn upon the industry for personnel; but he added that his appointees had "freed themselves of any previous affiliations" so that they were not advocating the petroleum process for selfish reasons. The farm bloc in Congress, however, championed the use of grain alcohol and criticized all those who failed to discern the advantages of using agricultural products. In the summer of 1942 Congress passed a bill sponsored by Guy Gillette of Iowa which would have created a rubber agency with overwhelming powers and given alcohol a favored position. A Congressman from North Carolina, convinced that "the action of the House was due to hysteria" and signified merely an "advertisement of our concern for Agriculture," urged the President to veto the bill, which he promptly did."[17]

As rubber supplies continued to dwindle, the President decided on a scrap drive as a last alternative to rationing. On June 12 he appealed to the people to turn in "old tires, old rubber raincoats, old garden hose, rubber shoes, bathing caps, gloves—whatever you have that is made of rubber." The petroleum industry managed the drive. Citizens deposited rubber at gasoline stations where it was picked up by tank wagons on their usual rounds. To provide some financial reward, the stations offered one cent a pound for old rubber which the government then purchased for $25 a ton; any profits went to charity. The industry also formed a "War Council" to kindle enthusiasm for the drive, to obtain newspaper and radio publicity, and to display the booster spirit. Among other things, the Council recorded the reaction of the manager of "Nat Jupiter's station in New York:" " 'A carload of girls from a musical comedy drove up here and they busted off garter straps, wriggled out of girdles and what not. This is fun!' . . . Sure is fun, ain't it Nat?"[18] In less than four weeks, Americans donated 450,000 tons of scrap rubber in every form imaginable, some of which was mailed directly to the White House. One person sent in a pair of rubber boots which, he said, had been in the family since 1896.

While this campaign caught people's imagination, it was at best a stopgap measure. To conserve rubber, nationwide gasoline rationing seemed necessary so that the supply of automobile tires would be stretched as far as possible. Yet Roosevelt was reluctant to challenge powerful groups opposed to the plan. Petroleum companies were prepared to battle restrictions on automobile use, and officials in many states which relied on gasoline taxes for revenue also expressed disapproval. The Governor of Arkansas warned that "drastic

rationing will wreck the financial structure of many states."
Cutting down on driving threatened to produce a political
whiplash. Democratic chieftains feared that the "over-all
rationing of gasoline in all states is loaded with political
dynamite." One high-ranking party official predicted that
gasoline rationing, like prohibition in the 1920s, would give
rise to bootlegging and racketeering. As service stations and
refineries shut down, the men thrown out of work "would
be subject to proselyting [sic] by the anti-administration
forces, with an almost certain loss of many Democratic
seats." At least a decision could be deferred until after the
November 1942 elections. "An appeal by the President for
voluntary cooperation will get patriotic support," he noted,
"and will be politically safer."[19]

Buffeted by conflicting pressures, Roosevelt hit upon the
idea of a nonpartisan investigation of the rubber shortage.
If rationing was required, this might remove some of the
stigma from the administration. When Chief Justice Harlan
Fiske Stone declined to head the investigation on the grounds
that it would compromise the Supreme Court's impartiality,
the President turned to Bernard Baruch. Baruch, one observer
later commented, "was girt about with a kind of Wall Street
homespun," and he stood high with influential congressmen.
"Let me handle the Senators and fellows on the Hill," Baruch
said, "they're mostly good friends of mine."[20] The other members of the group—James B. Conant and Karl T. Compton,
presidents of Harvard and M.I.T.—were glad to oblige. The
Baruch Committee reported in September, proposing expansion of synthetic rubber output largely on the basis of
petroleum, urging appointment of a Rubber Director to "bull
through" the program, and calling for nationwide gasoline
rationing. With Baruch's blessing, the administration imposed full-scale rationing in December, a few weeks after the
elections; in January 1943 it placed a ban on all pleasure
driving, even within allowable quotas. This ban was quickly
relaxed, however, and while gasoline rationing did cut down

on tire use—each car was driven on the average one-third fewer miles in 1943 than in 1941—consumption tended to exceed quotas throughout the war.

Only the mushroom-like growth of the synthetic rubber industry ultimately enabled supply to overtake demand. Much of this buildup was supervised by William Jeffers, president of the Union Pacific Railroad, whom Roosevelt appointed Rubber Director late in 1942. Jeffers' office, like most wartime agencies, drew its personnel from the industry involved, and while he was criticized for giving "members of the rubber industry complete control over their fellow members and over the national economy so far as it affects rubber," he obtained results. The government spent $700 million to construct fifty-one plants, which it then leased to rubber companies for a nominal fee and operated on a cost-plus-a-management-charge basis. The plants were chiefly located in Texas, Louisiana, southern California and the Akron-Toledo area. One of the largest was built in West Virginia and run by the United States Rubber Company. Sprawled over seventy-seven acres, it could produce 90,000 tons a year—the equivalent of about twenty million rubber trees. By 1944 synthetic rubber capacity had soared to one million tons; actual production exceeded 800,000 tons and accounted for 87 percent of all the rubber used in the United States. Bernard Baruch could at last breathe with relief, "Oh, boy! How I had my fingers crossed on the making of butadiene."[21]

As industrial output surged ahead, a massive burden was imposed on the nation's transportation system, particularly on the railroads. In 1943 twice as much freight and more than three times as many passengers travelled by rail as in 1940. War also distorted normal operations since much of the traffic was destined for new military bases, defense plants and coastal ports. Unlike World War I, when the government had taken over the railroads, a system was devised under which the industry voluntarily submitted to centralized direction. Compliance warded off the bogeyman of nationalization. To provide a clean flow of traffic, the railroads pooled their resources, agreed to permit rerouting among competing lines, and generally improved efficiency by adding cars onto engines, loading them more heavily and hauling them longer distances. Use of centralized traffic control (CTC) jumped three times during the war. By automatically transmitting information about train movements to dispatchers, CTC eliminated the need to stop cars and throw switches by hand; it made for striking increases in speed.

Starting in 1942 railroads supplied oil to cities along the eastern seaboard. In the past this had been done by tankers, but that spring German submarines preyed on merchant shipping along the coast with deadly effect. Railroads tank cars were called into service, and by September they provided more than 800,000 barrels a day, or 70 percent of the total. But this was at best a makeshift; pipelines offered the only long-range solution. Without them, Ickes told Roosevelt, "we would be as helpless before the Axis powers as were Holland and Belgium and Norway." In March the major oil producers met in Tulsa, Oklahoma and agreed to construct pipelines if the government would assure "freedom of action with protection against loss on the huge expenditures involved." The War Production Board then doled out the necessary steel (after toying with the idea of building a short line across Florida and "barging the oil up the inland waterway in wooden barges and wooden tugs"), and the government agreed to defray construction costs.[22] Work on the "Big Inch," running 1250 miles from the Texas oil fields to the New York-Philadelphia region, began in the summer of 1942 and took a year to complete. Twenty-four inches in diameter, it was three times the size of any other pipeline, and could carry 335,000 barrels a day. While pipelines eventually shouldered the greatest share of the load, railroads continued to cart oil throughout the war.

The policies adopted in recruiting manpower resembled those applied in mobilizing industry: wherever possible the government relied on incentives to elicit voluntary compliance. Although it had always been difficult to fill hot, dirty jobs in copper mines or lumber camps, manpower at first caused trouble. Of more than fifteen million people who entered the labor force or armed services from 1940 to 1943, many were drawn from the ranks of the unemployed or else were women and teenagers lured by the magnet of high wages. Even so, labor supply demanded attention: in the spring of 1942 Nelson learned that "manpower pirating" threatened to stall production in Detroit, and Sidney Hillman called for a "national policy for the orderly transfer of workers from civilian occupations to war jobs." In April, Roosevelt set up the War Manpower Commission under Paul V. McNutt, a former governor of Indiana who had headed the Federal Security Agency since 1939. The Commission, which was supposed to determine where workers were needed and how they should be apportioned between industry and the Army, was designed to coordinate rather than control. It could not prescribe selective service policy regarding deferments, had no voice over labor relations, and lacked power to enforce its decisions. The President believed that control over a man's job must be approached gingerly, for if workers grew resentful their morale would drop. For this reason he clung to the notion of "voluntary cooperation."[23]

By the end of 1942 the inadequacies of this approach were all too apparent. Not only were labor reserves being milked dry, but absenteeism and rapid turnover were also posing formidable problems. The unwillingness of the Army and Navy to funnel orders away from established contractors who were located in areas in which there was a general scarcity of labor further aggravated the situation. As early as October 1942, one official found that Americans were not giving enough of their energies to war. He grumbled that "all of the men and women whose services are used to produce large editions of magazines such as *Vogue* and *Harper's Bazaar* are hardly being used for direct war purposes" and urged that people be compelled to take essential jobs. At about the same time McNutt requested that the War Manpower Commission be given control over labor utilization, new hirings, and selective service. By December many recognized that sanctions "bordering on compulsion" could not be put off much longer.[24]

Consequently, the administration took the first tentative steps in the direction of regimenting manpower. In December the President ended most Navy enlistments to prevent the draining away of skilled workers. He also transferred selective service to the War Manpower Commission over the strong opposition of the War Department. Stimson had warned against making the draft subservient to a civilian manpower system, which he angrily termed "an untried experiment full of political hazards [which] contains the certainty of bitter controversy." But his objections were brushed aside.[25] Then, in January 1943, McNutt issued a "work or fight" order. Wielding the draft as a club to move people into jobs related to the war, he ordered an end to deferments for all those, including men with children, in unessential work. At a time when four of every five draftees were unmarried, McNutt proposed substituting occupation for dependency as grounds for deferment. During the next few months the WMC valiantly attempted to channel the stream of manpower by drawing up lengthy lists of nondeferrable occupations.

Yet even these measures ran into a stone wall of political opposition. The proposal to draft fathers rubbed a particularly raw nerve in Congress. One Senator remarked that "slackers in the government bureaus" should be inducted "before American homes are broken up, before children are driven into the streets."[26] In December 1943, after a long controversy, Congress in effect prohibited taking fathers, however unimportant their jobs, before men without children, no matter how vital their work. McNutt then backed down and rescinded the work or fight order. Legislators proved equally responsive to the demands of the farm bloc. Disturbed by the shortage of labor and the high wages for farm hands that resulted, Congress accepted a scheme proposed by Millard Tydings to defer all essential farm workers. Its appetite whetted by this victory, the farm bloc moved in 1943 to obtain the release of any soldier who had worked on a farm within the last year. This bill passed the Senate but it died in the House when the promise of a looser interpretation of "essential" work appeased its supporters. By the fall of 1943 two million farm workers had received occupational deferments, and tobacco, the pet crop of important Congressmen, had been defined as an essential crop. This policy had a twin effect: it placed an unfair portion of the burden of providing soldiers on industry, and it encouraged inefficient use of farm labor.

Not until late in the summer of 1943 was a partial solution to the manpower dilemma discovered. Spurred to action by labor turnover in aircraft plants and shipyards on the West Coast—where hiring gates had come to resemble turnstiles, with four of every ten men staying on the job less than a year—the administration adopted a balance sheet approach to match production demands with labor supply. Local committees determined how many workers were available in each area, and firms could receive new contracts only if a sufficient supply of labor existed. As jobs were finished and workers freed, new orders could be accepted. Moreover, a system of controlled referrals ensured that new hiring would be done with the approval of a central employment service. The West Coast Manpower Plan went into effect in Seattle, Portland, San Francisco, Los Angeles and San Diego in the fall of 1943 and rapidly spread to cities across the country. It represented a halfway stage between voluntarism and compulsion: men could not switch jobs at will, but no worker was forced to change his job, no employer obliged to hire anyone to whom he objected, and no penalty imposed in case of defiance.

Manpower was closely connected with the broader issues of wage control and stabilization. By the spring of 1942, when the cost of living had climbed 15 percent above the 1939 level, Roosevelt and his advisors recognized that runaway in-

flation could wreck the economy. When one farm leader, re-
calling the rock-bottom prices of the depression, was in-
cautious enough to suggest that "a little inflation would not
hurt," the President replied that he was reminded of "a fellow
who took a little cocaine and kept coming back for more until
he was a drug addict." Many of these fears found expression
in the theory of an inflationary gap, defined as the difference
between disposable income and available consumer goods.
Economists in the administration reasoned that as the gap
widened, prices would skyrocket. The implications for labor
policy were spelled out by Leon Henderson, who held that
wage increases posed a double-barrelled danger: they increased production costs for each item, and upped prices by
boosting purchasing power. Since some decline in living
standards seemed likely, Henderson thought that the discrepancy between the wages of different groups should be
narrowed. "If wage increases are permitted according to
bargaining power, this spread will be increased," he noted.
"The stronger bargainers will hold their standard of living
at the expense of others, and these others will suffer a double
burden, getting an even smaller piece of a smaller pie."[27]

A simple, comprehensive plan for controlling wages and
prices was put forward by Bernard Baruch, who wanted to
freeze the conditions existing when the war began. Baruch
supported "an over-all ceiling in order to keep the same relationships between the various segments of society."[28] Once
retreat before the demands of any pressure group, he warned,
and a wild scramble for private gain would ensue. But Baruch's
proposal was far too strict to suit Roosevelt. Favoring a more
flexible system, the administration tried to appease labor by
imposing controls slowly and selectively. Incentives in the
form of wage hikes, provided they did not get out of hand,
would at the same time safeguard important political interests and make possible some gains for those at the bottom
of the ladder.

Even within the bounds of a more pragmatic approach

there was room for variation. One group of presidential advisors—centering around Budget Director Harold D. Smith and including Leon Henderson, Henry Wallace and Samuel I. Rosenman—backed a rather rigid anti-inflation plan. "Everyone admits that full conversion of the country to war makes sacrifices imperative, but each group tries to shift the sacrifices to others," noted Smith. It was necessary to make sure that "all interests are restricted at the same time" in order to "allay class bickerings." In March and April 1942 Smith's group urged Roosevelt to stabilize wage rates as part of a broad-gauged program that involved freezing prices, taxing war profits out of existence, lowering income tax exemptions, rationing scarce necessities, curtailing consumer credit, imposing a compulsory savings plan, and readying a sales tax for future use. Wage controls were at the heart of the matter, for "deep popular resentment would follow the exemption of labor from the general program." But labor could still be counted on for support, Smith argued, since the cost of living would be held down and the freeze would not prevent increases in substandard wages. Besides, Draconian restraints would be fastened on the well-to-do. In all seriousness, Smith and the others suggested that a ceiling of $50,000, after taxes, be set on all personal incomes, "thereby dramatizing the equality of sacrifice implicit in the over-all program."[29]

But Roosevelt was reluctant to take the route of strict control, and his doubts were strengthened by the advice of Henry Morgenthau. The Secretary of the Treasury accepted the need for price ceilings, rationing, credit restrictions and higher taxes, but he flinched at further action. Proposals for a sales tax or for lowering personal income tax exemptions, said Morgenthau, would shift the burden of the war to poor people; they were simply "spare the rich" measures. He also preferred voluntary bond drives to a compulsory savings plan. Above all, Morgenthau protested against a wage freeze, which he considered unnecessary and impractical: it would be taken as "a slap in the face of labor" and stir up a hornet's nest of resentment. When, on April 27, the President finally announced a stabilization program, he leaned in Morgenthau's direction. While he called for a heavy excess profits tax, a $25,000 salary limitation, price ceilings, rationing and restrictions on credit, the President supported a voluntary savings program and held that existing wage scales could be maintained without new legislation. "There is really everything in there that I fought for," chortled Morgenthau.[30]

Responsibility for putting a brake on wage increases fell to the National War Labor Board. Created in January 1942 to settle labor conflicts in war industry, the Board was headed by William H. Davis and had twelve members representing labor, industry and the public. After the President's April message it obtained authority over wage increases in cases involving labor-management disputes. In arriving at guidelines, however, the Board had to overcome the resistance of organized labor, which stubbornly opposed wage controls. Both the AFL and the CIO rejected the inflationary gap theory. Union spokesmen denied that wage hikes were always inflationary since workers would put added earnings in the bank and employers could absorb increases out of profits. Trade unionists bitterly resented any move to eliminate collective bargaining or diminish their own usefulness. Philip Murray told members of the CIO executive board that "if anyone here in this room is foolish enough to believe that national regimentation . . . will not give us a complete Fascist control over American workers during this war, then I say they are perfectly crazy." Destroy collective bargaining, he warned, "and see how effective you will be with your people back home. You will find out how quick they will tell you to go to hell."[31]

Despite these protests the War Labor Board moved to halt spiraling wages. In July 1942, faced with a demand by workers in the Bethlehem, Republic, Youngstown and Inland steel companies for a dollar a day increase, the Board adopted the "Little Steel" formula. Taking January 1, 1941 as a starting point, it approved a 15 percent increase to cover the rise in living costs to May 1942. Since steel workers had already received a raise, they were entitled to an additional hike of 5.5 percent, or 44 cents a day. The Board noted that in applying the formula to other workers, larger increases would be granted where necessary to correct substandard wages or other inequities. The Little Steel formula did not penalize workers who had not yet benefitted from boom times, but it was not inflationary since most workers had already obtained the permissible increase. As best it could, the War Labor Board was attempting to preserve peacetime standards.

The Little Steel formula cooled wages but by no means froze them. As a result, unions at first found it possible to live with the decision. Not only did the ruling permit some increase, but it also applied to hourly rates rather than weekly earnings. A fatter pay envelope could still be obtained through overtime, fringe benefits and travel allowances. Then too, wage boosts resulting from upgrading of job classifications commonly occurred and were not restricted. Finally, the Little Steel formula only affected dispute cases. Those employers who were willing to grant increases were free to do so. Where war contracts were involved and the government was footing the bill, employers were often quite willing to pay higher wages to attract labor. In many instances businessmen granted increases because the labor market was tight, government contracts covered labor costs anyway, and the price of the finished product meant less than having the working force to finish it.

In time the administration moved to close some of these loopholes. In October Roosevelt extended the jurisdiction of the War Labor Board to include voluntary wage increases. "When we got the executive order ... which in effect said 'No more wage increases'—I nearly dropped dead," recalled Davis, "because how do you settle a labor dispute with no more wage increase?" When even this proved inadequate, the President issued the "hold the line" order in April 1943 which deprived the Board of the power to revise the Little Steel formula, or to permit raises to correct certain inequities. But the Board retained the right to grant increases in "rare and unusual cases affecting critical war production" and in cases of substandard conditions. By the summer of 1943, while wages had largely been removed from the realm of collective bargaining, they were still not bound by iron-clad rules. "The idea of an absolute unbreakable wage ceiling is a fine slogan," Robert Wagner had noted, "but cannot be worked out . . . in actual practice."[32] The administration always had better luck in limiting hourly increases than actual earnings: whereas wage rates rose by only 24 percent during the war, weekly earnings spurted by 70 percent.

Wage controls could not curb inflation unless supplemented by a broad-based system of taxation. Taxes had met 30 percent of the cost of World War I, but while the Second World War was ten times as expensive as the First—indeed, the government spent nearly twice as much from 1940 to 1945 as it had in the preceding 150 years—taxes covered nearly half its cost. The President much preferred taxes to borrowing. "I would rather pay one hundred per cent of taxes now than push the burden of this war onto the shoulders of my grandchildren," he said in December 1942.[33] Taxes would not only help avert a mammoth national debt, but would siphon off excess purchasing power and obligate the wealthy to assume a heavy share of the burden. But when the United States went to war it had a rickety tax structure. In fact, most people paid nothing at all: in 1939 only four million returns were filed.

In March 1942 Morgenthau called for higher individual and corporate taxes, payroll deductions, increased social security taxes, and an end to oil depletion allowances and exemptions for interest on municipal bonds. But these proposals met strong opposition in Congress, which sat on the Treasury bill for seven months while it scheduled hearings and kept a wary eye on the fall elections. Moreover, even

Morgenthau was sensitive to the political implications of taxation. In May the Secretary agreed that it would be wise to postpone collection of withholding taxes. "I am more interested that we get a Democratic Congress than I am in inflation or anything else," he confessed. "If you should have this thing hit these people before election it will hit them like a ton of bricks and it may be very harmful to our Democratic congressmen."[34] Not until October did a bill emerge, and then only after the Senate had added some 500 amendments. Although Congress refused to plug glaring loopholes and provided only $7 billion in additional taxes instead of the $8 billion requested, the Revenue Act of 1942 brought nearly all Americans within the system, increased corporate taxes, and raised the excess profits tax from 60 to 90 percent.

Having thrown the tax net around millions of low and middle-income people who were unaccustomed to filing returns, the administration found itself under pressure to erase back taxes. Beardsley Ruml, an unorthodox New York financier, suggested that the entire 1942 tax be forgiven, and his plan won widespread support not only from the wealthy who stood to gain most but from all who owed back taxes. "Things would move along just the same as time moves on under daylight savings," Ruml promised. Republicans eagerly endorsed the Ruml plan, and a prominent Democrat, urging it on Roosevelt, said the Treasury "will lose nothing until the day of Judgment, and at that date no one will give a damn." The President, however, opposed the plan as a massive windfall for war profiteers and the very rich. The scheme, grumbled one Congressman, was "about as legitimate as horse-stealing."[35] Joined in opposition were liberals who resented write-offs for the wealthy and economy-minded southern conservatives.

Nevertheless, the Ruml plan gained momentum in the spring of 1943. To coax the House into defeating it, and then by the razor-thin margin of four votes, the Democratic leadership accepted a compromise forgiving half of all 1942 taxes; then, in May, the Senate accepted the plan in full.

The administration tried to salvage what it could in conference, but the House delegation finally caved in. As signed by
the President, the new Revenue Act wiped out all 1942 obliga-
tions up to $50, forgave 75 percent of the rest, and introduced
a withholding tax on most wage earners. By the summer of
1943 nearly all Americans paid taxes out of their weekly
earnings, and most were current in their payments. While
rates never climbed too high during the war—few ever paid
as much as 20 percent—a foundation for the modern tax
structure had been erected.

The sale of war bonds was still another prong in the attack
on inflation, and like wage controls and taxes it illustrated the
fine line between voluntarism and compulsion. In 1942 most
of Roosevelt's advisors favored a compulsory savings plan,
but the President followed Henry Morgenthau in relying on
voluntary bond purchases. Yet the term "voluntary" could
be deceptive. Those who wanted compulsory savings held that
if subtle social pressures were used in selling bonds a semi-
coercive system would result. Formal and impartial government coercion would in fact be less oppressive than hap-
hazard and unequal community pressure. Bond drives during
World War I, several advisors reminded Roosevelt, "extended
even to badgering school children, to vicious pressures, to
odious personal comparisons, and to painting yellow the homes
and barns of those who failed to subscribe. . . . Since coercion
is inevitable in any event, it should be placed upon an orderly
and equitable basis."[36]

Fear that the bullying methods used in World War I would
reappear was unfounded. Morgenthau, who believed that
bond campaigns would "make the country war-minded" and
"give people an opportunity to do something," put his faith
in advertising rather than strong-arm tactics.[37] To conduct
the drives, he recruited men from Madison Avenue who
relied on Hollywood hoopla and the hard sell. Their slogans
ranged from "Back the Attack" to "Smash 'Em With Sock
Showmanship." Entertainers also pitched in: Betty Grable's

nylon stockings fetched $40,000 at auction and, as one official related, "Kay Kayser played a Bondwagon performance to 10,000 people . . . Miss Loretta Young sold $40,000 in Bonds to a Kiwanis luncheon-meeting . . . The Jeep Tour, with Marlene Dietrich as the Hollywood attraction, visited 16 towns in the State of Ohio . . . The first Victory Pig sale in the country was held by the Sunset Victory Pig Club at Jonesboro, Arkansas . . . Publishers of *The Batman* magazine devoted their cover to a picture of their hero urging the purchase of War Bonds."[37] Spectacular displays and stunts were common. In Oregon, seven men set themselves adrift on a life raft in the Willamette River and refused to come ashore until Portland filled its quota.

Morgenthau pushed the sale of low-denomination bonds, which drew off money that consumers would otherwise spend on everyday items. The Treasury's Series-E bonds were far more attractive than World War I Liberty Bonds, for they were registered in the buyer's name and could be replaced if lost, and their value was guaranteed since interest was accumulated and paid at maturity. The first war loan netted $12.9 billion in December 1942, and was followed by six other drives each lasting about a month. As an anti-inflation measure, the voluntary program had mixed results. While sales reached $135 billion, banks, insurance companies and corporations bought most securities; individuals purchased only one-quarter of the total, and sales of $25 and $50 bonds were even more disappointing. Even worse, the redemption rate of $25 bonds doubled from 1942 to 1944. Nevertheless, twenty-five million workers signed up for payroll savings plans, and in 1944 E-bond sales alone absorbed 7.1 percent of personal income after taxes.

Chipping away at buying power could not stop inflation unless prices were controlled and scarce goods rationed. In January 1942, Congress authorized the Office of Price Administration to fix maximum prices, but since the agency considered some increases necessary to provide incentives for expanded output it was reluctant to take action. Not until late in April did it issue the General Maximum Price Regulation, requiring every merchant to accept as a ceiling the highest price he had charged in March 1942. The general freeze, while simple to invoke, was difficult to enforce and often unfair. It worked for standardized items like cigarettes, but failed to control the price of products whose style, design or packaging changed. Clothing manufacturers, for example, often stopped putting out inexpensive garments and concentrated on costlier lines; price rises were sometimes cloaked by deterioration in quality. The ruling penalized dealers who had not already raised their prices, and left in limbo those who started to handle new products. The cost of living, therefore, continued to creep upward.

Controls were also crippled for a time by the special favors accorded agriculture. Early in 1942 the farm bloc cajoled Congress into setting ceilings on farm prices at 110 percent of parity. During the summer rural interests fought a holding action against the administration's efforts to revise this formula, which effectively excluded many crops from control. "Did you ever read the *Merchant of Venice?*" Roosevelt asked one Senator bitterly, "I remember something about a fellow who wanted his pound of flesh." In September the President ordered Congress to give him added authority over farm prices and threatened to act on his own if it balked. While Congress resented his peremptory tone, the President had shown both restraint and political savvy. By taking Harold Ickes's advice and putting "this hot potato right where it belongs—in the lap of Congress," Roosevelt had escaped the charge of usurping legislative powers.[38] In October Congress gave the President most of what he wanted and the hold-the-line order in April 1943 prevented inflationary price increases. At about the same time, over the strong opposition of farm groups, the administration introduced a program of subsidy payments whereby it purchased crops to bolster farm prices and sold them at a loss to consumers to hold down living costs. By mid-1943 the tools needed to nail down prices were at hand; consumer prices advanced by less than 2 percent during the next two years.

To a great extent the success of price control hinged on rationing which, by substituting coupons for cash, demonetized currency for certain purchases. Rationing also distributed hard-to-get items fairly, and stopped consumers who were on friendly terms with the corner grocer or who could afford to stand in queues for hours at a time from gobbling up limited supplies of sugar or coffee. No form of regulation, however, conflicted more sharply with traditional American values. Not only was strict rationing unprecedented—it had been experimented with only casually in World War I—but it harshly narrowed the range of individual choice. Moreover, in a society that cherished the ideal of material abundance the resort to rationing seemed almost a confession of inadequacy.

Nevertheless, the OPA introduced ten major rationing programs in 1942 and others followed later. They served a variety of purposes: gasoline was rationed because of the tire shortage, coffee because of the diversion of ocean shipping, canned food because of the shortage of tin, and shoes because of military needs. Where commodities could be restricted to the few, individuals had to obtain ration certificates by demonstrating need; where commodities had to be broadly distributed, families received coupons or stamps for redemption. The Office of Price Administration injected control at the highest link in the chain of distribution. Each dealer, having reported his inventory, collected ration coupons as he sold goods, and could replenish his store only by presenting them to his supplier; as the coupons flowed up the line, rationed goods moved down. Since local boards administered the program the last word rested with men who had prestige in the community and whose decisions were difficult to challenge. But the system had disadvantages: uniform treatment across the nation did not prevail, boards did not always resist community pressures, and too lenient a policy often resulted.

Officials of the Office of Price Administration believed it their agency's task to champion consumer as opposed to producer interests. "A strong consumer minded public," they reasoned, was "the only democratic answer to the pressure groups of business, farm and labor." But in attempting to stimulate consumer consciousness the agency crossed swords with well-entrenched interest groups, each of which sought to protect itself by influencing OPA policy or, if necessary, by pressuring Congress to restrict the agency's authority. As price controls and rationing affected daily life more intimately the OPA became, in the words of its chief, "the special target of every 'producer' pressure group in the country," and it became enmeshed in politics.[39]

Political controversies swarmed about the OPA like so many angry insects: each interest group scrambled to get preferential treatment; rural and urban forces clashed over food prices; opposing factions struggled for the upper hand in local rationing boards; Congress resented what it considered the arrogant exercise of power by OPA bureaucrats; and state political machines sometimes fought to prevent OPA patronage from going to Congressmen. In addition, Democrats as well as Republicans charged that their opponents were seeking to control the agency for narrow partisan advantage. "The politicians in and around here are drooling at the mouth and smacking their jowls in anticipation of the pickings once they get their slimy claws into the price administration," muttered Fiorello La Guardia. He added that "prohibition was but a penny-ante game in comparison with the pickings, plunder, patronage and power" that partisan control of wartime agencies would make possible.[40]

The first price administrator, Leon Henderson, never escaped the quicksand of politics. A New Deal economist who once asked an audience to consider his remarks "as coming from a sort of impersonal calculating machine," Henderson

offended Democrats by turning to state officials, regardless
of party, to fill OPA positions. At this, the party faithful
raised an anguished howl. When a high OPA post in South
Dakota went to one of Republican Karl Mundt's cronies,
Democrats were reportedly "in arms" at a "most deplorable
example of recognizing and giving quarter to the enemy."
A loyal southerner complained that "Mississippi O.P.A. is
almost entirely in the hands of the Philistines." Elsewhere
Democrats grumbled that "the entire OPA set-up is being
used for the furtherance of Republican political purposes."[41]
Henderson fought a game but frustrating battle against the
patronage hounds. "Some of these members of Congress . . .
want to control or dictate my state personnel," he protested:
"Nothing could ruin our efforts so easily as to have OPA
become political, and to have the public feel that a right
political connection could get favors on rents, prices and
rations." Late in 1942 Henderson stepped down, citing reasons
of poor health; he warned the President that "control of
rationing should never be given to anyone who does not deep
in his soul believe in the Roosevelt aims."[42]

Administrative rivalries plagued the OPA as much as
political squabbles, and these rivalries were rooted in the
President's overall administrative technique. Roosevelt at the
outset of the war had favored a unified and functional approach to administration. He allocated powers according to
function—such as production or price control—and made an
effort to herd agencies under the roof of the War Production
Board. But as crises developed, he could not resist the temptation to create brand new agencies whose authority crossed
functional lines. The resulting twists and turns were revealed
in the dealings of the OPA with various "czars." Henderson
clashed with the Petroleum Administrator for War over
gasoline rationing, because the OPA wanted to assure an
equal distribution of supplies while Harold Ickes was concerned with maintaining competitive relationships within the
petroleum industry. Again, Henderson quarreled with the

War Food Administrator because each wished to develop plans for food rationing, and each responded to a different constituency—one to rural producers and the other to urban consumers. Even Donald Nelson and Henderson did not always see eye to eye since the WPB feared that certain price restrictions might jeopardize production goals.

To settle these disputes, Roosevelt in October, 1942 set up the Office of Economic Stabilization under James F. Byrnes. In choosing Byrnes—who had represented South Carolina in Congress for twenty-five years—and in locating his office in the White House, the President gave recognition to the political dimensions of economic regulation. While in theory he had authority over the stabilization program, Byrnes speedily assumed jurisdiction over any and all matters relating to the economy, and in May 1943 was put in charge of a new Office of War Mobilization. Byrnes' influence derived from his political stature and the knowledge that he spoke for the President. He never performed actual administrative chores but instead coordinated the policies of other war agencies. His aim, an assistant said, was to "try to get [a] reconciliation of what everybody is doing." Roosevelt came to rely on him heavily, yet as "the official whose duty it is to constantly say 'no' to farmers, wage earners and the people generally," Byrnes could not avoid antagonizing interest groups. "If the price of potatoes is at stake, the Senators and Congressmen from Maine to Florida and to Idaho wish to be heard," he told Roosevelt: "If I approved their requests there could be no stabilization program. When I daily have to refuse their requests, . . . I certainly do not extend my influence with the Congress."[43]

Of course, every time the administration said "no" to one interest, it was saying "yes" to another: when dairy farmers failed to get a price increase, workers paid less for milk and butter; when steel workers were denied wage hikes, farmers could buy tractors more cheaply; and when storeowners were told to freeze prices, housewives got a better break. Naturally, the group that was rebuffed raised the loudest political ruckus, but the task of stabilization was in fact to balance off competing interests in such a manner as to win general approval. In this, the administration achieved substantial success. Not everyone improved his status during the war, and controls sometimes worked unintended hardships—meat rationing led some restaurants to serve buffalo and antelope steaks or even beaverburgers—but most Americans benefitted from wartime controls and were therefore willing to submit to them. Even after goods were skimmed off to fill military needs, most people were better off during the war than ever before.

By mid-1943 the administration had introduced a coherent system of economic controls, but had done so in piecemeal fashion and with a heavy emphasis on willing consent. The hard fist of compulsion had usually been sheathed in the velvet glove of voluntarism. Actually, the contrast between "freedom" in peacetime and "control" in wartime can be exaggerated. War imposed some sort of regimentation on all social classes, but it removed other restrictions that had been felt keenly during the 1930s. Military contracts, for example, released many businessmen from the fetters imposed on their activities by the absence of a market or by the need to show a profit. Similarly, the war freed workers, at least temporarily, from the burden of unemployment. Men who had been turned away at factory gates through the depression years did not resent too bitterly a system of controlled referrals that "forced" them into war jobs. In this sense, the war substituted a different and more elaborate set of controls for those that had existed all along. The new regulations seemed most oppressive to those ordinarily bound by the fewest restraints; they were finally accepted because for most people economic freedom had always been a relative, not an absolute, condition.

CIVIL LIBERTIES AND CONCENTRATION CAMPS

THROUGHOUT WORLD WAR II restrictions upon civil liberty were measured against those imposed in 1917 and 1918. Civil libertarians were haunted by memories of raids on the headquarters of radical groups, mobs forcing immigrants to kiss the flag, 100 percent Americans prying into their neighbors' opinions, and Fourth of July celebrations that included the burning of German language books. Mention of World War I conjured up a host of villains and persecuted heroes: Woodrow Wilson sending Eugene Debs to prison, Judge Kenesaw Mountain Landis dealing out twenty-year sentences to leaders of the Industrial Workers of the World, and Nicholas Murray Butler firing Columbia University professors who did not share his view of the war. Yet there was no reason to suppose that wartime restrictions upon individual liberty would invariably assume old forms. Instead, controls were affected by the nature of the war, the kind of opposition that existed, the type of internal threat perceived, the relative strength of various immigrant groups, the composition of the Supreme Court, and the outlook of the Roosevelt administration. As a result, certain liberties enjoyed unprecedented protection while others were abridged in unimagined ways.

Unlike World War I, which some denounced as a needless war fought to protect the investments of American capitalists and to enrich munition makers, nearly all Americans accepted the necessity of taking part in World War II after Pearl Harbor. While many criticized the conduct of the war, few ever thought the war itself unjust. Most people viewed it as a conflict between the forces of light and darkness, even as "a crusade to save Christendom and Christianity from the Axis powers of paganism." The popular interpretation of the war revolved about a few unambiguous themes: Hitler had seized power in 1933 with an "insane desire to conquer and dominate the whole world;" Italy and Japan served as his "tools;" the Axis powers had pursued a strategy of piecemeal aggression based on "treachery and surprise" with the ultimate goal of conquering the United States; the war was being waged for "the right of all men to live in freedom, decency, and security." Obviously not all Americans accepted this version of world affairs, but the great majority did. "Never in our history," said one observer, "have issues been so clear."[1]

The harshest critics of war have traditionally been radicals, but most left-wingers, particularly the communists, enthusiastically supported the government during World War II. From the moment that Hitler attacked the Soviet Union in June 1941, communists had demanded American intervention against Germany; after Pearl Harbor they subordinated everything to winning a rapid victory. Under the leadership of Earl Browder the party opposed strikes that might impede production, called for the suppression of war critics, and fought side by side with the American Legion for universal military training. A leader of the Young Communist League asserted that "our objective was and is: every YCL member a *Produc-*

tion Commando," and the YCL newspaper ran a comic strip which told the story of a "regular guy who knew his job and gave it all he had . . . and how he gained the inspiring name of PRODUCTION YANK!" In keeping with the spirit of amity Browder asserted that the bourgeoisie contained progressive elements with which the communists could work to bring about peaceful change. "We have to find out how to make the capitalist system work," he said. "National unity can be achieved only through compromise between the conflicting interests, demands and aspirations of various class groupings." In 1944 Browder dissolved the party and replaced it with the looser and more informal Communist Political Association. While membership climbed to 80,000, less likely targets for repression could hardly have been found.

Nothing better illustrated the communists' identification with American nationalism or the government's unwillingness to persecute members of the party than Earl Browder's release from prison early in the war. In March 1941, having been convicted of fraud in connection with the use of a passport, Browder had begun serving a four-year prison term. The severity of the sentence disturbed many civil libertarians, and after Pearl Harbor the communists began a campaign to obtain his release. In March 1942, the Citizens' Committee to Free Earl Browder, a group consisting primarily but not exclusively of communists, sponsored a gathering in Manhattan attended by nearly 1500 delegates. Browder was portrayed as "a true son of the greatness that is America. . . . America—the country of Dorie Miller and Thomas Jefferson; of John Brown and Frederick Douglass and the boys on Bataan Peninsula; . . . the country of General MacArthur and Earl Browder." Separate sessions were held by workers ("Joe Hill would have been able to make a song about the trade union panel"), Negroes ("the spirit of Frederick Douglass and Sojourner Truth hovered over the discussion of the Negro Panel"), and the clergy ("held on Saturday morning in deference to Palm Sunday.") Six weeks later Roosevelt commuted Browder's

sentence with the hope that his action would promote national unity and allay any suspicion that imprisonment had
been politically motivated.[2]

To some extent, communist acceptance of the capitalist way
of life was matched by American admiration for the Soviet
Union. The wartime alliance went far toward muting the hostility Americans had felt as a result of the Nazi-Soviet pact,
the invasion of Finland, and the Russian neutrality agreement
with Japan, a hostility that had to a considerable degree survived Hitler's invasion of the Soviet Union. In 1942 a prominent member of the Daughters of the American Revolution
declared: "Stalin is a university graduate and a man of great
studies. He is a man, who, when he sees a great mistake, admits
it and corrects it. Today in Russia, Communism is practically
non-existent." Similarly, *Life* magazine informed its readers
that Russians were "one hell of a people" who "look like
Americans, dress like Americans and think like Americans;"
the NKVD was brushed off as "a national police similar to
the F.B.I."[3] Of course it would be easy to exaggerate the
strength of this sentiment. Although a widely cited poll in
September 1944 showed that 46 percent of the people thought
that Russia had a government "as good as she could have for
her people," the question was phrased so that a positive response did not necessarily imply approval of the Soviet
system. Even so, most Americans felt good will toward the
Russians during World War II, and relatively few considered
the Soviet Union a menace to American institutions.

With the United States and Russia joined against a common foe, the Roosevelt administration was embarrassed by
proceedings it had instituted against communists in a less ami-
cable era. Consequently, it would have liked to put aside charges
against William Schneiderman, a communist who had been
naturalized in 1927 and stripped of his citizenship in 1939 on
the grounds that as a member of the party he could not have
honestly believed in the principles of the United States constitution when he took the oath of loyalty. But the case had

already reached the Supreme Court, and Chief Justice Harlan Fiske Stone insisted that diplomatic and political considerations not interfere with the Court's jurisdiction. In 1943 the Court restored Schneiderman's citizenship in a 5-3 decision. The majority found that revocation of citizenship on account of a man's ideas would jeopardize the status of all naturalized citizens who had entertained unpopular opinions and that, in any event, the right of revolution had been defended by Jefferson and Lincoln. (Reference to the founding fathers greatly angered Felix Frankfurter, who admonished one colleague: "I think it only fair to state, in view of your general argument, that Uncle Joe Stalin was at least a spiritual coauthor with Jefferson of the Virginia Statute for Religious Freedom.")[4] By affirming that a distinction had to be drawn between advocacy and action, and by insisting that in the absence of an overt act membership in an organization did not necessarily imply acceptance of all its tenets, the Supreme Court ensured that naturalized Americans would not be considered second-class citizens.

Schneiderman was an immigrant as well as a radical, and his case illustrated how far Americans had travelled from the crude antiforeign nativism of World War I. In 1917, when one of every three Americans was either an immigrant or the child of an immigrant, there was a strong fear that war would encourage the emergence of old world loyalties and tear apart the fragile bonds of social cohesion. But during World War II few feared that people of German or Italian descent, unlike the Japanese-Americans, owed a divided allegiance. Closing the gates in 1924 had meant that there were proportionately fewer immigrants in the total population; many others had become more fully assimilated and, partly as a result of the New Deal, had acquired a substantial degree of political power and social influence. Most of the 264,000 German and 599,000 Italian aliens who lived in the United States had children who were citizens and therefore able to exert pressure for fair treatment. Finally, the ideological nature of the war permitted

Americans to make a distinction between fascist leaders on the one hand and the German and Italian people on the other.

In the past Americans had stressed the importance of assimilation and uniformity, but during the 1940s positive values were more often attached to pluralism and ethnic diversity. Patriotic rallies provided an excellent opportunity to assert the nation's commitment to these ideals. When the Illinois War Council staged a celebration at Soldiers Field, 3000 people representing twenty-four different immigrant groups performed folk songs and dances of their native countries. Reporting on a mammoth parade in New York City, newspapers noted that "among the cosmopolitan city crowds, with loyal German and Italian-Americans as well as those of almost every other national and racial strain, was a cross section of patriotic and invincible America." The government did its best to encourage these activities. In the spring of 1942 the Office of Civilian Defense arranged "town meetings for war" in several places; they were not spontaneous but staged with a view toward public relations. A report to the President on their outcome boasted that nearly all groups in the community had participated, including "old Americans and new Americans with traces of their homeland accents."[5]

Tolerance toward persons of foreign ancestry was displayed in a number of ways. Minimal restraints were placed on enemy aliens: they could not travel without permission, were barred from areas near strategic installations, and could not possess arms, short wave receivers or maps. But as the war progressed, restrictions tended to be relaxed and on Columbus Day in 1942 Attorney General Francis Biddle announced that Italian aliens would no longer be classified as "aliens of enemy nationality." Aliens could work in factories with defense contracts if they obtained clearance, and during the war forty applications were approved for every one rejected. The Supreme Court bolstered the legal status of resident aliens when it held in *Ex parte Kawato* that war did not suspend their right to sue for wages or damages incurred on the job. For the most part, citizens of German and Italian descent encountered little public animosity. When a representative of the Italian community testified before a congressional committee the first question was tailored to evoke a sympathetic response: "Tell us about the DiMaggios. Tell us about DiMaggio's father."[6] The contrast with 1917 could sometimes be startling: when a Lutheran minister in Illinois asked permission to conduct services in German he was advised to do so by the governor, who made appropriate references to the help Baron von Steuben had given Washington's army at Valley Forge.

Even if immigrants and aliens were not generally regarded with suspicion, fear of espionage and sabotage was never far from the public consciousness. Slogans such as "A slip of the lip may sink a ship" and "Enemy agents are always near; if you don't talk they won't hear" were plastered on the walls of factories, shipyards and beachfront resorts. Books entitled *Sabotage! The Secret War against America* and *Under Cover* offered an "Amazing Revelation of How Axis Agents and Our Enemies Within Are Now Plotting to Destroy the United States," and warned that "the ghosts of secret destruction are walking again through the American countryside." Works of this kind often followed a pat formula: enemy agents could invariably be recognized by a tell-tale sign ("Young, wealthy, aristocratic, 'handsome Franzi' gave the appearance of being a man utterly fearless and frank. Only a certain narrowness about the eyes suggested the other aspect of the man's character: his evil genius for intrigue") and their diabolical ingenuity knew no limits (" 'If that piece of candy was broken in two . . . and some combustible phosphorus were placed inside it, it would make a very effective, though small, incendiary bomb. But a better bomb . . . could be made from chiclets.' ") The books were filled with photostats of "secret" documents, suggestions that isolationists and conservative members of Congress were in cahoots with the fifth column, and recommendations that all "defeatist propaganda" be banned.[7]

That the fear of Axis subversion was held in check may be attributed in part to the action taken in a spectacular case of attempted sabotage. On June 13, 1942 four German saboteurs were dropped by a submarine off Amagansett Beach on Long Island; a few days later, four others landed at Ponte Vedra Beach in Florida. Each group carried explosives, detonators, forged credentials, and plans of railroad terminals, bridges and factories. But the agents who went ashore on Long Island inadvertently came on a coast guardsman who, after pretending to accept a bribe, reported the incident to the FBI. One of the saboteurs, George John Dasch, was arrested and he in turn revealed enough so that his accomplices could be taken into custody by June 27. The President was determined to act decisively. "This is an absolute parallel of the case of Major Andre in the Revolution and Nathan Hale," he said. "Both of these were hanged." Roosevelt denied the saboteurs access to the civil courts, where proceedings might drag along and where the only provable crime—attempted sabotage— carried a thirty-year sentence. Instead, he arranged a trial by a military commission; unlike a court martial, only two-thirds of the judges could impose the death penalty and the President alone had the power of review. As Biddle informed Roosevelt, a military commission had the "clear power to impose the death penalty in this type of case" and could proceed without being bound by "the technical rules of evidence or procedure." Few considered this arrangement too harsh. One senator thought that "some of the strong-arm boys in the FBI should be allowed to sock the Germans around a little" to obtain information; a government official, conversing with a friend in the Justice Department, suggested, "Let me shoot one of them."[8]

The trial before a special commission of seven officers began on July 8 and lasted only three weeks. While lawyers were assigned for the defense, proceedings were conducted in secret with a brief daily press release the only source of information. On July 29 the Supreme Court met in special session to consider the defendants' plea for a writ of habeus corpus; two days later the Court rejected the claim and found that *Ex parte Milligan*—in which Lincoln's use of military commissions to try civilians in areas remote from combat had been declared unconstitutional—did not apply. Sentence was pronounced on August 3; within a week six of the saboteurs had been executed, one sentenced to life imprisonment and another given thirty years. When the Supreme Court later rendered its formal decision upholding Roosevelt's action, Biddle chortled: "Practically then, the Milligan case is out of the way and should not again plague us."[9] Some constitutional lawyers had reservations about the trial procedure and absence of impartial review, but to the public at large, which had no inkling that the swift arrests were made possible by Dasch's confession, the FBI's work seemed uncanny and the speed with which the affair was handled proved reassuring.

The nearly universal support the war commanded, the commitment to cultural pluralism and the conviction that espionage was under control served to guard the liberties of immigrants and radicals, but other groups received no such protection. From the start, the administration was prepared to curb the freedom of speech of right-wingers. The President even thought that editorials in the Chicago *Tribune* and New York *Daily News* that discredited America's allies might warrant legal action. "The tie-in between the attitude of these papers and the Rome-Berlin broadcasts is something far greater than mere coincidence," he observed. In October 1942 he added: "I would raise the question as to whether freedom of the press is not essentially freedom to print correct news and freedom to criticize the news on the basis of factual truth. I think there is a big distinction between this and freedom to print untrue news."[10] Under the stress of war, Roosevelt preferred to stifle profascist propaganda rather than observe constitutional niceties.

A large number of American liberals endorsed the President's position. Freda Kirchwey, editor of the *Nation*, con-

tended that the traditional civil libertarian position—that all
ideas should receive an open hearing, that people could be
trusted to winnow truth from error, and that the line between
legitimate criticism and sedition was difficult to draw—was
no longer adequate. "The treason press in the United States,"
she announced, "is an integral part of the fascist offensive."
Such newspapers "should be exterminated exactly as if they
were enemy machine gun nests in the Bataan jungle." Even
the American Civil Liberties Union drew back from its traditional position in 1942 and decided not to defend persons
charged with acting on behalf of the enemy unless grave issues
of due process were involved. One veteran crusader for civil
liberties no longer dreaded government agents; "the men in
the FBI today seem to be a clean-cut, intelligent, college-
educated crowd," he remarked, quite unlike the "rough-
necks" formerly employed. Another prominent liberal told
the President: "The *right* of free speech carries with it the
obligation not to use it to aid the enemy. The Russians have
set a damn good example there."[11]

It would be simple to condemn civil libertarians who would
fight to the death only for the rights of those with whom they
agreed. Yet the relativist assumptions upon which they acted
were shared by nearly all Americans, including many of their
critics. The relativist position was advanced most forcefully
by Reinhold Niebuhr who, having moved away from his
earlier Marxist and pacifist position, was concerned with
achieving a "proper balance between freedom and order."
The problem, he thought, was that individuals had an inordinate lust for freedom and communities an inordinate
passion for order. Yet democratic societies could not survive
if they refused to recognize that community was as worth-
while a value as liberty. Niebuhr reasoned that it was impossible to "lay down absolute principles about the preser-
vation of liberty" without reference to the challenges facing
society and the degree of cohesion that could be obtained by
voluntary means. Since the survival of democracy required

national unity, and unity often had to be gotten through coercion, it followed that absolute liberty could not be preserved unless the nation was willing to accept defeat.[12] The debate over freedom of speech in wartime usually took place within the framework Niebuhr established: the question was not whether to draw a line between what could be said and what could not, but where to draw it.

Naturally the line was drawn in a different fashion in the 1940s than it had been during World War I. Far fewer people were prosecuted for sedition under Roosevelt than under Wilson, in part because local United States attorneys were not permitted to bring charges without Biddle's personal approval. The government had more luck in curbing antiwar propaganda when it relied on informal pressure than when it resorted to jury trial or when its efforts were subject to scrutiny by the Supreme Court. Moreover, the targets of attempted censorship were no longer romantic rebels such as Eugene Debs and the Wobblies, but would-be fuehrers and anti-Semites. Several of these themes are illustrated by the successful attempt to silence Father Charles Coughlin, the putative sedition trial of native fascists, and the fate of various measures taken against friends of the Nazi cause.

The Reverend Charles E. Coughlin, who had attracted a vast radio following during the depression, edged ever closer to a fascist position in the 1940s. While he could no longer obtain air time, his magazine *Social Justice* still reached 200,000 subscribers. In September 1941 it declared: "The Jew should retire from the field of politics and government. He has no more business in that sphere than has a pig in a china shop."[13] After Pearl Harbor Coughlin charged in effect that Jews and communists had tricked America into the war. In April 1942, citing the Espionage Act of 1917, Biddle asked the Postmaster-General to suspend the second-class mailing privileges of *Social Justice* because it echoed the enemy's line and could damage troop morale. Coughlin was willing to testify before a grand jury, but the last thing Biddle wanted was a sedition trial that might transform Coughlin into a martyr for Catholics and isolationists. The administration much preferred to maneuver behind the scenes. Biddle asked Leo T. Crowley, a prominent lay Catholic, to explain the situation to Archbishop Edward Mooney of Detroit; within three days Mooney ordered Coughlin to be silent and he complied. In the end the very source of Coughlin's strength—the immunity to outside pressure afforded by his position in the church—led to his downfall.

Whatever doubts Biddle had entertained about trying Coughlin in public were substantiated by the sedition trial of 1944. In July 1942, egged on by the president, Biddle indicted twenty-six "native fascists"—including Gerald B. Winrod, Elizabeth Dilling, and Gerald L. K. Smith—for sedition under the Espionage Act of 1917 and the Smith Act of 1940. The latter, which had originally been aimed at communists and aliens, made it a crime to conspire to advocate the violent overthrow of the government even if no overt act was committed. Although it could very easily be shown that the defendants had, in the prosecutor's words, "engaged in a mass propaganda campaign spreading hatred against the Jews, prejudice against the Negroes, fear of the communists and distrust of our public officials," it was nearly impossible to prove that they had conspired with one another and with the Germans, or that their intent had been to cause insubordination in the armed forces. In April 1944, after two more indictments were issued, the trial finally began in Washington. It dragged on for more than seven months, with the defendants acting in an unruly way, lawyers screaming at each other and the courtroom in tumult. "To win easy convictions," one of the defendants later snapped, "the government should have staged the Trial in the Bronx or on the East Side of Manhattan" and packed the jury with "readers of *New Masses, P.M.,* . . . or the B'nai B'rith's *Messenger.*"[14] By the end of the year the trial had become a source of embarrassment. After the judge died in November, the administration moved for dismissal; no convictions were obtained.

In several instances the Supreme Court thwarted attempts to handcuff those who openly or covertly sided with the enemy. By 1942 Roosevelt had appointed seven of the nine justices and several of them—particularly Frank Murphy, Hugo Black and William O. Douglas—had strong libertarian inclinations. In 1943 the Court (with, however, Douglas and Black dissenting) overturned the conviction of George Sylvester Viereck who, in registering as a foreign agent, had reported his activities on behalf of Germany but not those undertaken on his own initiative. The majority also reprimanded the prosecutor, whose inflammatory charge to the jury had been intended to stir up war hysteria. A year later, in the Baumgartner case, the Court unanimously set aside the denaturalization of a German-born citizen charged with continued loyalty to the Third Reich on the grounds that his 1932 oath of allegiance to the United States had not been proven fraudulent. Similarly, the Court decided in favor of Hartzel, a fascist sympathizer whose writings were streaked with Anglophobia, anti-Semitism and hatred of Roosevelt. In the absence of clear evidence that his intention was to foster dissention among servicemen, five justices held that "an American citizen has the right to discuss these matters either by temperate reasoning or by immoderate and vicious invective."[15] Finally, in 1945 the Court reversed the conviction of the leaders of the German-American Bund who had been charged with counseling resistance to the Selective Service Act. Even though these cases were often resolved on narrow procedural grounds and never required overriding an act of Congress, the decisions threw a protective mantle around freedom of expression.

Although it proved difficult to muzzle critics on the right, the government successfully instituted loyalty tests for federal job holders. The Hatch Act of 1939 had sought to exclude from federal employment anyone who belonged to an organization advocating the overthrow of the government, and during the war years, as the government payroll expanded, the Civil Service Commission stepped up the activities of its loyalty board. From 1940 to 1944, the number of agents climbed from 80 to 755; 273,500 individuals were investigated of whom 1180 were found to be ineligible. On occasion, disloyalty could be confused with nonconformity. In November 1943 the commission cautioned its investigators not to ask an applicant whether he read radical periodicals, attended racially integrated meetings or belonged to the ACLU, and added: "You are not investigating whether his views are unorthodox or do not conform with those of the majority of the people." Even so, investigations into the political beliefs of job applicants became a routine part of the examining process.

Early in 1943, disturbed by charges that government agencies were honeycombed with subversives, Roosevelt created the Interdepartmental Committee on Employee Investigations. The committee investigated those who advocated, or belonged to organizations that advocated, the violent overthrow of the government. (The Department of Justice listed the Communist Party, the German-American Bund and the Silver Shirt Legion as such organizations.) In entering uncharted waters the committee set several precedents: it accepted circumstantial as well as direct evidence concerning employee loyalty; it regarded membership in "fellow-travelling" organizations "as sufficient to warrant investigation of employees by the Federal Bureau of Investigation" although as insufficient in itself to cause dismissal; it decided that in cases involving past membership or advocacy, "unless casual and remote in time," the burden of proof would be on the employee who contended he had changed his opinions "to make a complete revelation of the facts asserted by him in support of the contention." The committee, however, adopted several procedural safeguards: it held formal hearings, insisted on written charges, provided adequate time for preparation of a defense, and granted the accused the right to be represented by counsel and to introduce evidence in his own behalf. Finally, the committee had power only to make recommendations; action in each instance was left to the discretion of the department involved.[16]

Just as the administration had tried to curb the advocacy of certain ideas, so it took measures to regulate the kinds of information generally available to the public; again, its efforts met with mixed results. In December 1941 the President asked Byron Price, a news editor for the Associated Press, to head the Office of Censorship. Price not only examined all communications between the United States and other countries, but also issued a Code of Wartime Practices to which publishers and broadcasters were asked to adhere. These codes banned news concerning troop movements, ship landings, and battle casualties and restricted certain radio broadcasts—such as man-on-the-street interviews, musical request shows and lost-and-found notices—that could be used to transmit coded messages. (One official even suspected that "the Star Spangled Banner can be played in a manner to convey a message from someone in Kansas City to someone in Mexico.") To prevent Germany from learning about weather patterns, newspapers printed only brief official forecasts; no radio bulletins—except storm warnings—were permitted. The distinction Price drew between the right to criticize the government and freedom "to be criminally careless with military information" seemed reasonable to most Americans and gave rise to little resentment.[17]

Persuaded that propaganda was hardly less important than censorship, Roosevelt set up an Office of War Information in June 1942 to explain government policies to the public and serve as liaison between the communications media and Washington. The OWI differed from its First World War counterpart, the Committee on Public Information, in important respects. Unlike the CPI which had supervised censorship as well as propaganda, the OWI had no jurisdiction over censorship and even lacked authority over several autonomous information agencies. Nor did OWI director Elmer Davis always receive presidential support in his efforts to extract information from the Army, Navy or State Department. After his first encounter with Secretary of War Stimson, Davis sensed that he had gotten "the polite brush-off."[18] The controversies that swirled about the OWI revealed some of the snags wartime propaganda encountered, the techniques favored to mold public opinion, and the limitations imposed on such programs by political rivalries.

The instinctive American aversion to propaganda—with its implied manipulation of the many by the few for unworthy purposes—had been strengthened by a reaction against the rhetorical excesses of 1917 and 1918. Consequently, the Roosevelt administration shunned the word "propaganda" and spoke instead of providing "information" or "facts and figures." Throughout the war, Elmer Davis insisted that his task was primarily educational and that he could "tell the truth and nothing but the truth" because "the truth is on our side." Yet this view left a good deal unclear, for at the very least the choice of which facts to play up and which to pass over was itself a decision that determined what the public would know. Archibald MacLeish, who directed the Office of Facts and Figures prior to Davis' appointment, conceded as much when he offered to "supply the country with factual information to demonstrate the necessity of decisions taken or proposed and the advisability of policies now adopted or proposed for adoption in the near future."[19] Although OWI steered away from blatant appeals, its aim resembled that of the propagandist: to inspire right-thinking and acceptable forms of behavior.

This could be accomplished in rather different ways. A group of liberal intellectuals within OWI reasoned that the agency should avoid oversimplification and put its faith in people's ability to make subtle distinctions. They complained that some radio announcements were "so phony and so hoked up that they stink violently," that there was "too God-damned much cleverness, sleight of hand . . . and too God-damned little straight talking over the table at an adult public."[20] But the OWI also employed advertising executives eager to apply their own experience in selling the war. They warned against a "tendency to keep the psychological war on a plane far above the understanding of the people;" while "it would be wonderful indeed if the psychological war would be fought on an intellectual basis," most Americans "unfortunately are not so educated. . . . We must state the truth in terms that will be understood by all levels of intelligence."[21] As this viewpoint came to prevail, liberals grew more disenchanted and their patience seemed to give out when a new administrator wanted to replace a Ben Shahn poster with one by Norman Rockwell. In the spring of 1943 many of the writers resigned, protesting that OWI had come under the domination of "high-pressure promoters who prefer slick salesmanship to honest information."[22] The dispute had centered largely on how to package information rather than on what information to provide, but victory went to those skilled in promotional techniques.

At the same time as liberals charged that OWI had fallen victim to business domination, conservatives in Congress regarded it as a propaganda vehicle for the Roosevelt administration. The most well-meaning statement offended some group or other. An OWI pamphlet suggesting the wisdom of a broadly-based system of withholding taxes antagonized certain legislators. Another pamphlet, which described the Negro's contribution to the war, was assailed by black leaders who detected an inference that Negroes were insufficiently patriotic, and by southern Democrats who considered it too complimentary and "filled with Negro pictures." Republicans expressed horror at a description of Roosevelt as "a visionary whose social and economic philosophies once before saved his country in a crisis."[23] Some Democratic politicians did, in fact, hope that the agency would serve a partisan purpose. One member of the Democratic National Committee thought that "when a sore spot develops any place in the country, OWI should, immediately, get on the job with counterpropaganda, so that the sore does not spread over the entire country." But fears that the agency would evolve into a New Deal propaganda bureau were not justified.²⁴ Nevertheless, congressional suspicion ran so deep that in 1943 the House voted to eliminate the domestic branch of OWI altogether; it was rescued in the Senate, but with its allocation reduced so sharply that its program was severely curtailed.

To an even greater extent than propaganda or censorship, the treatment accorded conscientious objectors suggests the manner in which personal liberties were affected by the nature of the war, the outlook of the administration and the position of the courts. Throughout the war the measuring stick against which claims of conscience were held was the Selective Service Act of 1940, which provided that no one was to serve as a combatant who "by reason of religious training and belief, is conscientiously opposed to participation in war in any form." An individual who obtained classification as a conscientious objector from his draft board could be assigned to noncombatant duties, or if he objected to military service of any kind, to "work of national importance under civilian direction." This arrangement, however, fell short of what pacifist groups had proposed for it covered only religious objectors, did not permit total exemption for those who could not in good conscience register for the draft, and left decisions to the draft board rather than some independent tribunal. Given the decentralized nature of the selective service system, local boards sometimes adopted wildly disparate standards for granting conscientious objector status.

In addition, the Selective Service Act left two questions unresolved: what constituted religious belief? and what provisions would be made for work of national importance? In each instance the law was interpreted so as to narrow the rights of objectors. The director of selective service in 1940, Dr. Clarence Dykstra, originally ruled that religious belief might be construed to include purely moral considerations, and the U.S. Circuit Court of Appeals later upheld this view when it defined religion as a "response to an inward mentor, call it conscience or God." But these decisions did not bind Dykstra's successor, General Louis B. Hershey. In March 1942 he asserted that religious belief, far from consisting merely of ethical imperatives, "contemplates recognition of some source of all existence, which, whatever the type of conception, is Divine because it is the Source of all things." Similarly, arrangements for civilian service worked out less advantageously than had been anticipated. In September 1940 selective service looked with favor upon a plan offered by the pacifist churches whereby objectors could work in government camps and receive military pay if they desired. But when the President expressed "instant and aggressive opposition to the plan," the churches agreed to shoulder the financial burden and permit selective service to set camp policy. Under the system of civilian public service established in February 1941, no wages were paid to those in the camps.[25]

The options available to conscientious objectors depended on the nature of their opposition to the war. Most objectors belonged to one of the three historic peace churches—Quaker, Mennonite and Church of the Brethren. A surprisingly large number of them put aside religious scruples altogether to enter the military (three of four Quakers did not even seek exemption) and most others accepted service as noncombatants. Perhaps 25,000 men served in this fashion and suffered no penalty; while at first they performed a variety of tasks, after 1943 they were limited to the medical corps. Those religious objectors who refused to put on a uniform were consigned to civilian public service camps. All told, 11,950 men took this path. They devoted much of their time to forestry and conservation, building roads, clearing trails, fighting forest fires, and digging irrigation ditches. Others worked in mental hospitals or helped bring public health facilities to depressed rural areas. About 500 objectors, who volunteered to be subjects of medical experiments, allowed themselves to be infested with lice or bitten by mosquitos to test cures for typhus or malaria.

While civilian public service satisfied some objectors, others came to despise the system. They deplored the control over camp discipline exerted by the military, and complained of work projects that were demeaning and often failed to utilize their skills. "While people live on inadequate diets and in tumbled-down shacks, we build picnic groves. While guns shatter homes, we landscape the park roadway," grumbled one objector. Worse yet, certain projects appeared to have military implications in that they aided war production, and the camp system seemed shot through with injustice. Since the men were not paid, and their families received no benefits in case of accident, the government seemed to be exacting a heavy price from those who adhered to religious conviction. Even when objectors were allowed to work outside the camps, the comptroller-general ruled that their wages had to be turned over to the government. "For the government to require unrequited service smacks of slavery to the state and is a bad precedent in these times," Norman Thomas informed the President.[26]

But the inequities of civilian public service do not fully explain this discontent. Precisely because the system, for all its shortcomings, conferred privileges upon conscientious objectors, it diluted the purity of their witness against war. In the past opponents of war had faced persecution or prison. In World War II many of them were absorbed by the apparatus of the state. Then too, since total war had obliterated much of the distinction between civilian and military work, many camp projects did in truth help the United States carry on the war. As the *Christian Century* noted, the government had "arranged the situation so as to becloud and largely nullify the witness 'against war' which the conscientious objector desires to make by undergoing suffering and social stigma;" civilian service so reduced the objector's burden "that his witness has been rendered ambiguous." While real grievances surely existed and some found civilian service rewarding, much of the unhappiness derived from the recognition that, as a group of West Coast objectors confessed, the system "compromised our position as pacifists."[27]

If civilian public service eroded certain pacifist principles, it posed an even more cruel dilemma for the peace churches. Having agreed to collaborate with the government in administering the camps, the churches found it necessary to enforce discipline even when this required acting in disagreeable ways. Despite a commitment to racial equality, community pressure in the South led the churches to accept segregated camps; in 1944 the Mennonites even operated a public health unit in Mississippi for whites only. When several men disobeyed selective service regulations and left camp to attend a conference in Chicago, the religious agencies agreed to consider them AWOL, even though prescribing punishment for an act of conscience contradicted their professed belief. When permission was finally granted for some men to work away from the camps, the religious bodies had to determine who had been "cooperative" and deserved the opportunity. If a strong case could be made for acceptance of these responsibilities—for otherwise the system might have been even more harsh—the churches nevertheless sacrificed much of their autonomy and freedom to act on moral grounds. Taking up the task of ameliorating evil in the world was not without cost.

To demonstrate their dissatisfaction, some objectors resorted to walkouts, slowdowns or even strikes. But the attempt to apply Ghandian tactics of nonviolent resistance served a mainly symbolic purpose: while the government could not force men to "behave themselves and perform an adequate days work," neither could the resisters obtain more favorable policies respecting military control, work projects, wages or family allowances. Pressure to preserve the system was simply too strong. Government officials at all levels were primarily concerned with public morale, and believed that civilian public service must not come to be regarded as a haven for draft dodgers. Indeed, forestry and conservation were favored precisely because they insulated the objector from public attention. Some congressmen called for even sterner measures, and veterans' groups groaned that "thousands of young 'men' . . . are being mollycoddled by 'sob-sisters' of the Selective Service System and State officials."[28] In rejecting a suggestion that Roosevelt speak on the rights of dissenters, a Presidential aide noted: "Only those interested in religious minorities or holding membership in them would be pleased by anything the President might say. The great majority of people, I fear, would be displeased."[29]

Still another stumbling block in the way of a more generous policy was the narrow manner in which the State Department defined national interest. In 1941 the Quakers recommended sending some conscientious objectors to Mexico to help rebuild towns destroyed by an earthquake. Although the Mexican government welcomed the Friends' offer, the State Department vetoed the proposal on the grounds that objectors symbolized national disunity and their presence would be exploited by German propagandists. "At the very moment we are trying to convince our neighbors in the other American republics that national unity exists in the United States," said Under-Secretary of State Sumner Welles (upon whom Roosevelt leaned heavily for advice on Latin American matters), "the effect in the other American Republics of our sending to their countries Americans who are not willing to fight for their country would not be in the interest of this Government."[30] Few questioned the assumption that the needs of the government took precedence over the individual's desire to perform useful service. Some objectors were permitted to work off camp grounds, but hopes for a program of foreign assistance were shattered.

For the most part, the Supreme Court refused to intercede in behalf of conscientious objectors. Not until January 1944 did the Court consider the matter of draft classification and then it held that judicial review of an individual's status could not take place until after notice of induction had been served, for otherwise litigation might disrupt the operation of the draft. Furthermore, in the case of Clyde Summers, the Court indicated that pacifists forfeited certain liberties in wartime.

Summers was a religious objector who was denied admission to the Illinois bar on the grounds that his opposition to war meant he could not live up to an oath to defend the constitution. In June 1945 the justices found by a vote of 5-4 that Summers had not been denied rights guaranteed by the Fourteenth Amendment. The decision came too late to have much effect, and only in rare instances did states move to exclude conscientious objectors from licensed professions or public employment.

Of course not everyone who claimed to be an objector was classified as such. Those who refused to register for the draft, whose objection to war rested on political grounds, or whose claim to religious opposition was not allowed, were imprisoned. Some 5,500 men went to jail, more than three-fourths of them Jehovah's Witnesses. Since Witnesses did not reject the use of force in all situations but eagerly awaited the final battle of Armageddon, draft boards consistently refused to honor their request to be granted ministerial exemption so that they might continue to preach God's word. Although most religious objectors believed that confinement gave adequate testimony to their unwillingness to cooperate with the war-making state, some thought that the struggle for social justice should go on behind prison walls. They engaged in work stoppages and hunger strikes to protest racial segregation, censorship of mail and parole restrictions. At Danbury prison, eighteen objectors who went on strike were confined to their cells for four months but finally caused the warden to eliminate Jim Crow dining facilities.

Even while Jehovah's Witnesses suffered under the draft, their right to worship as they pleased received unusual protection. In 1940 the Supreme Court had decided, in *Minersville School District v. Gobitis*, that schoolchildren could be required to salute the flag as a condition of attendance even if their religious beliefs prohibited honoring a secular symbol. "National unity is the basis of national security," reasoned Felix Frankfurter, and only Justice Stone dissented from this view. Within a short time several members of the Court had a change of heart. In 1942 the Court narrowly upheld a local ordinance forcing Witnesses to pay a license tax on the sale of their publications, but three dissenting justices confessed that they regretted *Gobitis* and were ready to reverse it. Then, in June 1943 the Court struck down the compulsory flag salute in *West Virginia State Board of Education v. Barnette* by a 6-3 margin. "Words uttered under coercion are proof of loyalty to nothing but self-interest," affirmed Hugo Black. "Neither our domestic tranquility in peace nor our martial effort in war depend on compelling little children to participate in a ceremony which ends in nothing for them but· a fear of spiritual condemnation."[31]

In 1944, when Attorney General Biddle told Roosevelt that "all the conscientious objectors to whom I have talked . . . agree that the system is far better handled than during the last war," he expressed a commonly held view and one that had much truth to it.[32] The pacifist press was allowed to criticize government policy, religious minorities found an ally against conformist pressure in the Supreme Court, and mob violence against dissenters seldom occurred. Some religious objectors undertook satisfying work in civilian public service. On the other hand, civilian service proved needlessly restrictive and no safeguards were provided for many opponents of the war. Nearly three times as many conscientious objectors were imprisoned, in proportion to those conscripted, as in the First World War. Individual conscience could be a casualty of the cooptive as well as the coercive power of the state: as civilian public service revealed, freedom not to serve in the armed forces could prove debilitating to the pacifist position.

Restraints imposed upon conscientious objectors were trivial compared with those placed upon Japanese-Americans. Unlike the objector, who had come to his position voluntarily and whose family underwent no direct persecution, Japanese men and women of all ages were victimized solely on account of ancestry. More than 110,000 people, two-thirds of them citizens, were forced to sacrifice their homes and businesses in 1942 and were herded into relocation centers hastily constructed in barren, desolate spots. Families found themselves crowded into one-room wooden barracks in camps enclosed by barbed wire and patrolled by armed guards. No individual had been charged with a crime; instead, a judgment of collective racial guilt had been made. Japanese-Americans were stripped of their freedom in a gradual way. At the outset, no one intended to build concentration camps; but given the political, military and racial assumptions upon which government officials acted, every step led logically toward that solution.

One fundamental decision was to treat Japanese aliens differently from German and Italian aliens. At first the government made no such distinction: travel restrictions applied to all persons of enemy nationality, and General John DeWitt, who headed the Western Defense Command, wished to treat all aliens with equal severity. In this instance civilian officials overruled DeWitt. Since Germans and Italians were numerous, politically influential, well assimilated and widely dispersed, Roosevelt and Biddle believed that it would be unwise to take action against them. "American citizens with German and Italian names are also worried [about evacuation]," Roosevelt said, "I am inclined to think this may have a bad effect on morale."[33] Japanese-Americans, however, were peculiarly vulnerable: they formed a relatively small group, were concentrated on the West Coast and could easily be singled out. Moreover, they lacked political power because the foreign-born Japanese (Issei) who had migrated before 1924 were barred from citizenship and most of their children—although born in the United States and therefore citizens (Nisei)—were too young to vote. Nor had the Japanese moved into occupations vital to national defense. Nearly four of every ten worked on small vegetable farms, and the rest engaged in domestic service or in businesses catering to a Japanese clientele. Discrimination had kept most out of professional, white collar or skilled blue-collar jobs. As a powerless and poorly assimilated group, Japanese-Americans lacked any shield.

Having placed the 47,000 Issei in a separate category, the government next widened the net to include 80,000 American citizens of Japanese ancestry as well. Military and civilian officials, most of whom recognized the revolutionary implications of what they were doing and conceded privately that it violated constitutional principle, came to this position with some difficulty. Late in December DeWitt reasoned that "if we go ahead and arrest the 93,000 Japanese, native born and foreign born, we are going to have an awful job on our hands and are very liable to alienate the loyal Japanese. . . . An American citizen, after all, is an American citizen."[34] Secretary of War Stimson believed that "we can not discriminate among our citizens on the ground of racial origin" for to do so would "make a tremendous hole in our constitutional system." Nevertheless, by mid-February the War Department had decided to press for a program covering "all persons of Japanese ancestry."[35]

What had once seemed unthinkable had suddenly become essential. By February General DeWitt and his superiors in the War Department had concluded that racial bonds were more important than nationality. "In the war in which we are now engaged racial affinities are not severed by migration. The Japanese race is an enemy race," DeWitt asserted. "To conclude otherwise is to expect that children born of white parents on Japanese soil sever all racial affinity and become loyal Japanese subjects, ready to fight and, if necessary to die for Japan in a war against the nation of their parents."[36] Furthermore, the Army assumed that it was impossible to tell a loyal Japanese-American from one who was disloyal. Earl Warren, Attorney General of California, expressed much the same view: "We believe that when we are dealing with the Caucasian race we have methods that will test the loyalty of them. . . . But when we deal with the Japanese we are in an entirely different field and we cannot form any opinion that we believe to be sound." Secretary Stimson confessed that the "racial characteristics" of Japanese-Americans required treating citizens and aliens alike.[37] An American citizen, apparently, was not necessarily a loyal American citizen.

Just as considerations of race and politics served to set Japanese-Americans apart, so they influenced the decision for relocation. At first the military preferred exclusion from certain strategic areas to total evacuation. "I'm only concerned with getting them away from around these aircraft factories and other places," DeWitt said.[38] But pressure to rid the coast of all Japanese-Americans proved irresistible. Various nativist groups had long agitated for exclusion and realized, as one Native Son of the Golden West put it, that "this is our time to get things done that we have been trying to get done for a quarter of a century." Some agricultural interests and small businessmens' associations also stood to gain from removal. "Those who regard Japanese as economic competitors tend to be more opposed to them," concluded one public opinion survey.[39] In the Capital, congressmen from California, Oregon and Washington who favored exclusion hounded the War Department. Subjected to these pressures, some military officials in Washington came to consider DeWitt overly cautious and indifferent to "the necessary cold-bloodedness of war."[40]

The Army, however, justified evacuation on the grounds of military necessity. According to DeWitt's report: "The continued presence of a large, unassimilated, tightly knit racial group, bound to an enemy nation by strong ties of race, culture, custom and religion along a frontier vulnerable to attack constituted a menace which had to be dealt with."[41] Even the absence of any overt act of sabotage caused suspicion, for it was taken as proof that plans had been carefully worked out and an "invisible deadline" was drawing near. Yet while the threat of Japanese forays against the West Coast was not in fact removed until after the Battle of Midway in June 1942, and while the supposition that all Japanese-

Americans were potential fifth columnists drew strength from a report on Pearl Harbor that erroneously ascribed American losses to espionage, the Army's decision to relocate all Japanese resulted as much from the clamor of pressure groups as from an appraisal of military risk. "There's a tremendous volume of public opinion now developing against the Japanese of all classes," DeWitt reported late in January. "As a matter of fact, it's not being instigated or developed by people who are not thinking but by the best people of California."[42]

Even so, the argument from military necessity swept all before it. President Roosevelt, concerned both with the possibility of espionage and public opinion on the coast, supported the War Department to the hilt. On February 11 Stimson consulted with Roosevelt and "fortunately found that he was very vigorous about it and [he] told me to go ahead on the line that I had myself thought the best."[43] The Justice Department, which had all along denied the necessity for mass evacuation, refused to block a military program. Attorney General Biddle—who had been charged with treating the Japanese "with all the severity of Lord Fauntleroy playing squat tag with his maiden aunt"—did not approve of the Army's decision but was unwilling to challenge it, especially in view of his personal admiration for Stimson, the President's wishes, and the readiness with which several of his subordinates embraced the military solution.[44] Congress also took the generals at their word and passed with literally no debate legislation that the military requested. Even some Japanese-Americans, in a futile attempt to demonstrate their patriotism, reluctantly expressed a willingness to relocate if military requirements so dictated.

By February 17 representatives of the Army and Justice Department had agreed to evacuate all Japanese-Americans from the West Coast, and two days later the President authorized Stimson to prescribe an area that would be off limits. Yet while the government had decided to treat the Issei differently from other aliens, to include the Nisei in the program, and to require evacuation of the entire coast, the policy was only half complete. It was still necessary to determine whether the evacuees could settle in the interior, and if not, what arrangements would be made for detaining them and what criteria would be used in setting them free. None of these matters had as yet been settled. Stimson noted of a cabinet meeting on February 27 that "there was general confusion around the table arising from the fact that nobody had realized how big it was, nobody wanted to take care of the evacuees, and the general weight and complication of the problem."[45]

Early in March the War Department ordered Japanese-Americans living in the western part of California, Oregon and Washington to leave. Within four weeks about 9,000 persons had moved to wherever they could find work in the interior; then the Army abruptly slammed the door. Officials in other western states had protested bitterly against serving as a "dumping ground for enemy aliens" and many people wrongly assumed that the Japanese-Americans were fugitives. Residents of Denver or Laramie saw little reason to welcome people whom the government considered too dangerous to remain in San Francisco or Los Angeles. "A good solution to the Jap problem," announced the Governor of Idaho, "would be to send them all back to Japan, then sink the island. They live like rats, breed like rats and act like rats." Milton Eisenhower, who directed the newly created War Relocation Authority, admitted that public antagonism made free settlement impossible. "Demands arose that the Federal Government take all people of Japanese descent into custody, surround them with troops, prevent them from buying land, and return them to their former homes at the close of the war," Eisenhower later reported. "Violence was threatened. Japanese were arrested. Mass meetings that warned of trouble were held."[46]

Accordingly, the Army began transporting Japanese-Americans to assembly centers, thrown up at race tracks and fairgrounds, where they were confined pending transfer to more permanent facilities. Evacuees took only some clothing, bedding and utensils. "No pets of any kind will be permitted," stated the order. "No personal items and no household goods will be shipped to the Assembly Center." Although the government offered to store personal property, it could not be insured and most evacuees sold their possessions for whatever they could get. In order to carry out evacuation in "a truly American way," the Army decided not to split up families or communities "where this could be avoided." Assembly centers functioned only on a provisional basis; they permitted rapid evacuation and served the further purpose of "acclimating the evacuees to the group life of a center in their own climatic region." Military officials took particular pride in their accomplishment, pointing out that "no precedents existed in American life" and "European precedents were unsatisfactory for many reasons." By June 1942 more than 100,000 persons had been evacuated.[47]

But the character of the relocation centers to which they would be sent was as yet undetermined. Milton Eisenhower envisioned "small C.C.C. sort of work camps" carrying out useful projects around the country, but abandoned this idea when state officials demanded confinement of the evacuees and the Army indicated that guards could be provided only for large clusters of people.[48] Accordingly, the War Relocation Authority erected ten camps, each accomodating 10-12,000 persons, in seven western states. By September nearly all the evacuees had moved to these sites. A typical camp contained wooden barracks covered with tar paper, each having several one-room apartments—furnished with army cots, blankets and a light bulb—to which each family or group of unrelated individuals was assigned. There were communal toilet, bathing, laundry and dining facilities. Schools were eventually opened, recreational areas cleared and religious worship (except for Shintoism) permitted, yet plans for making each camp economically self-sufficient fell through. The evacuees grew some of their own food and undertook small-scale manufacturing projects, but the land was too arid, the difficulty of obtaining scarce equipment too great, the unwillingness to compete with private industry too strong, and the wage scale of $12-19 a month too inflexible to permit much success. Even though the WRA encouraged the formation of community government to enforce daily regulations it had little power and less prestige since the project director could override it at any time.

The War Relocation Authority did not at first expect to detain all evacuees for the duration of the war. Dillon Myer, a former official in the Department of Agriculture who replaced Milton Eisenhower as director in June 1942, believed that the relocation centers were "temporary wayside stations" which offered a form of protective custody. They were "not so-called concentration centers but simply places for people to live until they become adjusted." Nevertheless, since the public would greet the release of potentially disloyal Japanese-Americans with hostility, the WRA concluded that it would be unwise to release anyone before "segregating those who may be dangerous to internal security."[49] By 1943 the agency had devised a system of granting permanent leave that placed the burden of proof on the evacuee. To gain his freedom, a Japanese-American against whom no evidence of disloyalty existed had to prove that he had a job waiting away from the coast, show that he would find acceptance in the community, and promise to notify the WRA of any change of address. During 1943 the WRA granted some 17,000 such leaves; by the end of 1944 a total of 35,000 evacuees, most of them youthful Nisei, had left the camps.

Yet even these mild concessions exposed the War Relocation Authority to criticism. Many congressmen and War Department officials favored a harder line toward the evacuees, and made much of two occurrences—a series of riots in the centers and the refusal of many evacuees to forswear loyalty to Japan. The most serious riot erupted in December 1942 at Camp Manzanar in California after several evacuees had beaten up a man they considered an informer and one of the alleged assailants had been arrested. When a large crowd demanded his release and taunted the soldiers called to restore order, shots were fired, gas grenades thrown and two Japanese youths killed. At about the same time, many evacuees proved unwilling to renounce allegiance to Japan. In February 1943 the War Department sought to register evacuees with a view toward enlistment. A questionnaire, which asked whether one renounced allegiance to the Japanese emperor, was given not only to citizens but to Issei who were barred from American citizenship and justifiably feared that they might be left with no nationality if they answered in the affirmative. Of 75,000 who replied, 8,700 either refused to give up allegiance to the emperor or somehow qualified their answer. These included one of every four male Nisei of draft age, who did not believe that their one right as American citizens should be that of military service.

The permanent leave policy, together with the riots and response to the questionnaire, provided ammunition for politicians eager to denounce the War Relocation Authority. "We are treating these Japanese like highly preferred American citizens instead of members of an enemy nation," charged one Republican. "These centers are a Japanese W.P.A. with gilded trimmings. Every possible service is provided in the best New Deal style. No group of Americans receive the complete free public services granted to these orientals."[50] A Democratic senator from Washington thought it suicidal to release a Japanese-American who seemed trustworthy. "You know, a Jap would be an awfully good dog right up to the point that he can pull something. . . . They might be able to go out some place and blow up maybe Coulee Dam or Bonneville, or maybe some large munitions plant."[51] Moreover, six states—Texas, Arkansas, Utah, Wyoming, Arizona and California—took steps to frighten away potential Japanese-American emigrants by limiting their right to vote, own land or obtain certain commercial licenses.

Critics of WRA also called for the segregation of "disloyal" evacuees and, as in the past, a policy that had at first seemed inconceivable gradually gained acceptance. As early as December 1942 DeWitt urged the WRA to segregate, without notification, all "potentially dangerous" evacuees, and warned the agency to prepare for "probable rioting and consequent bloodshed." WRA officials coldly rejected a scheme that would "treat the evacuees as though they were so many blocks of wood, with complete disregard of the rights and liberties, not to mention the fears and sensibilities, they share with other human beings." DeWitt's plan seemed "much more compatible with the Nazi psychology of our enemies than with the democratic psychology we are fighting for."[52] But by July 1943, after a Senate resolution had called for segregation, the WRA capitulated. In the fall those evacuees who had requested repatriation to Japan, who had refused to disclaim loyalty to the emperor, or who had suspicious records were shipped to Tule Lake in California. About two-thirds of the 18,500 segregants were American citizens, but many, particularly those who had received their education in Japan in the 1930s, responded to segregation by proclaiming their adherence to the Japanese way of life. Later, after Congress enabled the Nisei to renounce their citizenship by written request, some 8,000 Japanese-Americans, most of whom had been confined at Tule Lake, left for Japan.

By the spring of 1944 the Roosevelt administration recognized that there was no longer military justification for excluding Japanese-Americans from the West Coast, but political considerations still had to be taken into account. In May Stimson informed the President that terminating the program "would make a row on the California coast" and suggested that if riots against returning evacuees took place Japan might retaliate against American prisoners. In June Roosevelt decided against doing anything "drastic or sudden." He reasoned that "the whole problem, for the sake of internal quiet, should be handled gradually," and added that "a great method of avoiding public outcry" would be to distribute one or two Japanese-American families to each county in the United States. Finally, after Roosevelt's re-election, the administration concluded that "it was time to let them loose."[53] In December the exclusion order was rescinded and on January 20, 1945 nearly all Japanese-Americans in the relocation centers were allowed to leave at will. A policy of individual exclusion, which barred about 5,000 evacuees from the coast, remained in effect.

The relocation centers, however, could not be so easily dismantled. A substantial number of evacuees had come to look upon the camps as a refuge and were afraid to leave without some assurance that they could find a place to live and would be protected from mob violence. The government found that people whose pattern of life had been torn to shreds had incurred deep psychological damage and could not be expected to pick up again as if nothing had happened. Nevertheless, the camps had already cost $250 million and the expense could no longer be justified. In June 1945 the WRA decided to close the camps by the end of the year, and later established weekly quotas to be filled forcibly if too few volunteered to leave. In the end, little more than half the evacuees returned to the West Coast, where some were greeted by sporadic outbursts of violence and most found that their farms had been confiscated, their leases had expired, and their old jobs had disappeared. Japanese-Americans suffered income and property losses of about $350 million. For a time the WRA provided information about jobs and housing to ease the process of adjustment, but in May 1946 the agency declared that remaining problems "were largely the type which the individual must solve for himself in our society if he is to be a self-reliant and productive member of that society."[54]

Even while they had gone ahead with evacuation and relocation government officials had kept one eye on the Supreme Court. Yet the justices, choosing to rule on the narrowest possible issue, upheld the validity of exclusion (though not of permanent detention), accepted arguments founded on racial assumptions, and indicated that the military need not respect the ordinary requirements of law. The first case to reach the Supreme Court involved Gordon Hirabayashi, a student at the University of Washington, who refused to obey a curfew imposed by DeWitt and then failed to report to an assembly center. In June 1943, having decided to pass over the issue of exclusion, the Court unanimously found that DeWitt had authority to set a curfew and that in so doing he had not discriminated against Japanese-American citizens. In time of war, the Court reasoned, "residents having ethnic affiliations with an invading enemy may be a greater source of danger than those of different ancestry." The justices neither required military officials to produce evidence of actual danger nor to prove that no alternative existed to treating all Japanese-Americans as a class. "It is not for any court to sit in review of the wisdom of their action or substitute its judgment for theirs." The unanimous opinion cloaked bitter divisions on the bench. Justice Murphy circulated a dissenting opinion which found in the government's action "a melancholy resemblance to the treatment accorded to members of the Jewish race in Germany." Only after Felix Frankfurter pleaded with him to uphold "the *corporate* reputation of the Court" did Murphy back down.[55]

Once it had sanctioned a discriminatory curfew, the Court rather easily took the next step. On December 18, 1944, in the *Korematsu* case, the Court upheld the exclusion of Japanese-American citizens from the West Coast. Once again it appeared that evacuation was a reasonable military precaution and, as Chief Justice Stone told Hugo Black, "it is important for us to make it plain that we do not impose our judgment on the military unless we can say that they have no ground on which to go in formulating their orders." This time opposition could not be hushed. Three justices dissented, including Frank Murphy who challenged the Court's deference to military desires and termed the decision a "legalization of racism."[56] On the same day, however, the Court found in

ex parte Endo that the government had no right to detain
loyal citizens in relocation centers. Temporary detention was
permissible, but once a person's loyalty had been established
his detainment could not be justified by public hostility. By
unanimous vote, the Court ordered the release of Mitsuye
Endo two and one-half years after she had filed a petition of
habeas corpus and one day after the government announced
revocation of the order banning Japanese-Americans from the
West Coast.

The men who devised and carried out the policies affecting
Japanese-Americans during World War II were not motivated
by evil intent. Many would undoubtedly have been dismayed
had they known at the outset what the end result would be;
others in government saw clearly enough that evacuation
would someday be regarded with shame. Yet nearly all political and military leaders, as well as the great majority of
Americans, operated on certain assumptions—that public
opinion must be propitiated, that military necessity excused
just about anything, that racial distinctions were ultimately
insurmountable—that pointed inexorably toward concentration camps. If anything, the men who led the War Relocation
Authority tried to follow a generous and humane policy as
they defined it; like the church leaders who cooperated in
administering civilian public service they believed that if
camps were to exist, civilians rather than the military should
have jurisdiction. Nor did the relocation centers resemble
Nazi concentration camps: there were no mass executions, no
systematic starvation, no purposeful brutalization. The one
point Tule Lake had in common with Buchenwald was the
importance each attached to doctrines of race.

THE WANING OF THE NEW DEAL

SPEAKING TO A GATHERING of reformers in 1944, Archibald MacLeish voiced the widely-held belief that war had dealt the liberal cause a deadly blow. "Liberals meet in Washington these days," he said, "if they meet at all, to discuss the tragic outlook for all liberal proposals, the collapse of all liberal leadership and the inevitable defeat of all liberal aims." All through the war years reformers noted signs of a conservative resurgence and looked on helplessly as Congress jettisoned New Deal programs and businessmen displaced New Dealers in positions of power. When in December 1943 President Roosevelt declared that "Dr. New Deal" had outlived his usefulness and should give way to "Dr. Win-the-War," liberal morale hit rock bottom. Nor was it much restored by speculating about what the future might hold. As MacLeish observed, "It is no longer feared, it is assumed, that the country is headed back to normalcy, that Harding is just around the corner, that the twenties will repeat themselves."[1]

To some extent the notion that World War II crippled the New Deal depended on the assumption that it had been healthy when the war began. The reform program had in reality limped along for some time. A series of events in 1937 and 1938—particularly the Supreme Court packing plan and a devastating recession—had produced widespread dissatisfaction with the Roosevelt administration, and after the Republicans chalked up large gains in the congressional elections (winning 81 new seats in the House and 8 in the Senate) liberals and conservatives had battled to a standoff. Congress had passed no major piece of reform legislation since the Fair Labor Standards Act of 1938. With the outbreak of war in Europe, preparations for defense rather than proposals for social betterment absorbed the energies of an increasing number of government officials. By the time the United States entered the war, New Dealers were fighting a rear-guard action against the onslaughts of conservatives in Congress.

In fact, liberal disillusionment after 1941 derived in part from the belief that war might breathe new life into social reform. Throughout the 1930s many reformers were less interested in how World War I had weakened progressivism than in how, by allowing Americans to put aside the ethic of individualism, it had strengthened the movement. Only in 1917 and 1918 had large numbers of people been willing to accept full-blooded regulation of the economy; only then had planning in the national interest been possible. The war, Rexford Tugwell explained in 1939, had released Americans from the tyranny of the competitive system and gotten them to accept a form of "disciplined cooperation." Surely war had its terrible aspects, but "the fact is that only war has up to now proved to be such a transcending objective that doctrine is willingly sacrificed for efficiency in its service." Of course liberals were of two minds about the probable consequences of a future war: many pacifists feared that mobilization would lead to dictatorship, but it was not at all unusual for New

Dealers to predict that social gains would be extended for only in the event of war would men be "prepared to take the risks of the positive state."[2]

At first the war seemed to nourish these hopes, for it drew some reformers who had supported isolationism back into the New Deal fold and broke down resistance to the enlargement of presidential authority. A number of progressives had remained bitterly critical of the President's foreign policy until December 7, 1941, but Pearl Harbor removed some of their mistrust and improved chances for cooperation on domestic programs. One of Roosevelt's assistants, who had not spoken to Senator Robert La Follette, Jr. of Wisconsin for several months, dined with him "as soon as he voted correctly" on the declaration of war. "Bob is now 100 percent O.K.," he reported, "I am sure there isn't a thing Bob wouldn't do for the President right now." Just as the war enabled reformers to put aside differences over foreign policy, so it caused many Republicans to recognize, however grudgingly, that Roosevelt required sweeping powers to meet the emergency. Even while insisting that war not serve as a pretext for social reform, Herbert Hoover admitted, "To win total war President Roosevelt must have many dictatorial economic powers. There must be no hesitation in giving them to him and upholding him in them."[3]

Nevertheless, expectations founded on memories of World War I and on the mood of unity following Pearl Harbor were not fulfilled. Instead the war weakened American liberalism in many ways, some temporary and some lasting, some small and others large. The war obliged reformers to grant priority to military objectives, provided an excuse to liquidate certain New Deal programs, and revealed that powers lodged in the welfare state could be put to illiberal uses. The war raised other barriers to reform by creating pressure to cut domestic expenditures, to halt the inflationary spiral and to staff emergency agencies with businessmen. Finally, by injecting new issues into the political arena, the war splintered the electoral coalition upon which Roosevelt had relied. This is not to say that the war invariably worked against the interests of reformers. It solved many problems which had baffled New Dealers and made possible the implementation of particular reforms—such as the GI Bill of Rights—that could be justified on military grounds. Nevertheless, the reform movement was in a weaker condition at the end of the war than at its start.

From the beginning, most liberals agreed to put aside social reforms that could interfere with the military program. Few protested when rural electrification was trimmed back to free copper for military purposes, or when the working day was lengthened in order to boost industrial output. "Progressives should understand that programs which do not forward the war must be given up or drastically curtailed," wrote David Lilienthal, head of the Tennessee Valley Authority. "Where a social service doesn't help to beat Hitler, it may have to be sacrificed," observed another reformer. "This may sound tough—but we have to be tough."[4] Roosevelt and his advisors took much the same approach. Although he believed that existing reforms should be preserved where possible and that others would undoubtedly be required when peace came, Roosevelt thought that "the weaknesses and many of the social inequalities as of 1932 have been repaired or removed and the job now is, first and foremost, to win the war." Even Bruce Bliven, an editor of the *New Republic*, concurred. "If it were true that continued devotion to the New Deal hampered the war effort, then the New Deal should be laid on the shelf."[5]

Of course the key to Bliven's remark was the word "if." Very often liberals denied that reform was incompatible with wartime requirements and argued instead that it would con- tribute to victory. New Dealers supported job training pro- grams "not as a social gain, but as a wartime necessity," upheld collective bargaining on the grounds that it fostered industrial harmony, and defended payroll deductions in an expanded social insurance system as "an effective weapon in the wartime battle against inflation." Sometimes they carried this argument to the point where it seemed that every reform would help win the war because, by advancing social justice, it would make American society that much more worth defending. Again and again reformers employed military metaphors; in urging Roosevelt to sponsor a postwar economic plan Henry Wallace even suggested the title "Lend-Lease on the Domestic Front."[6] Reform, in a sense, was considered guilty until proven innocent. Liberals had to show how each reform was related to victory, and unless they could provide an iron-clad case it stood slim chance of survival.

Nothing better illustrates the way in which wartime needs forced a postponement of reform than anti-trust policy. Beginning in 1938 the Roosevelt administration had made a vigorous effort to enforce the Sherman Act. But by 1940 officials began to think twice about prosecutions that might hamper defense production and were quite reluctant, for example, to bring suit against large oil companies suspected of fixing prices and compelling service stations to handle their products exclusively. One New Dealer, admitting that anti-trust action would not disturb gasoline deliveries, nevertheless feared that it might have an adverse "psychological effect" upon an industry vital to the production of synthetic rubber and hi-octane gasoline. After much hesitation the Justice Department decided to proceed with the suit. The Attorney-General, who still thought that "the question of national defense is more important than the settlement of the theory on which the oil industry is to operate," did not want his department to "be placed in the position of saying it will let down the bars." Also, he expected that the case "would sink into an argument between lawyers and disappear from the newspapers." That is exactly what happened.[7]

Once the United States entered the war, however, anti-trust prosecutions virtually ceased. Not only did businessmen receive immunity if the War Production Board certified proposed arrangements in advance as being in the national interest, but the demand to relax the law even for suspected violators proved irresistible. Although Thurman Arnold, who headed the Anti-Trust Division of the Justice Department, maintained that the Sherman Act did not diminish business efficiency and should be stringently enforced, most officials responsible for production believed that anti-trust actions antagonized businessmen and caused them to fritter away valuable time preparing legal defenses. Secretary of War Stimson came to consider Arnold a "self-seeking fanatic," and reported a prevalent feeling in his department that rigorous enforcement "frightened business" and had "a very great deterrent effect upon our munitions production." Harry Hopkins, voicing the general desire to suspend the anti-trust laws in certain instances, affirmed that the President would have to "take [Arnold] in hand and stop his interference with production."[8]

To settle the matter, Roosevelt called on Samuel I. Rosenman who, after listening to all sides, found a solution that gave Stimson most of what he wanted. Any anti-trust investigation, prosecution or suit that might obstruct vital production would, at the discretion of the Attorney-General and the Secretaries of War or Navy, be postponed until after the emergency. In the event of disagreement between Justice and War "a letter from Secretary Stimson would be controlling." Arnold had tried to salvage at least his right to initiate investigations (if not prosecutions) but met with no luck. On March 30, 1942 the President approved the agreement, pointing out that "the war effort must come first and everything else must wait." During the next few years twenty-five suits involving such concerns as Bendix Aviation, General Electric and ALCOA were deferred at Stimson's request, and early in 1943 Thurman Arnold moved from the Justice Department to the Circuit Court of Appeals. A few old-style progressives wailed that anti-trust enforcement stood in greater peril than "when the New Deal went off courting the NRA," but most accepted the need to subordinate the competitive ideal to wartime requirements.[9]

Similarly, meeting the manpower shortage took precedence over protecting child labor. The Fair Labor Standards Act of 1938 had, by providing for effective regulation of child labor in interstate commerce, capped a twenty-five year crusade by social reformers. But during the war youngsters poured into the labor market. From 1940 to 1944 the number of teenage workers jumped from 1 to 2.9 million; four times as many fourteen-and fifteen-year old girls held jobs at the end of the war than at its start. Not only were more young people employed, but they were also performing heavier work. Fewer fifteen-year olds ran errands and more worked in retail trade; fewer seventeen-year olds were found in grocery stores and more on assembly lines. As a result, over a million teenagers dropped out of school.

Breaches of the child labor law occurred repeatedly. In North Carolina inspectors found more than twenty times as many violations in 1944 as in 1940. In New York the number of boys and girls illegally employed climbed by nearly 400 percent, and a survey of pinsetters in bowling alleys revealed that "boys as young as 9 years go to the alleys after school, eat supper in an upstairs or back room, and work until midnight on school nights and until 3 or 4 o'clock in the morning on Sunday." When violations of the law became too common, states simply watered down their laws. In 1943 fifteen states extended the hours that children might work, and the following year four others followed suit. Yet when reformers proposed a law banning the employment of anyone under sixteen during school hours or in any type of manufacturing, they agreed to permit "deferred effective dates" so as "to avoid any possible objection to the raising of State child-labor standards during the period of war production."[10]

Just as the war shouldered aside certain reforms, so it provided an excuse to abolish various New Deal relief agencies. During 1942 and 1943 Congress and the administration snuffed out the Civilian Conservation Corps, the Works Progress Administration and the National Youth Administration. In each instance the defense boom altered the character of the agencies' clientele, which had come increasingly to consist of those last to be hired—Negroes, women, very old and very young workers. Then, wartime job openings and draft calls had reduced the agencies' importance still further. Consequently, while the CCC, WPA and NYA often tried to justify their continuation by undertaking projects of military value, they could no longer count on strong backing from the Roosevelt administration. The point at issue was not as much the function of relief in wartime as its role in the reconversion period that would follow. Reformers wanted to preserve these agencies in at least a skeletal form for future use. Conservatives thought they "should be dropped, not only for the duration of the war, but forever after."[11]

The first relief agency to walk the plank was in some ways the most popular. The Civilian Conservation Corps had always attracted broad political support, in part because it was run by conservative administrators and brought revenue to communities in which camps were located. As late as 1940 Congress had allocated more for the CCC than Roosevelt had requested. From then on the agency took an active role in national defense, ordering drill for enrollees, providing instruction in reading blueprints, and performing tasks for military reservations. Its director affirmed that the CCC contributed to the war by building up boys' stamina and accustoming them to barracks life. Nevertheless, by early 1942 enrollment fell sharply, reaching a low point in March of little over 100,000, just one-third of what it had been a year before. A Gallup poll found that public opinion had turned against continuation, CCC officials were themselves unsure about whether to go on, and the President no longer showed much interest. He suggested maintaining camps "for only very nominal purposes, such as looking after parks, historic places, and forests," and opening them only to boys below draft age, preferably those "with slight defects which might be corrected." In June 1942 the House voted not to grant any funds for the CCC, and the Senate barely approved a small amount.

The compromise appropriation bill provided just enough to liquidate the CCC in an orderly manner.[12]

Unlike the CCC, the Works Progress Administration had been embroiled in controversy from its creation in 1935. Opponents of the New Deal had always opposed work relief, particularly for white-collar workers, and suspected that the WPA would create a political machine that would keep the Democrats in power indefinitely. But as wartime jobs opened up, the WPA experienced an abrupt decline, losing two-thirds of its enrollees in the year after Pearl Harbor. Conservatives saw a golden opportunity to abolish the agency and few liberals thought it worth defending. By mid-1942 one welfare official understood that "WPA's days are numbered," and most hoped merely that the program would last through the winter so as not to create hardships for "the Negroes, older workers, and women." In December 1942 Roosevelt asserted that a national work relief program was no longer needed and gave the WPA an "honorable discharge." Although a few New Dealers believed that it deserved a "wartime furlough" instead, the WPA mailed its last relief check in April 1943, ten years after Roosevelt first took office.[13]

The National Youth Administration became a third casualty of the war. In much the same manner as the CCC had turned to wartime tasks, so the NYA after 1940 had stressed vocational training programs that contributed to national defense. Spokesmen for the agency asserted that "the N.Y.A. is now exclusively for defense training," and professed their readiness "to liquidate everything that does not have to do with the winning of this war." The NYA enjoyed the support of many businessmen, since it taught needed skills and simplified worker recruitment by bringing boys from widely scattered rural areas to a central location. According to one manufacturer, the NYA had taken "strong mountain boys" and provided work experience so that they were "shop broken" and ready to take their place on the production lines. Given this, the agency survived the 1942 session of

Congress. But as NYA director Aubrey Williams admitted, obtaining an appropriation "really becomes a great game of tightrope walking."[14]

As the war progressed, the balancing act became impossible. Not only did the manpower shortage whittle down the NYA's clientele, but it ultimately forced manufacturers to hire untrained workers and provide instant on-the-job instruction. One official informed the President that "the pressure on production had changed the whole aspect of pre-employment training." As the need for NYA programs lessened, opponents of the agency took the offensive. State education officials, who had always disliked the NYA because it competed for funds and students, claimed that it opened the door to federal control of education. Arguing that the NYA "runs in competition with us and is not needed," they urged congressmen to "kill this octopus before it kills us."[15] Conservatives in Congress were eager to comply, for many regarded the NYA as a hotbed of radicalism. A Republican member of the House from New York reported his outrage at observing a Negro boy and a white girl walking side by side from an NYA training center in his home town; he also suspected that the school had destroyed property values in the surrounding area. By June 1943 pressures had grown to such an extent that Congress abolished the agency. Aubrey Williams attributed the action mainly to Republicans and "the school clique," which he likened to "a pack of wolves, nipping at the NYA's heels."[16]

In addition to shunting aside various reforms and putting New Deal relief agencies out of commission, the war demonstrated that the government might use its power in ways that reformers had never intended. Throughout the depression years, liberals had fought to expand government authority and had confidently assumed that this authority would be used for humane ends. But the war revealed that even well-intentioned programs were susceptible to other uses. "The United States Government is a vast machine that could be used for other purposes than national defense and furthering the common welfare," reflected Malcolm Cowley in 1943. He added ominously, "It is possible that a fascist state could be instituted here without many changes in government personnel, and some of these changes have been made already."[17] Although most reformers did not share these fears, the war at least raised questions in the minds of some about the benevolence of the state.

That federal authority could be a double-edged sword was nowhere more clearly illustrated than in the evacuation of Japanese-Americans from the West Coast, a process facilitated by a number of New Deal welfare agencies. The Farm Security Administration supervised the evacuees' agricultural property, the Federal Security Agency provided health services in the relocation centers, and former WPA personnel applied the knowledge gained in setting up work projects to administering War Relocation Authority camps. Nor could other reform agencies, even one so archetypical as the NYA (before its demise), be counted on to soften the blow. In the spring of 1943, still under heavy attack in Congress, Aubrey Williams refused to permit young Japanese-American citizens to leave the relocation centers in order to attend NYA schools. The issue, he remarked, was loaded with dynamite and his agency was too vulnerable.[18] The ease with which relief programs could serve the cause of relocation suggested that such a massive and efficient movement of people would have been immeasurably more difficult before the advent of the social service state.

The desire to trim nondefense expenditures loomed as another important obstacle to reform in wartime. As military costs mushroomed it became all the more difficult to justify spending for domestic programs not directly related to the war. Throughout the 1930s conservatives in Congress and spokesmen for the business community had favored a balanced budget; now that the war made gargantuan deficits necessary, they sought partial compensation by cutting back domestic spending. "The plausible argument that the nation cannot

afford to buy both guns and social security," wrote one reformer, "is all the Roosevelt-baiters have left and they are
making the most of it."[19] Republican victories in the 1942
elections greatly bolstered the drive to prune costs. The call
for economy, of course, often served as a cloak behind which
various interest groups concealed more substantive objections to reform measures. This was made evident in the dissolution of the National Resources Planning Board, the erosion
of the Farm Security Administration, and the unwillingness
of Congress to extend social security and unemployment
insurance benefits or to provide for comprehensive medical
care.

Unlike New Deal relief agencies which grew less important
as unemployment fell, the National Resources Planning
Board could have exerted considerable influence over economic
policy during the war and after. But the Board, which analyzed economic trends, formulated plans regarding resource
utilization, and evaluated priorities for public works projects,
was always subject to conservative suspicion. If anything,
distrust of "long haired planners" increased early in 1943
when the NRPB proposed an elaborate postwar expansion
of medical care, education, housing and social insurance
to help "the degraded and impoverished of our country, the
disinherited and despised." The Board's chairman, Frederic
A. Delano, noted "a strong disposition in Congress to cut
our appropriations to the bone," and although Roosevelt
pointed out that planning saved money ("I am definitely
opposed to the principle of 'Penny wise, dollar foolish'," he
told party leaders) Congress in the spring of 1943 ap-
propriated only enough for the NRPB to wind up its affairs.[20]
Even one conservative member of the House thought that
his colleagues might become too free in wielding the economy
axe. "Having 'tasted blood', I am now a bit fearful that its
zeal toward economy and toward disrupting New Deal
agencies may be excessive and in the end injurious."[21]

That is exactly what occurred in the case of the Farm

Security Administration. As with other reform agencies, the FSA had for some time emphasized its role in national defense. The agency claimed that by helping marginal farmers purchase land and equipment it boosted crop production. Its defenders praised the FSA as a "first-line war agency" that would "help in meeting the food needs of wartime America." One official, who insisted that he was "not normally disposed to place social considerations precedent to considerations of winning the war," nevertheless reasoned that farm workers were "the lowest paid, least organized group in the country," and deserved whatever protection the government could provide.[22] The FSA also retained a symbolic as well as economic value. "FSA is the very symbol of the New Deal for small farmers," commented one reformer. "It is the agricultural equivalent of the Wagner Act." Calvin B. Baldwin, a staunch liberal who headed the FSA, boasted that it "has always been proud to be known as a New Deal agency."[23]

For a time the FSA's reform instincts found an outlet in the Mexican farm labor program. In 1942 farmers in Texas, California and Arizona had urged the government to allow importation of *braceros* to ease the labor shortage. In August the United States and Mexico reached an agreement which required American farmers to pay prevailing wage rates, absorb transportation costs, furnish housing and medical facilities equal to those available for American workers, and provide protection against periods of unemployment. For about a year the Farm Security Administration supervised the program, but American farmers complained bitterly that the agency imposed impossible standards. Landowners in the Southwest believed that the FSA consisted of "social uplifters" who "look to the guidance of [the Mexicans'] spiritual welfare, their entertainment, physical well-being and happiness, see that they are fairly well taken care of with food and housing." "I get tripped every time I turn around," groaned one Arizonan, "My Mexicans are all happy." Farm owners thought they should be trusted to provide decent facilities, and wanted the matter handled at the state level by the agricultural extension services with a minimum of interference. Congress moved in that direction in the spring of 1943 by requiring the approval of county agricultural agents before farm laborers could be transported across state lines. Then, on July 1, control of Mexican farm labor was transferred from the FSA to the War Food Administration.[24]

In addition, Farm Security faced a threat to its very existence from a band of hostile forces: southern conservatives who thought that the agency was controlled by "social gainers, do-gooders, bleeding-hearts and long-hairs who make a career of helping others for a price and according to their own peculiar, screwball ideas;" Republicans who considered the agency communistic because it required farmers "to sign agreements with the laborers to pay them certain amounts and to provide them with meals costing at least $1.00 a piece and nothing but the highest grade of delicacies—no veal, little pork, plenty of lamb and beef and chicken, all sorts of fresh fruits and fresh vegetables;" and established farm organizations such as the American Farm Bureau Federation whose leaders thought that the FSA "promoted socialistic land policies."[25] With these groups united under the banner of economy, Congress cut the FSA budget to ribbons, slashing it by 30 percent in 1942 and by 36 percent more the following year. Indeed, the 1943 appropriation of $111.7 million went through only after Baldwin promised to resign. Within a short time his place was taken by a former Democratic representative from North Carolina whom conservatives found unobjectionable. The FSA lingered on with its funds depleted, liberal leadership gone, and program much reduced.

In much the same way as the budget squeeze victimized the NRPB and the FSA, so it worked against congressional enactment of new social welfare measures. Throughout the war liberals in the administration pressed for reform of the social security and unemployment insurance systems so as to cover more workers and liberalize payments.[26] Many of their proposals were embodied in the Wagner-Murray-Dingell bill introduced in 1943 which would have set up a national insurance system to replace the existing federal-state arrangement, extended coverage to 15 million agricultural and domestic workers, and increased unemployment benefits. In addition it proposed a federal system of health insurance under which each worker's family could obtain medical and hospital care. The individual would select a physician from among those agreeing to participate, provided the doctor was willing to treat him. Although it did not cover dental treatment or maternity costs and was to be financed by employer and worker contributions, this was the most ambitious plan of health insurance yet proposed.

Such proposals, however, made no headway during the war. President Roosevelt occasionally spoke in favor of social welfare measures, but he lent no support to Wagner's legislative endeavors. On one occasion he asked Frances Perkins, who was preparing a speech in behalf of expanding social security, to emphasize "that this is not, what some people call, a New Deal measure." The President also recognized that health insurance was widely resented by doctors who saw in it the specter of socialized medicine. "We can't go up against the State Medical Societies," Roosevelt concluded, "we just can't do it."[27] The President undoubtedly assessed the balance of political forces correctly. Given the conservative mood in Congress, the opposition of the medical profession, and the rather widespread prosperity, there was little inclination to undertake potentially expensive new programs. Congress not only failed to broaden social security coverage, but from year to year it froze the rate of contributions at 1 percent thereby postponing a small scheduled increase.

If social welfare schemes stood little chance in wartime, proposals to help those on the bottom of the ladder stood even less. Although most Americans enjoyed higher incomes during the 1940s than ever before, for some the depression had never really ended. In 1944 ten million workers—one-

fourth of those engaged in manufacturing—received less than
60 cents an hour. Moreover, white collar wages lagged far
behind those of industrial workers. But the people who suffered most were those on fixed incomes (such as the elderly
on social security), state employees, and unskilled workers.
Congressional committees investigating substandard conditions heard from a New York City sanitation worker, a
Pittsburgh cleaning woman and a Boston nurse, none of whom
could support their families. "I have no fresh meat for my
family," lamented one woman who received 50 cents an hour
for canning tomatoes and whose husband worked in an automobile plant. "We do not have milk; I cannot afford milk
except for only the baby." In January 1944 a group of senators
reported that twenty million Americans "dwell constantly in
a borderland between subsistence and privation, where even
the utmost thrift and caution do not suffice to make ends
meet."[28]

Nevertheless, the Roosevelt administration opposed across-
the-board wage increases on the grounds that they would increase inflationary pressures. When Senator Claude Pepper of
Florida sought to aid those in the greatest distress by allowing the War Labor Board to permit voluntary wage hikes to
65 cents an hour (rather than the 50 cents allowed in 1944)
he received a chilly response. Asserting that "you cannot wish
65 cents out of the air," WLB chairman William Davis suggested that raising the wages of the lowest paid was like
tossing a stone into a pond: inflationary ripples would spread
through the economy since, to preserve wage differentials,
adjustments would be made all along the line. Higher prices
would eventually rob the worker of any benefit. "Unfortunately," said Davis, "you cannot fix that substandard bracket
in our present economy at the level which really represents a
decent standard of living with security for the future."
The President strongly endorsed this view. In defending his
anti-inflation drive Roosevelt remarked that every group
would have to accept a cut in its standard of living during the

war. The government could do no more than see that "those on the lower rungs of the economic ladder are not ground down below the margin of existence."[29] Not until 1945 did the War Labor Board authorize a wage increase to 55 cents an hour, and then only in certain instances.

Having argued that the danger of inflation precluded gains for the working poor, the administration attempted to deal with the very rich by limiting salaries to $25,000. Roosevelt first advanced this idea in April, 1942 and after the Price Control Act passed in October he empowered Stabilization Director James Byrnes to hold salaries at $25,000 after taxes "insofar as practicable." But congressional opposition, particularly in the House Ways and Means Committee, soon put an end to the plan. A Treasury official noted that when he informed congressmen of his work on the limitation, "I received a Bronx cheer, and was told by many that I could spare myself that work."[30] In the spring of 1943, ignoring Roosevelt's pleas, the Committee attached a rider ending the salary limitation to a bill authorizing an increase in the public debt, and the President had no choice but to go along. In a sense the issue had greater symbolic than fiscal meaning: since maximum salaries were computed after taxes the limitation ordinarily affected earnings over $67,200; exceptions could be permitted to meet life insurance premiums, mortgage payments and contributions to charity; and income from interest or investments was not touched. At most the plan had affected some three thousand people. Even so, its repeal contrasted vividly with the treatment of those who eked out a marginal existence during the war.

Changes in the composition of the federal bureaucracy worked to the disadvantage of social reform no less than did the need to give priority to military projects, to limit domestic spending, or to curb inflation. During its early years the Roosevelt administration had drawn into government service a group of economists, lawyers, social workers and reformers motivated largely by the desire (in Rexford Tug-

well's phrase) to make America over. But during the defense
buildup a number of conservative lawyers and businessmen—
such as Edward R. Stettinius, James V. Forrestal, Henry L.
Stimson and Dean Acheson—began moving into Washington,
and in the early 1940s the federal service underwent a major
overhaul. Some New Dealers remained but usually their influence was greatly reduced. Many left government employment altogether: some enlisted in the armed forces, others became sacrificial offerings to congressional conservatives, and
still others resigned when their objectives were frustrated or
they became physically exhausted. Often their places were
filled by business executives who possessed the skills needed
to manage war production but who had little interest in
social reform. As one observer explained, "The mere fact of
passing from a state of peace into a state of war is marked
by a change in the prestige of professions which is perhaps
most clearly symbolized by the influx of production experts
into Washington and the simultaneous exit of the social
engineers."[31]

The new prestige accorded businessmen did much to re-
fashion their attitude toward government. During the 1930s
the business community had resented the Roosevelt administration not because it jeopardized capitalism, but because it
deprived them of status and authority. It was not so much
that New Deal policies were harmful as that businessmen felt
they had literally no voice in decision making. This changed
dramatically during the war. As the government called on
industrialists to staff production agencies, business once again
basked in the warm glow of public admiration. A chairman of
the National Association of Manufacturers noted happily
that "the public is turning again with confidence to business
leaders." *Business Week* declared that the war had placed a
premium on "business talents," that the administration could
no longer afford the "amateurism" of "braintrusters and
theoreticians," and, best of all, that businessmen were "moving up in the New Deal Administration, replacing New

Dealers as they go." Since government was destined to play a cardinal role in economic affairs, it followed that business-men should discard the idea that the state was their enemy and make sure it remained responsive to their interests. "The management men who have gone to Washington during the war should be the opening wedge for the participation of man-agement men in peacetime government."[32] Politics had be-come too important to be left to the politicians.

Nothing infuriated liberals more than this steady move-ment of businessmen into positions of authority. "The New Dealers are a vanishing tribe," wrote James Wechsler, "and the money changers who were driven from the temple are now quietly established in government offices."[33] Reformers, how-ever, saved their sharpest darts for the "dollar-a-year" men. To recruit executives for national defense, the government often permitted them to remain on their company's payroll for they might otherwise refuse to sacrifice their normal in-comes in order to accept temporary federal employment. Ultimately, dollar-a-year men made up three-fourths of the War Production Board's executive force. Even though such employees were supposedly prohibited from ruling on cases directly involving their own firms, liberals claimed that they looked after their own interests. But at bottom the issue was less one of individual selfishness than of the fundamental outlook and ideals of an entire class of government adminis-trators. Reformers saw clearly enough that war had bestowed power on many men who held the New Deal in horror and were likely to make judgments based on their past experience.

World War II weakened liberalism in still another respect: it raised issues that ruptured the New Deal coalition. Through-out his presidency Roosevelt had tried to hold together such diverse groups as southern white farmers, urban blue collar workers, middle-class intellectuals, and members of ethnic and racial minorities. Like every political coalition this one had always contained unstable elements, and signs of strain were apparent after 1937 when rural elements balked at proposals to aid northern industrial groups. The war both exacerbated existing tensions and introduced new ones. Foreign policy was one source of division: the administration found it increasingly difficult to retain the loyalty of Irish-Americans as a result of its collaboration with the Soviet Union, and of Polish-Americans after the Yalta settlement. Civil rights was yet another problem: as wartime manpower shortages forced the federal government to support, even in limited fashion, equal employment opportunities for Negroes, southern whites talked openly of bolting the Democratic party. But most of the difficulty stemmed from the competition between interest groups at a time when the government had to withhold economic favors rather than hand them out. For example, the imposition of price controls on agricultural products provoked a dispute between farmers who favored high food prices and consumers worried about their weekly budgets. By setting the farmer's interest against that of the urban dweller the war made it impossible not to alienate some part of the New Deal's constituency.

Similarly, the war caused some liberal intellectuals to re-examine their attitude toward the labor movement. During the 1930s reformers had occasionally criticized union tactics but had warmly endorsed labor's goals of union recognition, job security and improved conditions. Then the war enormously complicated what had formerly seemed a simple matter of justice for the underdog. As unions gained members and workers' conditions improved, the problems posed by disruptive strikes, racially exclusive membership policies, and inflationary wage demands became more difficult to resolve. A prominent liberal told Victor Reuther of the United Automobile Workers that if the demands of striking workers were met, "it will be at the expense of some other group. Higher wages will not result in greater production of consumers goods as heretofore." The *New Republic*, noting that labor "has the highest real wages, the greatest extent of employment and the best working conditions it has had in its history," suggested that the time had come for unions to turn away from their "immediate interests" and concern themselves instead with liberalizing American national life. While the war did not disrupt the alliance between liberals and the labor movement, it surely subjected it to severe strain.[34]

As they observed the setbacks dealt to social reform in the early 1940s, liberals quite naturally grew pessimistic about the future. Many concluded that a postwar depression would occur and became obsessed with the menace of domestic fascism. Often they expressed such fears in terms bordering on the apocalyptic. "America is today more reactionary in its prevailing mood than any other country where the fascists are not openly in power," wrote one. "The counterrevolution is gathering its forces in America."[35] Despite these complaints the war did not in all respects impair the reform movement. Not only did it solve some pressing social problems, but it demonstrated the efficacy of Keynesian economics, inspired reforms related to labor efficiency and troop morale, and provided an opportunity to incorporate into the liberal program ideas which had largely been ignored in the 1930s.

"What are we liberals after?" asked a writer in *Common Sense* in September 1943. "Do we just want words which will run our way in neat ideological packages? Or do we want a better break for the common man?" Since the latter was surely the case, liberals would have to recognize that the war meant a higher standard of living than any had dreamed possible a few years before. "The honest minded liberal will admit that the common man is getting a better break than ever he did under the New Deal." The war, in fact, pushed farm income to new heights, reduced tenancy as individuals left the land for factory jobs or enlisted in the armed services, strengthened trade unions, and literally ended unemployment. Although not everyone shared equally in the new prosperity, wartime hardship where it existed differed qualitatively from depression hardship: it was not a matter of having no job, no food, and no place to live but rather of having less nutritious food, poorer housing and lower wages than people thought they deserved. In 1943 the Women's Christian Temperance Union in Illinois failed to find a single needy family to whom it could distribute Christmas baskets.

The war, moreover, exerted a modest levelling influence. Because the well-to-do paid heavy taxes and goods were rationed, class differences were felt somewhat less keenly. "Rockefeller and I can now get the same amount of sugar, gasoline, tires etc., etc., etc.," said one reformer, "and the etc's will soon fill many pages."[36] Between 1939 and 1944 the share of national income held by the wealthiest five percent of the American people declined from 23.7 to 16.8 percent. The pyramid of social stratification was by no means entirely flattened, but far fewer could be found at the very bottom. In that sense, the war remedied problems that had plagued reformers even before the crash of 1929.

Since it was abundantly clear that government spending had created this prosperity, Keynesian economic thought acquired new converts. Followers of Keynes asserted that fiscal policy, in the form of deficit spending and the control of taxes and interest rates, held the key to prosperity. By stimulating investment and boosting purchasing power, they said, the government could insure high levels of employment. This argument, which a growing number of New Dealers had found appealing in the late 1930s, now seemed wholly substantiated. "The war has proved to us that it is possible to have full employment," wrote Alfred Bingham. "It was achieved by making available to the government sufficient spending power to put all our productive resources to use." If the government could spend vast sums for war, surely it could spend a fraction of that amount for constructive social purposes in peacetime. Keynesian economics became sanctioned fiscal policy with the Employment Act of 1946, an early version of which had been introduced in 1944. Although watered down considerably in that it did not establish methods of dealing with future downturns or instruct the President to lift federal expenditures to a

level necessary to insure full employment, the act recognized
the responsibility of the federal government for the prevention
of mass unemployment. "We have seen the last of our great
depressions," said Chester Bowles, "for the simple reason that
the public [is] wise enough to know it doesn't have to stand
for one."[37]

The war afforded greater scope to reformers in the area of
housing. From 1940 to 1945 millions of Americans moved to
new homes, many to be near defense plants. To ease the strain
of migration, the government often assumed responsibility for
housing defense workers (as well as for providing health facilities and day care centers for the children of working mothers).
In February 1942 Roosevelt created the National Housing
Agency which, along with other production and manpower
boards, determined the nature and location of the necessary
dwellings. In all, public and private sources provided housing
for more than nine million migratory war workers and their
families. The government spent $2.3 billion for this purpose,
much of which necessarily went for temporary facilities. Even
though building standards were diluted to conserve materials
and manpower, government construction of low-cost housing
far exceeded anything contemplated before the war.

Since most people did not live in public projects, it was
essential to prevent landlords from taking advantage of war
workers by hiking rents. In March 1942 the Office of Price
Administration froze or rolled back rents in twenty defense
areas; in April three hundred additional areas were included,
and eventually 86 million tenants benefitted. Wartime rent
control proved both popular and successful. Unlike businessmen who could frequently evade price control by turning out
a new product and finding a customer willing to pay the price,
landlords dealt with relatively unalterable products and with
tenants who moved quickly to obtain OPA assistance when
threatened by a rent hike or eviction. Of course means were
devised, legal and illegal, to get around rent control. Since
commercial rents were not affected landlords attempted to

convert dwellings to business purposes. Even worse, tenants were obliged to give a nonreturnable deposit, purchase furniture already in the apartment, or assume responsibility for repairs. Nevertheless, rents paid in large cities rose only fractionally after OPA controls took effect.

To a much greater extent than war workers, soldiers and veterans benefitted from social legislation. Although broad-gauged proposals for national health insurance made no headway, maternity and pediatric care were provided for families of servicemen in the lowest pay grades. More than one million mothers and infants eventually received medical, hospital and nursing care; at its peak the program covered one of every seven births in the United States. Then in the fall of 1943 the President called for liberal unemployment, social security and education benefits for veterans. In January 1944, after several bills had been introduced along these lines, the American Legion proposed an omnibus measure thereafter known as the GI Bill of Rights. It sailed through the Senate by a unanimous vote in March, and then made its way more slowly through the House where it was modified to suit John Rankin of Mississippi, chairman of the Committee on World War Veterans' Legislation. Rankin feared that overly generous education or unemployment benefits might weaken the incentive to find work. "We have 50,000 negroes in the service from our State," he said, "and in my opinion, if the bill should pass in its present form, a vast majority of them would remain unemployed for at least a year, and a great many white men would do the same thing." Rankin succeeded in partially diluting the measure, but as signed by the President in June 1944 it provided generous educational benefits, readjustment allowances for veterans during the transition to civilian life, and guarantees of mortgage loans.[38]

The GI Bill of Rights revealed much about the character of wartime social reform. In many ways the bill proved an exception to the rule: in this instance, congressmen—whether from gratitude, considerations of troop morale, or knowledge

that financial outlays would not begin until the war's end—
were willing to distribute benefits denied to other groups.
Unlike the Wagner-Murray-Dingell health insurance bill or
the activities of the Farm Security Administration, veterans'
legislation affronted no major interest group. On the contrary, it had the backing of a powerful lobby headed by the
American Legion, which saw a chance to put returning
veterans in its debt and was anxious to centralize services in
the Veterans' Administration rather than see them divided
among various government bureaus. Moreover, the bill passed
only after John Rankin had whittled down some of its most
liberal features by tightening eligibility requirements for
educational grants. Above all, the GI Bill of Rights was construed wholly as a veterans' measure rather than as part of a
broader scheme of social reform. New Dealers had wanted to
link veterans' benefits to expanded social insurance, aid to
education and home loans for the entire population, but had
met with no success.

If liberals failed to provide most Americans with the advantages offered to veterans, the war nevertheless brought
into prominence ideas which had either not been part of the
reform tradition or had been regarded as inessential. The depression had fastened attention on problems of economic
security, unemployment, business regulation and conservation of natural resources. Given these concerns, reformers had
paid scant regard to health insurance, federal aid to education, and civil rights. But as the war cleared away economic
problems, each was incorporated into the liberal platform.
Roosevelt accepted the proposition, first advanced by members of the National Resources Planning Board, that the
political liberties guaranteed by the Constitution needed
supplementing by an Economic Bill of Rights, that the right
to adequate medical care and a good education was no less
important than freedom of speech or trial by jury. Liberals
also asserted more positively that Negroes as well as whites
were to enjoy these benefits. In the 1930s a man like George

Norris could oppose an antilynching bill and still be counted a liberal in good standing; by 1945 support for civil rights had become an acid test of one's liberal credentials.

The relationship between the war and social reform depended on reformers' goals and the degree to which those goals contributed to the military or economic conduct of the war. To the extent that American liberalism was identified with expanding the scope of governmental activity in behalf of underprivileged groups, it lost strength during the war. Liberals had relegated many reforms to a back seat, had seen New Deal projects dismantled and wartime agencies taken over by businessmen, and had found that pressure to prevent inflation often precluded assisting the poor. Yet the war also had a more positive long-range effect, for it solved old problems even as it created new ones. By liberating the economy from the grip of depression, the war permitted more attention to be paid to other issues—federal aid to education, civil rights, medical insurance and a compensatory fiscal policy— that would comprise much of the liberal agenda for the next twenty years.

THE STRUGGLE FOR EQUAL RIGHTS

IN AUGUST 1940 a black man living in New York City bitterly described the many forms of discrimination found in the United States. "We are still deprived of proper education, robbed of our vote and ruled by lynch law in the South," he said. "In the North we are discriminated against in business: forced to live in ghettos like Harlem, through housing restrictions and prejudice. We are 'undesirable' socially. We can take no pride in our armed forces. . . . We can become no more than flunkies in the army and kitchen boys in the navy."[1] Within the next five years, however, the war altered the political, economic and social status of Negro Americans. These changes in status depended on the interplay of several forces: the reaction of articulate elements in the black community to the war; the outlook of the Roosevelt administration, the War Department and the Supreme Court; the response of the South and its congressional spokesmen; and a manpower shortage that grew increasingly severe as the

war progressed. By disrupting traditional patterns of racial
behavior the war broke down many barriers to equality. Precisely for this reason, however, it gave rise to the most intense
sort of racial conflict.

During World War I, most Negro leaders—conscious that
their position was weak, that Wilson had proven unfriendly
to their cause, and that widespread anxiety over divided
loyalties might victimize blacks as well as immigrants—
counseled unqualified support for the war. By demonstrating
their loyalty, the argument ran, Negroes would earn the good
will of white America. "Let us, while this war lasts, forget our
special grievances," W. E. B. DuBois advised members of the
NAACP.[2] But the policy of conciliation had not worked very
well: at the end of the war most of the economic gains made
by Negroes evaporated and a wave of race riots swept the
country. Even in 1918 DuBois's position was attacked, and
by the 1940s it commanded little support. Not only had experience demonstrated its inadequacies, but most black
leaders believed that a militant posture would be more likely
to win concessions from the Roosevelt administration.

Consequently, the theme running most insistently through
the Negro press was that the war must not be allowed to
divert energy from the struggle for equality. Nothing less than
the end of racial oppression would insure Negro backing for
the war since "only a fool would fight for continued enslave-
ment, starvation, humiliation and lynching." Most blacks
had nothing but contempt for the lip service paid to high-
sounding principles, complaining that the government did
"nothing but mouth mystic words about fabled four freedoms." Just as they thought it necessary to reconcile democratic war aims with the treatment of minority groups at
home, so they believed that the United States should avoid
at all cost any trace of racism in its approach to Japan. Blacks
objected strenuously to the allegation that the Japanese were
inferior and deplored the racial motivation behind relocating
the West Coast Nisei. Roy Wilkins attributed the disaster

at Pearl Harbor in part "to the stupid habit of white people of looking down on all non-white nations."[3]

For a few blacks, the bonds forged by color and racial oppression proved stronger than those of nationality. During 1940 and 1941 street corner speakers in northern ghettoes preached the unity of colored peoples throughout the world, and exploited Negro resentment at Jewish merchants in Harlem and British imperialists in Africa. In the fall of 1942 the government took action against several religious cults, such as the Peace Movement of Ethiopia and the Brotherhood of Liberty for the Black People of America, which had promised that "Japan is going to liberate the dark races" by eliminating white rule in Asia. Sedition charges were brought against more than eighty blacks, including Robert Jordan who had told a Harlem audience that the Japanese "wanted to help you and give you back your culture" and who dreamed of "an Africa ruled by 20,000,000 American Negroes under the benevolent protection of a Japan, after the Rising Sun Empire had conquered all Asia and over-ridden the United States."[4] Supporters of the Axis, of course, never won more than a tiny following; a more common response among blacks was to take vicarious pleasure in the military success of nonwhite peoples.

Even though less hostility toward Japan existed among Negroes than whites, literally no pro-German sentiment could be found in the black community. The war demonstrated in a particularly cruel way that Negroes were in, but not yet of, American society, but nearly all who asked if the conflict was "a white man's war" answered that it was not. "If Hitler wins, every single right we now possess and for which we have struggled here in America for three centuries will be instantaneously wiped out," said the NAACP. "If the Allies win, we shall at least have the right to continue fighting for a share of democracy for ourselves."[5] What spokesmen for civil rights emphasized was not the bond of color between blacks and Japanese but the need for unity among American Negroes, not the success of the Japanese navy but the heroic exploits of Negroes when given the chance to fight. Black Americans did not seek an Axis victory but the right to contribute to an American victory.

Perhaps nothing better illustrated this insistence on full participation—as well as the use of the emergency as a lever for reform and the willingness to experiment with new protest techniques—than the March on Washington Movement that occurred in the summer of 1941, several months before the United States entered the war. The march, which was proposed by A. Philip Randolph of the Brotherhood of Sleeping Car Porters, originated in the discrimination against Negroes practiced both by defense contractors and the armed services. Randolph believed that a massive protest would, by pointing up the discrepancy between America's professed ideals and actual practice, embarrass the administration and force a change in its policies. In Randolph's view, "The Administration leaders in Washington will never give the Negro justice until they see masses—ten, twenty, fifty thousand Negroes on the White House lawn!" In May 1941 he called for a "thundering march" to "shake up white America."[6]

The March on Washington Movement differed from existing forms of protest in important respects: it attempted to mobilize the Negro masses rather than the middle class, it sought concessions through direct action and publicity rather than quiet back-stage negotiations, and it worked for reforms that would benefit northern urban Negroes as much as those living in the South. But it departed most radically from the practice of other civil rights organizations by excluding white people altogether. Starting from the premise that "no one will fight as hard to remove and relieve pain as he who suffers from it," Randolph concluded that "Negroes are the only people who are the victims of Jim Crow, and it is they who must take the initiative and assume the responsibility to abolish it." Although he welcomed the support of white liberals and the labor movement (but not of communists whom his membership policy was meant to exclude), Randolph did not trust them to lead the struggle. Furthermore, to the extent that blacks relied on white philanthropy and leadership they relinquished control over their own destiny. A number of whites, including Norman Thomas, A. J. Muste and Roger Baldwin defended Randolph's followers against the charge of racism in reverse. "At this stage of their development they need to assert a kind of sturdy independence in certain areas to prove to themselves and others that they are competent to handle their affairs without white leadership."[7]

While the March on Washington Movement adopted a separatist organizational structure, its goal was in every respect to achieve full integration. This was made clear in June 1941 when Randolph presented Roosevelt with a list of demands; significantly, all but one could be satisfied by presidential action. They included executive orders withholding defense contracts from manufacturers who discriminated in hiring, authorizing the government to seize any plant which proved refractory, abolishing "discrimination and segregation" in all branches of the armed forces and departments of the federal government, ending discrimination in vocational training courses, and instructing the United States Employment Service to refer workers without regard to race. Only one point required legislative as well as executive approval: Randolph wanted the President to ask Congress to deny collective bargaining rights under the Wagner Act to trade unions that barred Negroes from membership.[8]

The Roosevelt administration responded to the threatened march first by issuing statements in behalf of equal opportunity, then by exerting pressure upon Randolph to cancel the demonstration, and finally, when neither tactic proved successful, by making concessions on some points in order not to give up others. On April 11, 1941 Sidney Hillman and William Knudsen, the directors of the Office of Production Management, had urged defense contractors to hire workers without regard to race. A few weeks later Roosevelt suggested what would have been a revolutionary step: that the OPM require the employment of a stated percentage of Negroes in each factory. Replying that "if we set a percentage it will immediately be open to dispute," Knudsen and Hillman promised instead that they would "quietly get manufacturers to increase the number of Negroes on defense work."[9] Then, in mid-June, just two weeks before the march was scheduled to take place, Roosevelt went on record in support of the OPM letter to contractors. While the President's statement affirming that the United States must refute "at home the very theories which we are fighting abroad" was itself faultless, black leaders were unwilling to place much faith in pious announcements of hope unaccompanied by the power of enforcement.[10]

Even while it tried to appease the organizers of the march, the administration did everything possible to dissuade them from proceeding with their plans. Not only did the march call to mind the unhappy experience of the Bonus Army in 1932, but since Washington was very much a southern city it also carried a potential for violence. On June 7 Roosevelt asked that black Americans be informed that "the President is much upset to hear that several negro organizations are planning to March on Washington on July first, as he can imagine nothing that will stir up race hatred and slow up progress more than a march of that kind." Nearly every New Dealer with any standing in the black community fell in step. Eleanor Roosevelt, perhaps the white person most admired by Negroes, warned Randolph that the march would be "a very grave mistake;" the times were too "tense," she added, and an ugly "incident" might occur.[11] The President's press secretary hoped that Fiorello La Guardia could be induced "to exercise his persuasive powers to stop it. The Mayor has, of course, great influence with the New York negroes."[12] But these pleas counted for no more than had declarations of good intent. At Randolph's insistence, the President and several advisors met with a delegation of Negroes on June 18. In the week that followed an executive order was drawn up that satisfied some of Randolph's demands without requiring the administration to go further than it thought safe.

On June 25, 1941 the bargain was sealed: Roosevelt signed Executive Order 8802 and Randolph agreed to cancel the march. The executive order stipulated that government agencies, job training programs, and manufacturers accepting defense contracts put an end to discrimination in hiring. In addition, it created a Fair Employment Practices Committee to investigate complaints and attempt to enforce the ruling. Although the executive order failed to provide for integrating the armed forces, Randolph could hardly have held out for this point. Not only would he have jeopardized important economic gains but he was not at all certain that 50,000-100,000 Negroes could in fact be mobilized or that the administration would give any more ground if they were. Randolph's weapon was the threat of a march; to carry out the threat, particularly if it proved empty, would largely disarm his movement. The Negro press rightly construed Roosevelt's action as a victory and concluded that "we get more when we yell than we do when we plead."[13]

Even though no marchers paraded down Pennsylvania Avenue in 1941, Randolph decided to keep his organization intact. His own militancy did not diminish after Pearl Harbor —in planning the program for a Chicago rally in May 1942 he noted, "We don't want any spiritual song that indicates resignation or weakness"—but was, if anything, reinforced by his conception of the war. "This is not a war for freedom. It is not a war for democracy," he wrote, "it is a war to maintain the old imperialistic systems. It is a war to continue 'white supremacy,' . . . and the subjugation, domination, and exploitation of the peoples of color."[14] Certain that only agitation for democracy could transform the war into a people's revolution, Randolph called for mass marches on city halls and protest rallies to center attention on civil rights. In 1943 he advocated disciplined acts of civil disobedience. Negroes in the South should boycott Jim Crow railroad trains and keep their children out of school for a week; in the North, blacks should enter places they customarily avoided, "such as going into the downtown sections of cities as patrons of the hotels, restaurants and places of entertainment with their white Christian friends." In the summer of 1943 the March on Washington Movement laid plans for demonstrations in twenty-six cities. As Randolph framed the question:"If we don't demand now,when are we to demand?"[15]

Not all Negro leaders responded as Randolph would have liked. As his movement explored new forms of protest it sacrificed considerable support. Most other civil rights leaders had always regarded the movement's nationalist overtones with suspicion; now they objected to Randolph's socialist analysis of the war and denounced his call for civil disobedience. Randolph, said the *Pittsburgh Courier*, was "guilty of the most dangerous demagogery on record" for proposing a plan that would expose southern Negroes to violent retaliation from segregationists. Fear of such reprisal was exceedingly strong: one poll indicated that while seven of ten northern blacks thought segregation should be attacked, only one of ten southern Negroes took that position. The race riots in northern cities in the summer of 1943 contributed further to the disinclination to adopt radical tactics. The March on Washington Movement was, in addition, a victim of its own success. As jobs opened up for black workers much of its original impetus was lost. "The March on Washington Movement has lost ground rather than gained it," one sympathizer told Randolph in March 1943. "I get the impression from reading the press that you are a leader without a movement."[16]

At least one new civil rights group, however, took a stance similar to that of Randolph's movement. The Congress of Racial Equality, which was founded in 1942 by pacifists affiliated with the Fellowship of Reconciliation, endeavored to apply the same tactics of nonviolent resistance to the cause of racial justice that Gandhi had used in the movement for

Indian independence. Although CORE was an interracial organization, it stressed "nonviolent direct action" and concentrated on the economic aspects of racial injustice. Its goals, as set forth by James Farmer, were "not to make housing in ghettos more tolerable, but to destroy residential segregation; not to make Jim Crow facilities the equal of others, but to abolish Jim Crow; not to make racial discrimination more bearable, but to wipe it out."[17] In 1943 CORE sit-ins helped eliminate segregation in several movie theatres and restaurants in Detroit, Denver and Chicago; as yet the group did not test Jim Crow in the South.

Most civil rights activity during the war was channeled through the National Association for the Advancement of Colored People and the Urban League which relied on more traditional means of protest: exposure, propaganda, political pressure and legal action. Advocates of this approach conceded that it had inherent limitations. Thurgood Marshall, for example, recognized that "the NAACP can move no faster than the individuals who have been discriminated against. We only take up cases where we are requested to do so." Nevertheless, most of these civil rights leaders believed that progress was gradually taking place, that the political process could be made responsive to the will of the majority, that the courts would ultimately render impartial justice, that prejudice could be eliminated through education, and that without white support their movement had no future. By 1945 when the March on Washington Movement had gone into eclipse and CORE was still a tiny pacifist fellowship, membership in the NAACP had risen substantially and its monthly journal, *The Crisis*, reached 70,000 subscribers.[18]

The outlook for civil rights, however, depended not only on what the Negro wanted but on what the Roosevelt administration was willing to give. The President's sympathy for the victims of discrimination had always been matched by a dual conviction: that racial problems could be solved only through a gradual process of education, and that progress hinged on the Democratic party's ability to win votes both from southern whites and northern Negroes. After the United States entered the war, Roosevelt assumed that military needs took priority over everything else. Where the cause of racial justice served the conduct of the war—as in permitting more efficient use of Negro labor—the President supported it; where it seemed likely to disturb matters—as in starting a congressional filibuster over the poll tax—he would not lift a finger in its behalf. In December 1943 Roosevelt admitted, "I don't think, quite frankly, that we can bring about the millenium at this time." Always he endeavored to soothe southern sensibilities. When someone proposed using "The Battle Hymn of the Republic" as a national rallying-cry, Roosevelt responded: "There is still real objection in the south to some of the words. . . . I wish somebody would eliminate those verses and substitute something else."[19]

For the most part, northern liberals were more demanding than the President. However, even those who criticized the administration for compromising on the civil rights issue often drew the line quite sharply at militancy in wartime and affirmed that while blacks must not relent in their struggle for freedom, they must not struggle too hard. Otherwise they would alienate whites, cripple the war effort and sacrifice their position of moral authority. Writing in a series entitled "If I Were a Negro," Eleanor Roosevelt said she would continue to work for political and economic rights "but other things such as social relationships might well wait until certain people were given time to think them through and decide as individuals what they wish to do." She would be grateful for every forward step but "would not do too much demanding" and "would not try to bring those advances about any more quickly than they were offered." Oswald Garrison Villard, a founder of the NAACP, would "refrain from any acts which will unduly arouse or antagonize white people." "I would not go too fast in enforcing social rights," he added, "age-long conditions of prejudice and of deliberate white supremacy cannot be cured by legislation or government fiat." "If I were a Negro no hunger and bitterness inside me would be eased by the promises of a white liberal telling me forever to 'take it easy, take it easy,'" said an editor of the *New Republic*, who added a moment later, "I believe the Negro should take care to keep his race militancy below the danger point of violent reaction."[20]

Although Roosevelt's northern liberal constituency supported the civil rights movement as long as it stayed within moderate bounds, southern Democrats regarded the movement with horror. The most striking feature of white southern opinion during the war was its stubborn adherence to the code of behavior sanctioned by segregation. Convinced that the existing order was marked by harmony, white southerners explained away dissatisfaction as the product of outside agitation. "Anyone who hears Delta Negroes singing at their work, who sees them dancing in the streets, who listens to their rich laughter, knows that the Southern Negro is not mistreated. He has a care-free, child-like mentality, and looks to the white man to solve his problems and to take care of him," stated the Memphis *Cotton-Trade Journal* in August 1943. "To stir up sullen discontent and misguided hatreds is dangerous and wrong." This view was not confined to the least enlightened quarters; most southern liberals, while admitting the justice of many of the Negro's demands, were hardly less critical of those who pressed for full equality in wartime. Ralph McGill of the *Atlanta Constitution*, for example, savagely denounced black leaders who were "willing to pull the house down" if their demands were not met.[21]

The intensity of the southern response may be attributed to the increased militancy of civil rights groups, the criticisms voiced by northern liberals, the wartime upheaval in social and economic relations, and, possibly, a heightened discomfort at the charge that Jim Crow resembled the racial practices of the Nazis. Often the resulting uncertainty took forms that bordered on paranoia. Throughout the early 1940s a tidal wave of rumors swept the region, exploiting fears of sexual inadequacy, race warfare, and the unwillingness of Negroes to accept an inferior status. As white men were drafted, people said, blacks would take control of the South in general and white women in particular ("every Negro man will have a white girl when the white boys go off to war"); blacks, people whispered, were purchasing ice picks and storing guns in order to massacre whites during the next black-out (in August 1942 Senator John Bankhead of Alabama requested that the Army assign northern Negroes only to northern training camps); Negro women, it was commonly thought, would no longer work as domestic servants but were forming "Eleanor Clubs," named for the President's wife, whose goal was "a white woman in every kitchen by 1943." "The story was told that a lady asked a Negro 'wash woman' if she would do her wash that week, whereupon the woman replied, 'I'll do yours this week if you'll do mine next week.'"[22]

Because southerners played so pivotal a role in the Democratic coalition they demanded that the President pay attention to their grievances. Without the South, one congressman reminded the White House, "there would be no Democratic Party now and President Roosevelt would not have his position as President and I would not be in Congress. It will be very difficult to break up a solid South and there is only one thing that will really do it, and that is this race question." An Alabaman warned Roosevelt that if the government tolerated challenges to segregation "we are going to face a crisis in the South, [and] witness the annihilation of the Democratic party in this section." Unless white supremacy were maintained, Negroes would "become impudent, unruly, arrogant, law breaking, violent and insolent."[23] There was little variation in the theme: the South could settle its own racial problems, northern meddling would do no good, law-abiding citizens of both races were making slow but visible progress, the South could only fight one war at a time. Roosevelt's grip on the South had always been most secure when economic

issues overshadowed racial concerns; as the war reversed this
situation, white southerners became openly rebellious.

In April 1944 a Supreme Court decision abolishing the
white primary added to this unrest. The white primary, which
disenfranchised Negroes in eight southern states, had with-
stood several challenges. As recently as 1935 the Court had
unanimously declared in *Grovey v. Townsend* that the Democratic Party in Texas, as a private organization, might exclude
blacks without violating the Fourteenth Amendment. But in
1941 the Court cleared the ground for reversal by deciding
that primaries were an integral part of the election process,
and in April 1944 it ruled in favor of Dr. Lonnie E. Smith, a
Houston dentist, who had been refused a ballot by an election
judge named S. E. Allwright. Eight justices now concluded
that political parties were agents of the state and could not
nullify the right to vote by practicing racial discrimination.
Fearful that the decision would set off an explosion in the
South, Robert Jackson urged the Chief Justice not to assign
the majority opinion to Felix Frankfurter who, as a northern
liberal and a Jew, would "grate on Southern sensibilities."
Jackson suggested that the case would "be much less apt to
stir ugly reactions if the news that the white primary is dead,
is broken . . . by a Southerner who has been a Democrat and
is not a member of one of the minorities which stir prejudices
kindred to those against the Negro."[24] Stanley Reed of Kentucky wrote the majority opinion and only Owen Roberts,
who had spoken for the Court in 1935, dissented.

This gesture failed to mollify most southerners. While
editorial writers in states such as Virginia and North Carolina
which did not have white primaries seemed resigned to the
inevitable, newspapers in the deep South regarded the Court's
ruling as part of a broader campaign "to ram social equality
down the throats of the white people of the South." Politicians
of every stripe—from New Dealer Claude Pepper who commented "the South will allow nothing to impair white supremacy" to conservative Cotton Ed Smith who declared "all

those who love South Carolina and the white man's rule will rally in this hour of her great Gethsemane to save her from a disastrous fate"—denounced the Supreme Court.[25] The most defiant response occurred in South Carolina where Governor Olin D. Johnston called a special session of the state legislature to circumvent the decision. With rebel yells resounding in the chamber, the legislature attempted to evade the Court's finding that parties were agents of the state by repealing all laws regulating the conduct of primaries. The Democratic party then barred Negroes from voting in primaries. The Court of Appeals later disallowed this procedure.

The Supreme Court decision enfranchised some educated, middle-class Negroes, especially those living in cities. In 1946, 75,000 Negroes voted in the Texas primary and sent delegates to the county convention in Dallas. For the first time Negro poll tax deputies were appointed in Houston and Negro leaders chosen in colored precincts. Congressman Wright Patman first responded to *Smith v. Allwright* by saying that blacks would vote in his district "over my dead body;" two years later he was shaking hands at Negro church picnics. In South Carolina, where the decision was resisted, it still encouraged greater political involvement. Negroes formed the Progressive Democratic party and sent delegates (who were not seated) to the 1944 national convention to protest the state's lily-white policy and to force "the issue of Negro admission into the Democratic party."[26]

Nevertheless, most barriers to Negro voting remained as high as ever. Even when primaries were supposedly open, black applicants could be kept waiting in line all day, or made to pass literacy tests that required them to read, write and interpret sections of the state constitution to the satisfaction of the registrar. Moreover, the poll tax still existed in eight states. It prevented an estimated three million blacks and six million whites from voting, for while the tax was ordinarily one or two dollars, payment could be made retroactive. Finally, the administration showed little desire to support the

Court's ruling. In September 1944 when the Justice Department had to decide whether or not to bring suit on behalf of Negroes excluded from the Alabama primary, Roosevelt was informed that intervention "might be the fact which would translate impotent rumblings against the New Deal into an actual revolt at the polls."[27]

To a considerable extent, then, the standing of black people depended upon their own efforts to secure justice, the consideration Roosevelt and his liberal supporters gave to civil rights, the position taken by the Supreme Court, and the pressure exerted by white southerners. But what happened to the Negro during the war, especially after mid-1943, was also influenced by the manpower requirements of industry and the Army. How did wartime developments affect the Negro's economic prospects and what function did the Fair Employment Practices Committee serve? How did changing views in the War Department affect the Negro's place in the military? What impact did wartime changes have on the pattern of race relations?

As late as 1940 Negroes lived with more insecurity than most whites had known in the worst year of the depression. Unemployment remained high—one out of every five black workers was jobless at the end of the year—and those jobs that were available ordinarily involved hot, dirty work, paid badly and offered little security or chance of promotion. The surge in defense production failed to improve these conditions. In 1940, of 100,000 aircraft workers, only 240 were Negroes and those mainly janitors. Blacks comprised less than 1 percent of the work force in electrical machinery and less than 3 percent in the rubber industry. More often than not, white people filled the jobs available in national defense and Negroes took over the less desirable ones that whites had vacated such as hotel bellhops, short-order cooks, elevator operators and garage attendants. The proportion of blacks in all branches of manufacturing was lower in 1940 than it had been in 1930. Nearly two out of every three Negro workers, compared with one of five whites, were domestics, unskilled agricultural or industrial laborers, or in service industries. Similarly, blacks faced discrimination in government employment. The government hired Negroes as custodians but seldom as secretaries or clerks.

For a variety of reasons the door to economic opportunity remained locked during 1941. The depression had driven nearly half of all skilled black workers from their usual employment and many who had taken unskilled jobs could not easily pick up skills that had rusted with disuse. The large pool of unemployed white labor made it that much more difficult even for skilled Negroes to obtain defense jobs. Nearly all vocational training programs discriminated against blacks who, when they received instruction at all, were often taught to repair shoes or sew dresses rather than to operate complicated equipment. In addition, management often refused to consider blacks for other than low-level jobs on the grounds that they made poor workers and that white employees would resent their presence. In September 1941 a survey of employment prospects in armament factories showed that blacks would not even be considered for more than half of the new positions expected to open up and that the least opportunity existed at the highest level of skill. Firms were often brutally explicit. "The Negro will be considered only as janitors and in other similar capacities," stated North American Aviation. "Regardless of their training as aircraft workers, we will not employ them."[28]

Technological change created still another roadblock to advancement. By eliminating some unskilled jobs altogether and by demanding mastery of unfamiliar skills, the mechanization of industry often worked to the Negroes' disadvantage. Since black workers usually performed heavy, back-breaking work they were most easily replaced by machines. In southern coal mines, for example, Negroes had always done manual loading; but the advent of mechanical loaders displaced them, for operating such machines was considered white men's work.

In shipbuilding, where many Negroes had always found employment, the new skill of welding excluded those who had not received the necessary training. Similarly, conversion of the automobile industry directly threatened many black workers. Most of the Negroes employed by Ford and General Motors worked in the foundries, where the greatest cutbacks occurred. Foundry workers either had to take jobs on the assembly line or go without work.

The upgrading of Negro workers, however, met with stubborn resistance from sectors of the labor movement. Ill-concealed hostility had always marked the relationship between black workers and the AFL. In the past employers had recruited Negroes (who were often excluded from craft unions) as strikebreakers; black workers frequently saw the boss as benefactor and the union as foe. The discrimination practiced by craft unions derived from their fear of job competition, their origin as fraternal societies in which membership was a badge of social equality and, perhaps above all, from their racial biases. "Any Negro, any white man, or Chinaman or anybody else that would step forth and say they want social equality and intermingling of races," commented an AFL official, "couldn't be acting within his religion and he would be dissatisfied with God, and he would be denying everything God intended to be."[29]

Trade unions used a variety of methods to deprive black workers of a living. The railroad brotherhoods and the machinists excluded them through constitutional provisions or ritual. The boilermakers and shipbuilders placed Negroes in separate auxiliaries: while black members paid the same dues, they could transfer only to another segregated branch, had no voice in union affairs, had no grievance committee, received smaller death and disability benefits than whites, and could not be upgraded without the consent of the supervising white local. Negroes had always received fairer treatment from the CIO. Composed of industrial unions that needed to organize entire plants and led in some instances by communists or socialists, the CIO always took a public stand for equal rights. Even so, at various times in 1941 and 1942 white automobile workers in Detroit, many of them recent migrants from the South, resisted efforts to upgrade Negroes by walking off the job.

But as the manpower pinch grew tighter in 1943, many of the obstacles to Negro employment collapsed. With labor shortages becoming more acute each day and the government considering plans for manpower allocation, employers began to relax the bars to hiring and unions found it more difficult to maintain restrictive policies. Negroes, who accounted for just 3 percent of all war workers in the summer of 1942, comprised more than 8 percent three years later. The number of skilled workers doubled, and even larger gains took place in semi-skilled positions. Ultimately, one million black Americans, nearly two-thirds of them women, took jobs during the war. Lured by the promise of steady work, black people by the hundreds of thousands left the farm for the factory. For the most part, those from southern rural areas sought work in the steel mills or shipyards of Norfolk, Savannah or Charleston and those with an urban background more often migrated to the North and West. Although the war afforded new opportunities in industry, patterns of occupational discrimination persisted: the percentage of unskilled black workers remained constant, and most white collar and managerial positions were still reserved for whites.

The progress of Negro workers depended heavily upon how much support war agencies were willing to provide. Not only did the federal government itself hire more blacks—the number increased from 60,000 to 200,000—and employ them more often in higher classifications, but in 1943 it took three giant steps toward assuring fair opportunity: in June the War Labor Board outlawed wage differentials based on race, in September the United States Employment Service reversed existing policy by refusing to honor requests that specified the race of applicants, and in November the National Labor

Relations Board stated that it would refuse to certify unions excluding minority groups. But the agency that could have aided Negro workers most effectively was the Fair Employment Practices Committee, which Roosevelt had created in June 1941 in response to the demands of the March on Washington Movement. The pressures exerted upon the FEPC, the hurdles placed in its path, the decisions it made and the resulting response—all revealed that the path to economic equality even in wartime was anything but smooth.

From the beginning lack of funds, personnel and authority impeded the Committee. During its first year it spent only $80,000, hired twenty employees, and failed to set up any regional offices. Although it had jurisdiction over firms holding defense contracts, the Committee could not act even in blatant cases of discrimination unless a formal complaint was made. Many workers were reluctant to file charges or unaware of their right to do so. When Negroes knew that a plant hired only whites they often did not ask for jobs; yet when a plant that did hire Negroes turned one down it might be charged with discrimination. Consequently, the FEPC sometimes acted not against the worst offenders but against those whose policies were relatively fair. Even when allegations of bias were proved true, the FEPC had little authority to act. Lacking any statutory power, it could not require compliance with its orders; rather it relied on moral suasion and help from other war agencies with enforcement power. Its ultimate weapon—requesting cancellation of a defense contract—was no weapon at all, for the administration was unwilling to jeopardize war production. Even one friend of the FEPC admitted, "For the government to terminate an important war contract by reason of the contractor's indulgence in discriminatory employment would be highly impracticable."[30]

Cases that might complicate international relations were declared off limits. In June 1942 the Committee scheduled public hearings on discrimination against Mexican-Americans in the copper mines, shipyards and oil refineries of the Southwest. The State Department immediately blocked the investigation. Such discrimination admittedly tarnished the nation's image in Latin America, Sumner Welles informed Roosevelt, but the solution would require "time, tact and patience." Hearings were unnecessary because everyone knew discrimination existed; and washing dirty linen in public would not solve the problem. Welles reported the Mexican government's view that "any publicity in connection with our efforts to combat racial discrimination against Mexicans in this country would be most harmful." Furthermore he suggested that an open inquiry would furnish material for Axis propagandists. The FEPC tried to answer these arguments by claiming that it was obligated to respond to legitimate complaints, that fair treatment would improve relations with Mexico, and that enemy agents would use cancellation for purposes of propaganda. But in July Roosevelt decided to suspend the hearings for "international reasons." The FEPC later reported that the private pressure it continued to exert had resulted primarily in "formal paper compliance," "token upgradings," and "open defiance."[31]

For much of its life the Committee's hands were tied by more powerful agencies. Located at first in the Office of Production Management and then in the War Production Board, the FEPC was shifted in June 1942 to the newly-created War Manpower Commission. Ignoring the protests of Negro leaders who understood how profoundly administrative location could affect the Committee's work and who lacked confidence in WMC Director Paul V. McNutt, Roosevelt asserted that since the FEPC's chief purpose was manpower utilization the transfer made sense. But under McNutt the agency withered. Precisely because of his concern with manpower, McNutt would not press racial demands that might anger labor or management. Eventually he even refused to forward complaints of discrimination to the FEPC. The NAACP learned that "there is no room for optimism as to the success of FEPC under its present set-up." In January 1943 when

McNutt postponed an inquiry into bias in the railroad unions, several Committee members resigned and the agency plunged to its lowest point of influence. Roosevelt finally granted a reprieve in May 1943 by creating a new FEPC, placing it in the Executive Office of the President where it enjoyed some measure of autonomy, increasing its appropriations, and expanding its authority to conduct investigations and insert anti-bias clauses in government contracts.

Yet even the relative security of the President's office did not immunize the FEPC against the virus of congressional hostility. Republicans did not lead the crusade against the agency. "It probably would not be wise politically to oppose the FEPC," one aide informed a Republican congressman. "Actually it is not a Presidential idea but one forced on him by the Negroes, and . . . which has already caused him considerable embarrassment."[32] But since southern whites regarded what one newspaper called "dat cummittee fer de perteckshun of Rastus & Sambo" as an attempt to foment racial discord, integrate the public schools and produce a "mongrel race," there was every reason in the world for southern Democrats to oppose the agency. To John Rankin the FEPC heralded "the beginning of a communistic dictatorship," to L. Mendel Rivers it implied "bloodshed," and to James Eastland it suggested a failure of understanding: "What the people of this country must realize is that the white race is a superior race, and the Negro race is an inferior race."[33] Early in 1944 southerners launched a two-pronged offensive. Howard Smith of Virginia turned an investigation of the FEPC into a public forum for segregationists and shortly thereafter opponents nearly destroyed the agency by denying it funds. After failing on a test vote, the FEPC appropriation squeaked through the House by a 123-119 margin.

Complaints that the FEPC desired to revolutionize race relations were exaggerated. The committee chairmen believed in gradualism and were reluctant to move more quickly than public opinion would allow. The first chairman, Mark

Ethridge, was publisher of the Louisville *Courier-Journal*. Like other southern liberals, Ethridge feared that the FEPC had been set up in response to the "agitators" who might not give it the necessary "elbow-room." Expressing opposition to anti-discrimination legislation, Ethridge hoped that the President "would point out that discrimination is as old as the world and its eradication cannot be brought about except by persistence and patience over a long time." In 1942 Malcolm S. MacLean, president of Hampton Institute, replaced Ethridge. MacLean, who did not wish to give "undue encouragement" to advocates of civil rights, was intensely loyal to the President. "As I see it," he wrote, "the job of me and the Committee is to keep the heat off of the 'Boss' and at the same time to make as steady progress in practical ways as we can."[34] MacLean was followed by the prominent Catholic educator Monsignor Francis J. Haas. Although his commitment to the cause of racial justice was unquestioned, Haas nevertheless told a presidential assistant in September 1943: "I understand fully what you mean when you question the wisdom of stressing the magnitude of racial discrimination and understate the gains achieved. Although the patient is very ill, the fact that he is improving is the significant thing and should be emphasized. . . . Emphasizing improvement rather than seriousness is good for the patient and for every one else." The last wartime chief of the FEPC, the newspaperman and public relations expert Malcolm Ross, shared this view.[35]

Guided largely by these assumptions, the Committee did not consider segregation, as opposed to discrimination, cause for action. "Segregation, per se, is of no concern to my committee," said Malcolm Ross in 1944.[36] When white shipyard workers in Mobile rioted because Negroes were promoted to jobs as welders the FEPC sanctioned an arrangement that set aside four segregated shipways on which blacks could become welders, riggers and riveters (but not electrical workers, machine operators or pipe fitters.) Again, when white employees demonstrated against the integration of dining and locker room facilities in a Baltimore defense plant—forcing the Army to take over—the FEPC accepted a settlement providing for de facto segregation. The company built a larger washroom and cafeteria; by an informal understanding, whites and Negroes stayed at opposite ends. Such compromises, however, were not always possible.

From the start the problem of discrimination by the nation's railroad unions plagued the FEPC. With the introduction of Diesel engines during the 1930s, jobs as firemen, which had often been filled by Negroes, became much more attractive to white workers. Consequently, the Brotherhood of Locomotive Firemen and Enginemen reached an agreement with most of the southern railroads that sharply restricted employment of blacks and prohibited their promotion to firemen. In 1941 the Railway Mediation Board gave this pact its stamp of approval. Responding to complaints from Negro workers, the FEPC called for open hearings. But in January 1943 the War Manpower Commission postponed them so as to avoid labor unrest and possible disruption of vital transportation. When hearings finally occurred nine months later, the union refused to appear and the owners insisted that they would continue to abide by local mores. The FEPC ordered that discrimination stop; both parties refused to comply. In December 1943 the case went to the President who disposed of it by appointing a special investigating committee. This group had not reached a decision by December 1944 when the Supreme Court finally found the union's practice unconstitutional. By flouting the FEPC's directive, the railroad brotherhoods had exposed the agency's weakness.

The FEPC, however, scored a major victory in the Philadelphia transit strike. By 1943 the barriers to hiring Negroes as street car conductors and motormen had broken down in Detroit, New York and Cleveland, but the Philadelphia transit company claimed that its union contract prohibited

giving platform jobs to Negroes. In December 1943, after
a month-long inquiry, the FEPC directed the company to
upgrade blacks but did not try to enforce the order pending
the outcome of union elections. In March the Transport
Workers Union, which favored racial equality, defeated the
existing leadership. The contract it negotiated contained no
discriminatory provisions, and in July the company selected
eight Negroes for training as streetcar operators. At that
point several leaders of the old union, whose sound truck
during the election had blared "A vote for the TWU is a vote
to give your job to a nigger!", saw a golden opportunity to
regain their influence.[37] They stirred up discontent by arguing
that the seniority of upgraded blacks would include the time
spent in lower grades. Although the claim was untrue, on
August 1 several hundred men went on strike and the company, asserting that it feared violence but probably hoping
to assist the old-line union leadership, shut off the power.
Public transportation ground to a halt; absenteeism at the
Philadelphia Navy Yard soared to 72 percent. The government moved in swiftly with overwhelming force: the Army
placed soldiers on the vehicles, the FBI arrested four strike
leaders, and the selective service system announced that
workers who did not return would either be drafted or fired
and denied unemployment benefits. Within forty-eight hours
the strike collapsed.

The FEPC clearly had greater freedom in dealing with the
Philadelphia strikers than with the railroad workers. In the
railroad dispute a powerful union could have paralyzed the
nation, troops could not have broken the strike, and the
administration had to consider southern sensibilities. By
contrast, the transit strike was called by discontented elements
within a divided union, was on a small enough scale so that
troops could have provided emergency transportation, and
was localized in a northern city. As a result the administration backed the Committee solidly. In other instances as well
the Committee pried open opportunities for black workers,

but most substantive gains seem to have occurred as a result of manpower shortages rather than FEPC action. Only one-third of the 8,000 complaints registered with the FEPC—and only one-fifth of those filed in the South—were resolved successfully. More often than not the Committee met with defiance. In all, employers and unions disregarded 35 of 45 compliance orders. Opponents of equality had the last word in the summer of 1945 when, after a fierce battle, Congress sliced the Committee's budget in half and provided for its dissolution within a year. Its career as a force for racial justice was ended.

The armed forces offered as much resistance to racial equality as had industry but once again the pressures of war forced a revision in policy. In 1940 the American military expressed open disdain for black recruits. Negroes could not enlist in the Marines or Air Corps. They could join the Navy only as messmen. They were accepted in the Army but segregated rigidly: "The policy of the War Department is not to intermingle colored and white enlisted personnel in the same regimental organizations."[38] Officially the War Department took blacks in proportion to their share of the population and assigned them to separate combat and noncombat units. White officers commanded Negro combat units; Negroes who attended officer training schools were always assigned to black service or reserve units. William Hastie, who advised Secretary of War Henry L. Stimson on racial problems, described the situation in September 1941: "In tactical organization, in physical location, in human contacts, the Negro soldier is separated from the white soldier as completely as possible."[39]

The Army's segregation policy threw the American color-caste system into bold relief. Among civilians occupational lines could easily become blurred. While Negroes often worked at jobs with the least status and lowest pay, and although white assembly-line workers outranked black foundry workers, the caste system was far from rigid. Some blacks did of course hold better paying jobs than some whites, a perfect correlation did not always exist between financial reward and social status, and the hierarchical structure was subject to some confusion. In the Army all such doubt was removed. No black officer assigned to a black unit could outrank or command a white officer in the same unit; that is, no Negro was allowed to hold a rank higher than that held by the lowest-ranking white officer. The distinctions between a corporal and a sergeant, between a sergeant and a lieutenant, were razor-sharp and strictly reinforced a hundred times a day.

The Army justified its position on theoretical and practical grounds. Military leaders believed that Negroes had not performed well in combat during World War I and attributed this to racial inferiority. "Leadership is not imbedded in the negro race yet and to try to make commissioned officers to lead men into battle—colored men—is only to work disaster to both," Stimson said in 1940. Another officer found a "general consensus of opinion that colored units are inferior to the performance of white troops, except for service duties," but thought this could be explained by "the inherent psychology of the colored race and their need for leadership."[40] The War Department, moreover, thought that it should not serve as a laboratory for social experimentation but conform to civilian practices. To desegregate the army would cripple morale, George Marshall told Stimson late in 1941, for "the War Department cannot ignore the social relationships between negroes and whites which have been established by the American people through custom and habit." There was finally the dual conviction that "the basic issues of this war" did not involve "the question of whether Colored troops serve in segregated units or in mixed units," and that, as Stimson put it, "what these foolish leaders of the colored race are seeking is at the bottom social equality."[41]

The Jim Crow practices of the armed forces infuriated most Negroes. They blamed the Army for improperly training and equipping black troops in 1918, and held that soldiers who

were asked to submit like lambs to segregated training facilities could not be expected to perform like lions on the battlefield. They particularly resented the Army's decision first to
reject Negro blood donors and then to segregate plasma according to the donor's race. Not only did discrimination by
the military derive from explicit assumptions of racial superi-
ority, but it also symbolized the Negro's second-class status.
Above all it cruelly limited one of the few avenues open to
advancement. Restricted on so many sides, Negroes had
traditionally been oriented toward military service which,
even under a segregated system, had offered some measure
of opportunity, recognition and professional standing. As
the draft dramatically increased the number of black soldiers—
700,000 were serving in the Army by the fall of 1944 compared
to 97,000 in December 1941—restrictive policies regarding
officer assignment, combat duty and the use of training facilities seemed even more onerous.

Only when it became evident that the existing system involved an unacceptable waste of manpower was it modified.
The Navy took the longest strides toward racial equality.
In April 1942 it agreed to accept Negroes for general labor
service and after James Forrestal was appointed Secretary
in May 1944 integration proceeded rapidly. By the fall 500
Negro seamen were serving as radiomen and gunner's mates
in integrated crews on twenty-five ships. The Army, too,
gradually broadened its policy. In June 1943 it lowered literacy
requirements and created a special unit to instruct the edu-
cationally deprived. Southern Negroes benefitted most from
this program. In 1944 the Army attempted to desegregate
training camp facilities, but the order was often disobeyed,
especially in the South. Even troop assignment policy underwent a change: black soldiers went overseas and saw combat
more often. Negroes made up almost half of the transportation
corps in Europe; twenty-two combat units engaged in ground
operations. In January 1945, during the Battle of the Bulge,
2500 Negroes who volunteered as infantry replacements

served in platoons assigned to white companies. That was the closest the Army came to integration on the battlefield.

To some extent these measures were intended to eliminate racial discord in the armed forces. In the summer of 1943 racial explosions rocked nine training camps, most but not all of which were in the South. These conflicts were rooted in the resentment of Negro soldiers, especially those from the North, who had been placed under southern white officers, assigned inferior facilities, exposed to community hostility and subjected to what they regarded as police brutality. Sometimes the normal hardships of military life were attributed to racial discrimination. In several instances Negro soldiers seized arms to protect themselves or retaliate against some outrage. At Camp Van Dorn in Mississippi, after a sheriff shot a soldier who was fleeing arrest, Negroes broke into a stockade, took a supply of rifles and exchanged fire with a riot squad. Blacks at Camp Stewart in Georgia, believing that white soldiers had raped a Negro woman, seized submachine guns; in the ensuing skirmish one military policeman was killed and four wounded.

The deadliest riots occurred not on Army bases but in cities where war had disrupted the prevailing pattern of race relations. The massive influx of Negro and white workers often strained transportation, housing and recreational facilities to the bursting point. Wartime overcrowding washed away the informal demarcation lines between Negro and white areas and multiplied the potential sources of friction. White workers often regarded the gains made by Negroes in defense industry as a threat to their own status and security. Then too, as the draft called up trained policemen the task of law enforcement became that much more difficult. The situation was further inflamed by increased minority group militancy at a time when most whites assumed that Negroes were satisfied with their treatment and getting the opportunities they deserved. Given these conditions, a rumor of rape, an allegation of police brutality or a dispute over the use of a public park could bring on race war.

No city was more deeply affected by the wartime boom than Detroit, and no city more nearly resembled a tinder box. From 1940 to 1943 half a million people, including some 60,000 blacks, had moved to Detroit. Migration placed an unbearable strain on housing: one of every two Negro families and one of every seven white families lived in substandard homes. An investigator reported that "a converted residence, where one family once lived, contains 150 Negroes, often one family to a room." Five times as many people died from tuberculosis and twice as many infants died in the ghetto as in the city as a whole. Yet every move to improve living conditions brought Negroes into conflict with various groups, particularly white workers who resented job competition, Jewish merchants who owned stores in the Negro district, and Polish Catholics who, according to a report prepared by the FEPC, "dislike the Negroes for having decreased realty values and for surrounding the expensive churches built by and for the Poles who formerly lived there." Unhappily, the maintenance of racial peace was left to the local police force, which had lost a large number of experienced men. By 1943 the fabric of the city's life seemed to be unravelling. "Detroit is a mining town, set in Michigan, instead of Montana," claimed one observer. "There is no strong public point of view except the booster attitude, loving everything big, including riots."[42]

The riot erupted on a hot Sunday evening in June 1943. Nearly one hundred thousand people had spent the day at Belle Isle recreation park, which was located near the Negro ghetto of Paradise Valley. Early in the evening, when sporadic fights broke out between white and black teenagers, rumors of rape and murder spread like prairie fire. Within a few hours race war had engulfed the ghetto. Negroes smashed windows, stoned cars and attacked white workers returning from a night shift. Whites dragged Negroes off trolley cars and beat them; policemen shot a number of looters and exchanged fire with rooftop snipers. By Monday afternoon, June 24, a large crowd of whites had gathered at the edge of Paradise Valley. "One Negro, angered because the mob of whites had stoned his home, rushed out of his house and blazed away at them with a shot gun, scattering the mob." By nightfall the streets leading into the ghetto "had been infiltrated by rioters armed with clubs, bricks, stones and other missiles with the avowed intention of invading 'Paradise Valley,' beating up the Negro population and destroying it by fire."[43] When it became apparent that the police had lost control the governor reluctantly requested federal assistance. Six thousand soldiers, who had been alerted earlier, moved into Detroit on Monday night and dispersed the crowd. For days troops patrolled the streets enforcing an uneasy truce that was occasionally punctured by violence. In the riot, twenty-five Negroes and nine whites were killed, nearly seven hundred people injured and $2 million worth of property destroyed.

No two groups drew the same lesson from all this turmoil. The explanation offered most often by liberals was that Axis agents had stirred up racial unrest in order to disrupt war production and destroy morale. Northern newspapers more frequently attributed the riot to fifth column activities than to poor social conditions. In addition, many Negroes blamed the Detroit police for failing to restrain white rioters and for shooting at blacks without provocation. City and state officials in Michigan, on the other hand, charged that the riot resulted largely from "the positive exhortation to be 'militant' in the struggle for racial equality." They attacked the Negro press and NAACP for "fomenting trouble with their crusades in the Negro neighborhoods." Attorney General Francis Biddle, who traced racial disturbances to deplorable conditions in the ghetto, nevertheless proposed an unfortunate solution: the government should prohibit the migration of Negroes to areas where "physical limitations or cultural background" would prevent their absorption. When this recommendation was leaked to the Negro press, it caused a furor and was quickly dropped.[44]

The frustrations of ghetto life also boiled over in New York City, but in a different way. On Sunday night, August 1,

1943, a rumor circulated that a policeman had killed a black soldier in a Harlem hotel. Thousands of Negroes then rampaged through the business district, hurling rocks, breaking into stores and looting. Unlike Detroit, there was no clash between blacks and whites, life in the rest of the city went on very much as usual, and the police won praise for their impartiality from Negro leaders. Fiorello La Guardia, who drove through Harlem urging people to return to their homes, deputized 1500 Negro volunteers, attempted to team white and black patrolmen and ordered the police not to shoot at looters. Even so, six Negroes were killed and three hundred were injured. Black spokesmen termed the riot a "mad, shameful, disgraceful orgy" and a survey indicated that fewer than one in three Harlem residents thought it justified. Yet if violence was not condoned, most viewed the outburst as a product of "deep resentment against oppression." White Americans, said the *Amsterdam News*, "give the Negro a complete feeling of not belonging . . . of being unwanted." For violence to end, "Negroes must be made to feel that they are a part of this country."[45]

Negroes were not the only ethnic minority in the United States, nor the only one involved in wartime racial clashes. In California and the Southwest, Mexican-Americans were also victims of discrimination. Set apart by language as well as skin color, they were often segregated ("For Colored and Mexicans" read a sign outside a church in Texas), forced to live in filthy shanties, barred from good jobs, and deprived of political influence. Many Mexican-American youths, caught between rival cultural traditions, sought security and status in "Pachuco" gangs and adopted a costume distinctively their own. The zoot-suit—broad felt hat, long key chain with pocket knife, trousers that were flared at the knees and tapered at the ankles, long hair—appealed to many lower-class white and Negro youths as well, but in Los Angeles it was most commonly associated with Mexican-Americans. To the middle-classes, the zoot-suiters spelled a threat to law and order, in part because newspapers played up gang warfare whenever it occurred.

Over a period of four days in early June 1943 sailors from the Chavez Ravine Naval Base invaded the Mexican sections of Los Angeles, ostensibly to revenge servicemen who had been attacked by zoot-suiters. While the police looked the other way, sailors roamed the streets, stripped zoot suits off teenaged Mexican boys and beat them. According to one account, "Procedure was standard: grab a zooter. Take off his pants and frock coat and tear them up or burn them. Trim the 'Argentine ducktail' haircut that goes with the screwy costume." The city was finally declared off limits to naval personnel and an unsuccessful attempt was made to ban the wearing of zoot suits. Similar flare-ups on a much smaller scale occurred in San Diego, Philadelphia and Chicago where the victims were more often Negroes."[46]

The riots in Los Angeles, Harlem and Detroit, as well as those at military bases, reflected some of the tensions produced by wartime changes in race relations. Yet violence remained the exception rather than the rule. For the most part the civil rights movement proceeded peacefully: Negro leaders hammered out new tactics revolving around the use of civil disobedience, the Supreme Court took the first step toward guaranteeing southern Negroes the right to vote, industry provided fresh opportunities for black workers, and the armed services edged away from their policy of segregation. Moreover, the war brought many Negroes into cities and thereby increased their potential political influence. While only the first cracks in the armor of segregation had appeared by 1945, the war had served as a catalyst in the struggle for equal rights.

THE SOCIAL IMPACT OF WAR

DURING THE 1930s THE MOST urgent social problems seemed to be an outgrowth of the depression. Poverty-stricken families, hungry children, ramshackle houses, the gnawing fear of the future—all were clearly enough the product of hard times, and most people assumed that if only the economy were set right all would be well. But the American experience in World War II showed that this was only half the story, for even as it solved some familiar problems the war gave birth to new ones. Hoovervilles may have given way to boom towns and the stream of Okies been replaced by defense workers, but the resulting disruption of family life and breakdown in community services suggested that wartime prosperity was not without its social costs. If the war offered many Americans a higher standard of living and a satisfying outlet for their energies, it just as surely subjected families and communities to severe strain.

For most Americans World War II spelled neither hardship

nor suffering but a better way of life. In part this was because
the war followed a decade of distress: high earnings and full
employment contrasted sharply with conditions during most
of the 1930s, and millions of people gained a chance to get
back on their feet, clear up old debts, and make a new start.
While these economic gains cannot be weighed on the same
scale as the loss of a husband or brother in battle, it is nevertheless clear that Americans suffered proportionately few
casualties. The one million soldiers who were killed, wounded,
or reported missing in battle comprised less than 1 percent of
the total population; the corresponding figure in the Soviet
Union was 8 percent. Midway through the war nearly seven
out of ten Americans could say something with which few
people in Russia, England, or France could have agreed: that
the war had not required them to make any "real sacrifices."

Indeed, many of the sacrifices that were made hardly seemed
to be sacrifices at all, for people frequently derived great
satisfaction from contributing to the common good. "In this
war all of us, civilians as well as troops, may come under
fire," warned an advocate of civilian defense, who added
quickly: "But the cheerful side of this fact is that this war
offers us stay-at-homes a greater chance for real service than
any war in the past." A newspaper columnist put her readers
on notice that "bridge clubs that last all day have no place
in your life any more. Neither have all day gabfests. You have
work to do. . . . You'll roll bandages and knit, . . . cooperate
in blackout practices, . . . learn about first aid." Similarly,
sociologists reported finding a sense of "unconscious well-
being" because "everyone is doing something to help in the
common desperate enterprise in a co-operative rather than in
a private spirit." The belief that everyone had to do his share
strengthened each person's sense of his own worth. To a large
extent, participation in a common cause tended to enhance
feelings of comradeship and well-being.[1]

The government, seeking to bolster morale and speed up
mobilization, did all it could to channel civilian energies into

war-related tasks. In addition to organizing corps of air-raid wardens, fire fighters, auxiliary police and nurses' aides, the Office of Civilian Defense maintained that people could, through discipline and self-denial, contribute to an American victory. "Every time you decide *not* to buy something, you help to win the war," the agency noted as part of its anti-inflation campaign. The least momentous act—such as driving a neighbor to work to conserve rubber, or refusing to hoard scarce commodities—was imbued with broad significance, because, as the agency put it, "the empty seat is a gift to Hitler" and "hoarders are on the same level as spies." The OCD also gave a "V Home Award" as "a badge of honor for those families which have made themselves into a fighting unit on the home front" by conserving food, salvaging vital materials, buying war bonds, and refusing to spread rumors.[2]

The activities undertaken by civilians often called for a high level of community cooperation and served an important integrative function. In large cities, for example, victory gardens were planted in vacant lots and whole neighborhoods took part in caring for them. (Dietary habits also changed as people learned to eat kohlrabi, Swiss chard and other uncommon vegetables they had grown themselves.) Drives to collect scrap metal, paper and rubber also joined people in a common enterprise. In Virginia men discovered a way to raise sunken ship hulks from the James River; in Wyoming a group dismantled an old 20-ton steam engine and built several miles of road to get it to a collection center. Children took a particularly active role in these drives. Banding together and styling themselves "Junior Commandos," "Uncle Sam's Scrappers," and "Tin-Can Colonels" they rummaged through attics, emptied garages, and made door-to-door collections. If the mood of the 1930s had been expressed by an old jalopy filled with migrant workers on their way west, that of the war was conveyed by an old jalopy on its way to the scrap pile with a sign reading "Praise the Lord, I'll Soon Be Ammunition."

The wartime sense of shared purpose was heightened by the use of certain images and symbols. Of these, none was more common than the "V" for victory. Throughout the war the opening strains of Beethoven's Fifth Symphony stood for the letter "v" in Morse Code: dot-dot-dot-dash. "Vivacious Victory" girls entertained soldiers in canteens, a Broadway musical included "Of V We Sing," and Louisiana State University erected a huge V on its memorial tower: at night, red, white and blue bulbs flashed on and off in a dot-dot-dot-dash rhythm. (The government balked only at calling overtime work "Victory Time" on the grounds that "all too often such a proposal might evoke a Bronx cheer.")[3] Civilians also gained a vicarious sense of participation in the conflict through their image of the American soldier. The media portrayed the GI as courageous yet antimilitaristic, a killer in combat yet essentially kind at heart, devoted to principle yet wanting nothing as much as the simple comforts of home. As John Morton Blum has observed, the stereotype of a "conscript yeoman—a competent but fundamentally an amateur and transient soldier" was one with which civilians could readily identify.[4]

Then too, Americans were brought together by a common sense of danger and hatred of the enemy. In the early days of the war people who lived along the East and West coasts did not rule out the possibility of invasion, bombardment or espionage. At rallies in New York City in the spring of 1942 detectives searched the speakers' stand "lest some warped mind might have secreted a bomb to ruin the patriotic occasion," and the airplanes flying in formation overhead carried full combat crews so that, in the reassuring words of the *New York Times*, they "could answer any call to duty in case an enemy air raid occurred during the demonstration."[5] Even after the fear of attack passed, concern for the safety of relatives in the armed services acted as a unifying agent. This emotion cut across class lines: people living in elegant homes and those in decrepit shanties took part in the same farewell ceremonies at train stations, scanned the same newspaper columns for information about local servicemen, and displayed the same flags in their windows.

As the war created socially approved ways of expressing hatred for the Axis powers it tended to drain off internal social antagonisms and, according to one investigator, served a "therapeutic" function and strengthened national unity. More often than not, hatred was directed against Hitler and Mussolini rather than the German or Italian people (although Rex Stout, chairman of the Writers' War Board, asserted in a controversial article, "I hate Germans, and am not ashamed of it,") but against the Japanese people as well as the Emperor. This distinction was illustrated by floats carried in one parade. A "Hitler—the Axis War Monster" display was a hundred-foot long mechanical monster driven by a skeleton around which were strewn the mutilated bodies of women and children; a "Tokyo—We Are Coming" float was much less specific and more frankly racist. "It showed a big American eagle leading a flight of bombs down on a herd of yellow rats which were trying to escape in all directions." A reporter noted that "the crowd loved it."[6]

Many of the sentiments that united Americans—the willingness to sacrifice, the urge to participate, the sense of peril and hatred of the enemy—were reinforced by newspaper, magazine and radio advertisements. With consumer goods in short supply businessmen were not primarily interested in motivating people to buy more, but by linking their product with the war they hoped to keep alive brand name preferences, build up postwar demand, and maintain good will. In a sense, war reversed the traditional themes of advertising: people were urged to do with less and defer gratification. Ford assured Americans that "truly there's a great day coming" when Fords would again be available; ALCOA advised people to buy war bonds so they would be able to purchase aluminum products after the war; B. F. Goodrich asked its customers to conserve rubber since "Hitler smiles when you waste miles."

One advertisement, depicting the face of a Japanese person, announced "there's only one way to exterminate the slant-eyes—with gunpowder." Another showed a bullet-headed Nazi leering at three young girls and raised the specter of a German victory: "You they may cast aside and put to some ignominious task, . . . But your daughter . . . well, if she's young and healthy and strong, a Gauleiter with an eye for beauty may decide she is a perfect specimen for one of their experimental camps. A high honor for your daughter."[7]

Government officials encouraged advertisers to emphasize these themes and use the war as a backdrop. Advertisers, said an official in the Office of War Information, faced a new kind of challenge: "The job is not to influence [the citizen] to the point of spending his money for a 'product', but to invigorate, instruct and inspire him as a functioning unit in his country's greatest effort." This could be done in part by stressing Allied war aims and the differences between life in Germany and the United States ("A room filled with heiling kids and . . . a busy class room with relaxed children.") While the war should not be dragged in "where it does not belong," he favored "ads explaining what each of the Four Freedoms means and tying them in with the message of the advertiser." A breakfast cereal manufacturer, for example, might contrast "the Hitler 'Jugend' creed" with "our Boy Scout oath." "The message would be: 'We want our sons to grow up according to our creed — fine, healthy, clean-minded and not like Nazi hoodlums.'"[8]

Whether or not the values of sacrifice, self-denial and co-operation which the government inculcated and to which advertisers paid tribute ever gained full acceptance is a moot point. Certainly the difficulty of encouraging new forms of behavior in a society that had always prized individual initiative and pursued the main chance should not be underestimated. Most likely some Americans never accepted wartime mores, others accepted them as long as they imposed only slight inconveniences, and still others accepted them at first but reverted to more traditional ways of behaving as the war progressed. Not everyone had a relative in combat, and few could become as enthusiastic about the seventh bond drive as about the first. As the initial wave of patriotic emotion passed, as sacrifices became more demanding, as the danger of invasion disappeared and victory grew more certain, people became more likely to look out for themselves. The longer the war lasted, the more the balance shifted from public and collective to private and personal concerns.

Perhaps nothing better illustrated the gap between selfless rhetoric and grubby reality than the black market. Rationing and price controls, although they held down the cost of living and enjoyed considerable public support, gave rise to countless means of evasion. Merchants charged consumers too much for scarce items; landlords demanded side payments before renting apartments; criminals sold stolen or counterfeit ration books. In 1944 one racketeer was found with counterfeit coupons worth 38,000 gallons of gasoline and 437 pairs of shoes. Black market operations were frequently compared with bootlegging, but in some respects it was more difficult to enforce price controls than prohibition: the black market involved not just one commodity which many people considered a luxury, but such essentials as meat, gasoline, shoes and coffee, and it implicated not just liquor dealers but highly respected members of the business community. Even when the Office of Price Administration believed it had evidence of wrongdoing, it rarely could take the time or trouble to prosecute businessmen but usually sought to prevent further illegal sales by obtaining a court injunction. The social stigma attached to buying and selling in the black market was never as great as the government would have liked. One in five Americans told interviewers that buying scarce goods at black market prices was sometimes justified.[9]

The war, which in so many ways brought people together, was also capable of stirring up old hatreds. As the suspicion grew that some groups were peculiarly skilled in avoiding wartime burdens, so did the need to find a scapegoat. The search ended where it had so often in the past—with the Jew. Public opinion polls indicated that anti-Semitism—as measured by a belief that Jews were greedy, overprivileged, and trying to get ahead at one's own expense—increased during the war. "Jews were more often charged than any other group with shirking their share of the war effort, with draft dodging and, once drafted, with avoiding front-line combat." At the same time as American troops were fighting the Nazis, Gerald L. K. Smith was ranting about a Jewish conspiracy, anti-Semitic sheets such as *X-Ray* and *The Broom* were appearing, and a Gentile Co-operative Association was formed in Chicago "to halt growing Jewish power." For the most part, anti-Semitism remained latent but ugly incidents took place in the Boston suburbs of Roxbury, Dorchester and Mattapan where, in mid-1943, gangs of teenagers desecrated synagogues, smashed store windows, and fought with Jewish youths. On a patriotic poster near Boston's city hall someone crossed out the word "united" and scribbled "Jewnited."[10]

Far more serious than the casual acceptance of illegal profiteering or even the sporadic outburst of anti-Semitism, and as damaging to the nation's social fabric, were problems deriving from family mobility. In the three and one-half years after Pearl Harbor, 12 million men left their homes to enter the armed services and better than 15.3 million civilians moved across county lines, most of them in search of jobs but some to be near military bases. Families found it necessary to adjust to separation and migration, and children had to adapt to the prolonged absence of their fathers or to diminished attention from parents working long hours. What was worse, these adjustments often had to be made in communities that had sprung up overnight, where housing was hard to find, medical and sanitary facilities overburdened, and schools and day care centers inadequate. Where towns were hit by an influx of war workers, acute tensions developed between the newcomers and older, established residents.

The stream of wartime civilian migration flowed through the same channels as in the preceding twenty years, but at a much faster rate. People moved from the country to the city, from south to north, and from east to west. This movement, however, was not all in one direction: while 5.4 million people moved away from farms, 2.5 million others moved to farms; while 1 million southerners went north, 600,000 northerners travelled the other way. Above all people migrated west—1.4 million to California alone—and to the cities where shipyards, aircraft plants, munitions factories and military installations were situated. A half-dozen urban centers, including Los Angeles, San Francisco, and Detroit attracted two million migrants and cities along the Atlantic and Gulf coasts grew at a staggering rate: from 1940 to 1943 Charleston's population climbed by 37 percent, Norfolk's by 57 percent, and Mobile's by 61 percent. Migrants tended to be somewhat younger than nonmigrants, with the highest rate for those in their early twenties; since many men were in the Army, three of every five civilian migrants was a woman.

The path of migration was carved by the push and pull of economic forces: the concentration of people in cities reflected consolidation in agriculture and industry. Between 1940 and 1945 farm population declined by 17 percent, but at the same time the productivity of each person remaining on the land climbed by more than 25 percent. This resulted from increased mechanization—a million more tractors were in use at the end than at the beginning of the war— a dramatic rise in the use of fertilizer, and the consolidation of small farms into large ones. The process of industrial consolidation was even more striking, particularly in industries that relied heavily on defense contracts: iron and steel, nonferrous metals, ordnance, machinery and electrical products, transportation equipment, chemicals, petroleum, coal and rubber. In 1939 firms with fewer than 500 workers employed 52 percent of those engaged in manufacturing, but in 1944 accounted for only 38 percent; in 1939 firms with more than 10,000 workers employed 13 percent of the manufacturing labor force, but in 1944 accounted for fully 31 percent.

The social consequences of migration varied from place to place. Some areas were hardly touched. The war, for example, placed a relatively light strain on New York City where most people were employed in banking, trade and light manufacturing, and which experienced an exodus of workers rather than an influx. The situation, however, was entirely different in other large cities which grew still larger during the war, in small towns which blossomed into centers of war production, and even in largely rural suburban areas where factories were erected and "defense cities" appeared as if from nowhere. Of all the places transformed by the boom, perhaps none pointed up the difficulties of adjusting to migration more clearly than did Willow Run.

Before the war Washtenaw County, Michigan had a population of 80,000 of whom some 16,000 lived in and around the town of Ypsilanti in the area known as Willow Run. Located only 27 miles west of Detroit, Willow Run was a typical midwestern mixed farming community with a fair-sized sprinkling of industrial workers who commuted to the city. Early in 1941, however, Ford selected Willow Run, which was close enough to Detroit to draw manpower and where land could be readily obtained, as the site of a mammoth airplane factory. Architects hailed the plant as "a vast precision tool in itself:" raw materials flowed in one end, parts were fabricated in adjoining areas and fed onto the main assembly lines, and completed B-24s rolled onto runways at the other end. The main building alone covered 67 acres. Willow Run began manufacturing parts late in 1941, turned out the first bomber about a year later, and by 1944, after persistent problems of design were finally worked out, was producing a plane every hour. All told, the plant manufactured 8,685 planes and at its peak employed over 42,000 workers.[11]

If the Willow Run plant embodied the most modern technology, the conditions under which many workers lived seemed primitive by contrast. Before Pearl Harbor the planners assumed that workers would drive from Detroit along a special expressway, but shortages of gasoline and rubber soon precluded commuting on the required scale. Consequently, in April 1942 the government proposed building a model community: 6,000 permanent and 10,000 temporary units would be erected, each house would have grounds for a Victory garden, public buildings would be conveniently situated, and a green belt would encircle "Bomber City" to prevent the growth of shantytowns. But this plan ran into stubborn opposition from local property owners, real estate interests and politicians as well as from officials at Ford. These groups feared that Willow Run would eventually become a ghost town and the county would be saddled with a permanent relief burden, that property values would go down and taxes go up, that the existing water supply would be overburdened and the Huron River polluted. Some also suspected that a predominantly working-class town would decisively shift the balance of political power in Washtenaw County, which had voted Republican all through the 1930s, and give the CIO and the Democrats the upper hand. Ultimately the government modified its plan. It built "Willow Village" and "Willow Lodge" with fewer than half the number of homes originally proposed; they never accommodated more than 5,000 people.

Despite the shortage of adequate housing, workers poured into Willow Run. More than 32,000 people moved to Washtenaw County and, when nothing else was available, they crowded into one-room trailers. Since trailer camps were often located beyond town jurisdictional lines they were not covered by health codes. The result was rotten sanitation, impure water, and unrelieved fear of fire and epidemic. "Privies and septic tanks literally deposit their contents in the same puddle from which drinking water is drawn." said one reporter.[12] Houses, although more comfortable than trailers, were also strained to the bursting point. In one frame house five men lived in the basement, a family of five occupied the first floor, four men slept on the second floor, nine men slept in the garage, and four families parked their trailers in the yard. For those who had left impoverished areas in the South conditions at Willow Run were no worse, and were sometimes better, than what they had known; for others, life at Willow Run brought unaccustomed hardships. All agreed that the housing crisis added to the problem of labor turnover.

Prejudices held by oldtime residents of Willow Run worked against the provision of adequate community services. Just as they had fought large-scale federal housing, so many natives opposed raising taxes in order to expand facilities for health, recreation and education. Many oldtimers, who resented the tidal wave of war workers and the destruction of a more leisurely and simple way of life, tended to glorify the past. "Before the bomber plant was built, everything was perfect here," said one. "Everybody knew everybody else and all were happy and contented. Then came that bomber plant and this influx of riffraff, mostly Southerners. . . . You can't be sure of these people." This attitude found expression in a reluctance to expand the school system. In 1942 the town decided not to build a new school but grudgingly agreed to add four rooms to the existing one; within a few months the building had nearly twice as many students as it was designed to hold. Children had to attend a morning or afternoon shift. Not until a year later when the government stepped in and built three new schools was overcrowding relieved.[13]

The advances in technology and the accompanying social turmoil at Willow Run served as literary themes for several writers during the war. One novel about the construction of a B-24 endowed the plane with near-human qualities: "B-24 needs eyes. B-24 has five eyes: Nose Turret, Pilot's Window, Top Gunner's Turret, Tail Turret, Lower Gunner's Turret. . . . B-24 must be strong. . . . They are building wings for B-24! . . . They are building a body for B-24!" This provided the background for the story of five men and a flirtatious girl who

commute to the factory in a car pool. The men, when
they learn that she is deceiving them, react in tragic ways.
One, a former playwright, suffers a mental breakdown and
unfairly accuses a German-American welder of sabotage
("My liddle village iss nod Nazi. It iss schust like a liddle
village here," the accused had protested. "Dese Nazis—dey
are nod real Chermans.") Another decides to prove his man-
hood by smoking in the rest room; after noting the grafitti
("To hell with Ford!") he is caught cigarette in hand by a
guard and later discharged. Still a third pierces a rival's
skull with a power drill but makes it appear an accident. To
weave together the twin themes of creation and destruction
the author explains that B-24 "is made of living and dying
and loving and hating and aluminum alloy."[14]

Many of the real rather than fictional problems that plagued
Willow Run cropped up elsewhere. In 1940 the 6,000 residents
of Pascagoula, Mississippi lived by fishing, gathering oysters
and growing pecans. But Pascagoula had a shipyard and a fine
harbor and by 1944 a swarm of workers had nearly quadrupled
its population. Families, particularly those from backwoods
areas who spilled into trailers and tents, often found it difficult to cope with the demands of urban life. "In the grocery
stores they are lost, because they do not know what to buy,
cannot make up their minds quickly in the crowd, and get
jostled around by the others, who know their own minds and
can push for the things they want." They were, moreover,
ostracized by older residents; as one reporter was told,
"Folks in houses think trailer people are vermin." The city
had no public transportation and an inadequate sewage system; waste, discharged into the river after insufficient treatment, endangered the oyster reefs. Doctors were overworked
to the point of exhaustion. The wife of a shipyard worker
explained what had happened shortly before her two-year
old son died: "He was sleeping and he waked up and began
crying, so I carried him in the living room, and his hands
began drawing, and his feet, and I thought he was going into

convulsions. . . . My husband . . . went to call the doctor . . .
and told him the baby was going into convulsions, and the
doctor told him to give him the medicine . . . and he thought
the baby would be all right. And my husband told him he was
vomiting it up just as fast as we gave it to him, and the doctor
said he was tired and had to go to bed and get some sleep,
and he didn't come."[15]

The disruption of family life, the sense of impermanence,
the absence of traditional attachments, the competition for
scarce facilities—all increased the tension between newcomers
and oldtimers and made for anything but social cohesion. A
sociologist who studied Seneca, Illinois, a town whose population grew fivefold as it became a center of ship construction,
found that migrants took little if any part in the religious,
political and social life of the community. One newcomer explained that when she attempted to attend church, "nobody
ever spoke to me or looked at me." Although the older residents tended to put aside their own differences and "feel as
though they all belonged together when they faced the horde
of strangers moving in upon them," there was very little
interchange between the two groups. Instead parallel social
structures emerged, each with its own class system, and the
boundary between them, particularly at the lower levels,
remained fixed.[16]

Nor was there always much fraternization among the migrants themselves who, after all, came from dissimilar ethnic,
religious and educational backgrounds and who regarded their
stay in the boom town as temporary. People sometimes found
ingenious ways to clarify lines of social stratification. In
Seneca, for example, the government provided housing for
better than two out of every three residents. All homes were
alike in cost, style and quality and were supposedly open
on a first-come, first-serve basis regardless of social status.
But shipyard executives made an informal arrangement with
the Federal Public Housing Administration whereby the block
of homes nearest the town was set aside for their use exclusive-

ly. The block became known as "Gold Coast Row" even
though its homes were just like all the others. In this way
people with high social standing—as measured by income,
training or occupation—could set themselves apart and, to
some extent, escape the levelling tendencies of war.

Migration led to tensions not only between diverse social
groups but within families as well and, when added to other
wartime strains, often produced a good deal of instability.
One indication of this was the mounting divorce rate. Contrary to predictions that divorce would become less common—
since men whose marriages were failing could find at least a
temporary solution by enlisting, and since servicemen were
not required to answer a divorce summons—marriages broke
up more often during this period than before the war. In 1940
16 couples were divorced for each 100 who married; in 1944
there were 27 divorces for each 100 marriages. In some cases,
of course, the war strengthened and unified families: parents
and children sometimes drew together in the face of danger
or privation, and many of the worries associated with unemployment disappeared. Nevertheless, many other people—
those who migrated as well as those who did not—found
that the war seriously disrupted their normal pattern of life.

By far the most difficult adjustment families had to make
was to the loss of a husband to the armed services and the consequent anxiety about his safety and well-being. Although the
government postponed drafting fathers as long as it could,
the number of dependency deferments declined sharply as
the supply of manpower dwindled; by the end of 1944 only
80,000 men held such deferments compared with 8 million
in mid-1943. The emotional costs of the long-term separation
of wife and husband, or of father and child, have never been
adequately measured and perhaps never can be. When grade-
school children whose fathers were in the armed forces were
given dolls to play with they made up stories about family
life that should have surprised few psychologists. More than
children with both parents at home, father-separated children

produced an "idealistic fantasy picture of the father, who has a good time with his family and who is enjoyed by them," who gave and received much affection, and who showed little hostility.[17]

Still another wartime change that led in some instances to family instability was the increasing frequency with which women, particularly those with young children, took jobs. During the war the number of women workers spiralled from 12 to 16.5 million; women eventually constituted 36 percent of the civilian labor force. At first they took light jobs that men had given up, but by 1943 women began to enter heavy industry. One survey of steel plants found that women, who made up 10 percent of the labor force, were working in coke plants, blast furnaces and rolling mills. Another survey revealed about the same percentage of women employed in shipyards which, it was noted, had once been "so thoroughly male that any woman who ventured into a yard was greeted with hooting and whistling."[18] Many states amended their labor laws to permit women to do heavier work and work more than eight hours a day. As long as the work week did not exceed 48 hours, there was no difference in either the productivity or efficiency of men and women.

War jobs, while providing many women with an exhilarating sense of economic independence, gave rise to both real and imaginary concerns. Those who had struggled to protect women workers feared that carefully constructed safeguards regarding hours and working conditions would be abandoned. The Labor Department's Women's Bureau, supporting the view that "women are not able to work where marked spurts of strength and energy are necessary at times," urged employers to make adequate provision for rest and job rotation and not to assign women heavy or arduous tasks. Others feared to the contrary that women would become too strong. They foresaw the emergence of a class of "new Amazons" who would dress like men, talk like men, and develop powerful biceps. To some extent such fears may have fed on a wartime cult of masculinity. A number of middle- or upper-class women who wrote about taking war jobs did so in a mild locker-room vernacular. One book was entitled "Hit the Rivet, Sister." Another was written by a fashion designer who decided that "the world was busted wide open," that "pink ribbons and rosebuds, a penthouse studio and fashion shows, seemed to have become awfully stale when headlines and by-lines were telling you about hell broken loose." "To hell with the life I have had," she swore: "This war is too damn serious, and it is too damn important to win it."[19]

Even more common than the fear of exploitation or loss of femininity was the belief that working mothers would reject their children. One well-known social worker complained that women were "repudiating their children in their newly found freedom." Jobs at high wages, she added, offered women more excitement than did housekeeping. "Many of them are rejecting their feminine roles. They wish to control their own fertility in marriage, and say they never wanted the children which had been thrust upon them." This statement, however, may reveal as much about the outlook of social workers as about the behavior of working women. Undertaking activities outside the home permitted a number of women to overcome what a group of psychiatrists termed "the boredom of mothering" or "the guilt of being less maternal than they feel they should be." The war gave work a patriotic sanction it would not otherwise have had.[20]

Working mothers were more likely to neglect than reject their children, and to do so out of necessity rather than choice. Not only did signing up for a war job, and sometimes working a late-night shift, take women away from the home, but the need to queue up for rationed goods, the curtailment of home deliveries and the shortage of electrical appliances all made housekeeping more time-consuming. Several studies indicated that children of working parents often had difficulty in accepting their mother's absence. They became anxious and tense, found it hard to get to sleep, and regressed to infantile patterns of behavior such as bed-wetting and thumb-sucking. Experience with disturbed children led a committee of the American Orthopsychiatric Association to recommend that "mothers of infants up to age 3 should be barred from factory work. Mothers of the preschool child should be allowed employment only during the period in which a nursery school, properly inspected, takes over." Even compulsion, the committee argued, might be necessary to protect children from the consequences of maternal neglect.[21]

If "latch-key children" and "eight-hour orphans" were war-time social casualties, the fault rested in part with over-crowded public schools and the inadequate use made of child-care facilities. Many schools, particularly those in con-gested production areas, simply could not squeeze everyone in; children were able to attend only half a day. Nearly all schools faced a shortage of qualified teachers. As the turnover rate for teachers doubled during the war, standards had to be lowered and emergency certificates issued. Not all schools were equally affected: rural schools suffered more than those in big cities, and elementary grades more than the high schools. Teachers left the classroom for social as well as financial reasons. In many places teachers were still subjected to nag-ging social pressures: they were required to dress appro-priately in public, participate in community activities, and attend church regularly. In most American cities married women could not hold regular licenses. Also, teachers' salaries, which had been relatively high during the 1930s, began to lag further and further behind earnings in private employment; by 1944 teachers were paid on the average $500 less than workers in private employment. During the war Americans spent perhaps 1.5 percent of their national income on public education.

Under the 1940 Lanham Act, which provided federal funds for aiding war-boom communities, the government helped build and operate some 2,800 child-care centers, but the majority of working mothers did not use them. Often, facilities were not ready when and where they were needed. Applying for aid under the Lanham Act meant struggling through a jungle of red-tape, competing for funds with other types of facilities, and convincing the community to share in the cost. Nevertheless, the problem was less one of obtaining money to build centers than of getting parents to send their children to them. "There is a positive aversion to group care of children in the minds of working women," said a government official. "To some it connotes an inability to care for one's own; to some it has a vague incompatibility with the traditional idea of the American home; to others it has a taint of socialism." Group care, he concluded, "violates the mores and sentimentalism that has grown up around the young."[22] Even where facilities were available, working class mothers often boycotted them, especially when young children could be left to the care of a neighbor or an older brother or sister.

Unhappily, the older brother or sister was no less likely to be experiencing a difficult adjustment period. One indication of this was an extraordinary increase in juvenile delinquency during the war. Statistics that showed soaring juvenile crime rates must be taken with more than one grain of salt: particularly in towns which had an influx of war workers and their children, police were more likely to arrest juvenile offenders whom they did not know, and adults tended to be more stringent in defining permissible conduct. There was not only a change in adolescent behavior, then, but a change in what adults considered acceptable adolescent behavior. Even so, the rise in criminal activity among those under eighteen years of age, particularly when contrasted with declining crime rates among adults, was unsettling. Still more unsettling was the increase in aggressive crimes such as forcible entry and assault, and the greater frequency with which teenage girls ran into trouble with the law, usually as a result of what the courts termed "sex delinquency." Virtually everyone agreed that the old explanations for

delinquency—poverty, unemployment, the lack of opportunity for meaningful work—were no longer tenable, but few
could agree on a new diagnosis. Sociologists worked out
graphs showing that juvenile arrests varied directly with the
level of business prosperity and employment (wartime delinquency, while higher than during the 1930s, was not
higher than during the 1920s) and concluded that a causal
relationship existed. Psychologists affirmed that a society which
stressed martial virtues would of necessity trigger aggressive
impulses in teenagers. "War releases predatory impulses
among [adolescents], for . . . the lid seems to be off and there
is an implied sanction for aggressive action." Youth workers
pointed to the absence of parental supervision, the lack of
customary social restraints in boom communities, inadequate
housing and overcrowded schools, and the employment of
minors in bowling alleys, dance halls, beer parlors and other
places that posed "special moral hazards."[23]

Whatever their understanding of the cause of juvenile delinquency, many Americans regarded it as symptomatic of a
more general collapse in moral standards. This was perhaps
most vividly expressed in the concern over promiscuity among
teenage girls. People worried about "uncontrolled girls who
hang about the streets until late at night or frequent undesirable dance halls and taverns," and expressed alarm at the
appearance around Army and Navy bases of the "victory
girl," who out of "a misguided sense of patriotism . . . believes
she is contributing to the war effort by giving herself to the
man in uniform." (The problem of the man in uniform who
gave himself to the victory girl was, however, approached
more from a medical than a moral viewpoint.) More than
twice as many girls under the age of twenty-one were arrested
for sexual offenses other than prostitution or commercial vice
in 1942 as in the preceding year. It was widely believed during
the war that youngsters were being led astray, that "specific
biological sexual urges" were no longer being "held in check
by convention," that the tide of promiscuity was rising and
the dikes of respectability giving way.[24]

These fears, when combined with the recognition that venereal disease represented a dangerous threat to men in the armed services, led to a massive drive against organized prostitution. The May Act of July 1941, which enabled localities to shut down brothels located near military installations, became the chief weapon in the hands of reformers. "Like the threat of the atomic bomb," one recalled in 1945, "the knowledge that such a law existed caused many prostitution characters to forsake their haunts." Advocates of legal prostitution continued to say that periodic medical examinations would prevent the spread of venereal disease and that brothels allowed decent women to walk the streets without being raped, but these arguments carried less weight every day. Reformers contended that the "slimy dives" had to be closed for in wartime syphilis and gonorrhea were "enemy agents within our midst. At present they are working with the Axis." By 1944 some 700 cities had closed their red-light districts, and the percentage of communities that the American Social Hygiene Association rated "bad" had diminished greatly. Reformers told of their victories in articles entitled "Blitzing the Brothels."[25]

The battle against prostitution was only one maneuver in the war on venereal disease. In 1940 twenty states required blood tests before marriage; by 1944 thirty did so, and an equal number insisted on seriological tests for expectant mothers. The federal government—through the Social Protection Division of the Federal Security Agency and the Venereal Disease Control Division of the Public Health Service—published pamphlets, produced films and prepared radio scripts dealing with protection against, symptoms of, and treatment for venereal disease. More important, the government set up thousand of clinics to care for victims; in 1944 they treated 560,000 civilians, and state health departments distributed more than 18 million recently-developed sulfanilamide tablets for the treatment of gonorrhea. Soldiers contracted venereal disease less often than in World War I. The rate of infection, however, was higher among those stationed in the United States than those sent overseas, and while the rate of syphilis declined during the war that of gonorrhea rose.

The change in public attitudes was little short of revolutionary. In the mid-1930s the word "syphilis" was rarely mentioned in public; in the mid-1940s millions of Americans learned in clinical detail how to detect the early signs of the disease. Perhaps nothing did more to break down the old taboos than the Army's instruction in prophylaxis, a program that shocked those people who expected soldiers to remain continent. Gene Tunney, in an article called "The Bright Shield of Continence," argued against the notion that "indulgence is physically necessary" and for the view that continence, as any boxer knew, helped a man "keep at the peak of physical force." "Any man above the emotional level of a tomcat must realize that the professional's embrace is not only a menace to health but a shameful desecration of ideal love." The Army, however, proceeded along more practical lines. Since men's sexual habits were largely formed before entering service, since some would inevitably expose themselves to infection, since there was no way of knowing who would and who would not, it therefore followed that every soldier needed instruction in prophylaxis. To withhold such information, the Army concluded, would be equivalent to depriving him of a vaccination against smallpox.[26]

There had for some time been a link in the public mind between venereal disease and liquor, between prostitution and the saloon, and between war and prohibition. Not surprisingly, a Baptist convention and a Presbyterian women's group went on record in 1942 as favoring prohibition and some, including Henry L. Stimson, thought it unwise to underestimate "how much dynamite there is latent and dormant in the antisaloon sentiment of the country." Prohibitionists dusted off familiar arguments but added new twists: liquor was responsible for Pearl Harbor because the Japanese knew that American sailors would be in no condition to fight on a Sunday morning after the Saturday night before ("strong drink rendered the island helpless, befuddled, off-guard and at the mercy of the heartless Japs"); whiskey, which "weakens self-control and stimulates unholy desires," was corrupting American soldiers; liquor manufacturers were wasting precious quantities of tin, barley, sugar and rubber; drunkenness was responsible for much of the absenteeism in war plants. Three states—Kansas, Oklahoma, and Mississippi—and many counties in the South continued to prohibit the sale of liquor in law if not in fact, but local option elections during the war revealed no groundswell of sentiment for national prohibition. Nor did it have much political support either. If the past taught any lesson at all, it was that the social costs of attempting to regulate American drinking habits were exorbitant.[27] The failure of prohibition demonstrated not an absence of concern with moral problems, but a recognition that simple solutions to such problems were inadequate.

World War II freed both unifying and disunifying forces in American society; in some ways it made for cohesion, in others for fragmentation. The war years were a time when many people freely made sacrifices of the most generous sort and when others callously sought to benefit from those sacrifices, a time when many Americans experienced a sense of true community and when others succumbed to virulent racial, religious and class hatreds, a time when factories were models of modern technology and when factory workers sometimes lived in decayed or decaying homes. It was, above all, a time when society, having rid itself for the moment of large-scale poverty, was faced with the realization that wartime affluence brought troublesome problems of its own.

CHALLENGES TO ECONOMIC REGULATION

BY MID-1943 THE ROOSEVELT administration had devised a system of controls designed to stimulate the production of vital supplies and to slow down inflation. Although it relied to a considerable extent upon voluntary compliance rather than compulsion, the system irritated workers who feared that they were being left out of the prevailing prosperity and businessmen who believed that they were being unfairly restrained. During the last two years of the war, therefore, the administration faced direct challenges to the application of economic controls at the very moment when mounting war needs forced a tightening up. In particular, disputes arising over a nationwide coal strike, the seizure of Montgomery Ward, and the attempt to enact national service legislation revealed a good deal about these grievances, the kinds of pressure labor and management could apply, and the limitations placed upon the coercive power of government.

In the year preceding the attack on Pearl Harbor organized labor had made spectacular gains. As defense contracts started the wheels of industry turning, union leaders found themselves in an excellent bargaining position. In 1941 the United Automobile Workers won a contract from Ford that provided for a union shop and dues check-off, the Steel Workers Organizing Committee made a successful settlement with "Little Steel" that included a ten-cent an hour wage boost, and the United Mine Workers eliminated wage differentials between northern and southern coal fields. Union victories sometimes came in the wake of bitter conflict: 2.3 million workers went on strike during 1941 and more walkouts occurred than in any year except 1919 and 1937. In some cases they were inspired by communists who, before Hitler's invasion of the Soviet Union in June 1941, sought to obstruct the defense effort. More often strikes grew out of labor's attempt to use the upturn to win long-standing demands and management's reluctance to make concessions that, once institutionalized, would leave unions with a strong hand even if economic conditions should take a turn for the worse. Whatever the cause, the result was plain: during the defense buildup unions signed 1.5 million new members.

Even so, the labor movement faced severe problems when the United States entered the war. There was, first of all, no federal agency authorized to resolve labor disputes. In March 1941 Roosevelt set up the National Defense Mediation Board with members representing business, labor and the public in an effort to prevent strikes through arbitration. Throughout the year the Board settled 96 cases, but its recommendations were not binding and it was soon torn by dissension. This became apparent in the fall when a strike erupted in the southern Appalachian coal mines which, because they were operated directly by steel companies, were known as "captive" mines. In September some 53,000 men, 95 percent of whom already belonged to the UMW, struck when the owners refused to grant a union shop. On November 10 the NDMB decided against the union; the two CIO members dissented and then resigned. When the miners resumed the strike and were joined by 100,000 other UMW members, Roosevelt refused to uphold the Board and instead turned the matter over to an arbitration panel which eventually supported the union. In any event, the resignation of the CIO members combined with Roosevelt's action destroyed the NDMB.

Disunity in the labor movement proved an even more important source of weakness. In some ways war intensified the differences that had led the CIO to break with the AFL in 1935. As assembly line methods blurred old craft distinctions, jurisdictional disputes became more common; as unions expanded, competition for new members grew more fierce; as Washington assumed greater control over industrial life, the debate over labor's role in politics took on added meaning. Nor did the war reduce the personal animosities that had figured so heavily in the original split. Rivalry between William Green of the AFL and Philip Murray of the CIO, between John L. Lewis who loathed Roosevelt and Sidney Hillman who worshipped him continued to block moves toward reconciliation. Although Roosevelt appointed an advisory board with representatives from both the AFL and CIO it provided no more than a thin veneer over the deep-rooted division in the ranks of labor. When, on December 15, 1941 William Green said "we will fight against a movement which has vowed to destroy us and wipe us off the face of the earth" he was referring not to German fascism, nor even to the National Association of Manufacturers, but to the Congress of Industrial Organizations.[1]

These cat-and-dog squabbles together with the demise of the National Defense Mediation Board created grave difficulties for the Roosevelt administration and for the National War Labor Board, which inherited the task of preserving industrial peace. Created in January 1942, the Board was headed by William H. Davis and provided equal representation for labor, business and the public. Although resembling the old NDMB in some respects, the War Labor Board had greater authority: it could impose arbitration terms in any dispute and could call on the President to take over a plant if its orders were disobeyed. Unlike its predecessor, however, the WLB operated within a wage stabilization program: it could not simply expedite a settlement but had to see that union contracts did not violate wage guidelines. The tripartite structure created hazards in that the WLB could not solve disputes that arose between unions, could not function if one side withdrew in anger, and could not prevent labor and business from uniting to outvote the public members. At the same time the arrangement, by guaranteeing each party some voice in decisions and by ensuring that the public members would operate within a range acceptable to labor and management, fostered compromise and compliance.

In establishing the Board Roosevelt rejected the advice of those who wished to exclude interest groups from playing a direct part in formulating labor policy. James Forrestal and Robert Patterson, speaking for the armed services, had urged the President to appoint an impartial tribunal, with Wendell Willkie or Charles Evans Hughes as chairman and with two other members selected by the Senate and the House of Representatives. This, they reasoned, would make for unanimous and noncontroversial decisions and would "eliminate insofar as possible the friction and constant wrangling which is bound to take place between adversaries sitting on the same board."[2] But Roosevelt preferred to let labor and business resolve their own differences. At the same time he guarded against the danger of serious discord by choosing WLB members with an eye to their reasonableness. Secretary of Labor Frances Perkins assured Roosevelt that prospective labor appointees had been carefully screened: "They are good. Have been oked by Hillman, Anna Rosenberg, Will Davis and . . . by test questioning by Green, Murray, and several employers."[3] This method worked reasonably well. The WLB ultimately handled 17,650 disputes involving 12 million workers, though in 40 cases the President resorted to plant seizure.

The problem of union security put the War Labor Board to its harshest test. Trade unions demanded a closed, or at least a union shop, not only to give them greater bargaining power but also to offer protection against raids by rival unions and assurance that the millions of new war workers would be required to join. Employers argued, as they had for years, that the union shop deprived the worker of personal liberty and tempted labor leaders to misuse their power. Caught in what seemed an insoluble dilemma, the War Labor Board in the summer of 1942 accepted the "maintenance of membership" compromise. During a fifteen-day escape period workers could resign from the union and keep their jobs; after that, they had to remain members for the life of the contract. Whereas in a closed shop only union members could be hired, and in a union shop every worker had to join the union to keep his job, under the WLB plan every worker who did not leave the union within fifteen days had to pay dues while the contract remained in force. This preserved the principle of free choice and also protected the union in practice against any substantial loss of membership.

The public members, who had supported labor, believed that the decision would promote harmony and stability. "The maintenance of a stable union membership makes for the maintenance of responsible union leadership and responsible union discipline," they claimed.[4] In fact, the WLB found that it could discipline labor by withholding the privilege from unions which called strikes, failed to hold fair elections, or otherwise behaved "irresponsibly." Labor discovered to its chagrin that government protection exacted a price in the form of greater supervision of union affairs. But industry representatives remained unhappy with the maintenance of membership policy. They held that it amounted to a camouflaged closed shop, and in large part they were right. Certainly the formula spurred union growth: in 1943 the clause covered

3.9 million workers and from December 1941 to June 1945 union membership climbed from 10.5 to 14.75 million.

Despite these gains labor's dissatisfaction with wartime conditions reached a high point in 1943. Some grievances centered on the administration's anti-inflation program. Labor objected that the Little Steel formula, which permitted wages to rise only 15 percent above January 1941 levels, failed to account for increases in the price of food and clothing and discriminated against low-paid workers for whom such an adjustment meant little. Union leaders contended that the Bureau of Labor Statistics refused to take account of the black market or quality deterioration and consequently underestimated the rise in living costs. Other complaints derived from changes in working conditions, seniority and upgrading that often accompanied conversion to war production. As one worker put it, "the company goes out on the street hiring, hiring for the good jobs and leaving the people with seniority on those lower priced jobs." Those who were dissatisfied with their income or status often built relatively small annoyances—such as the failure to grant a ten-minute clean-up period, the padlocking of a tool room to prevent theft, the imposition of no-smoking regulations—into major disputes. In June 1943 labor leaders warned the President that "discontent and unrest are spreading among American workers."[5]

Much of this irritation resulted in growing impatience with the no-strike pledge. On December 23, 1941 spokesmen for labor and business had agreed to refrain from strikes and lockouts. But the no-strike pledge, which was at first widely observed, did not legally bind either side. As workers' indignation at spiralling living costs mounted, union leaders often had to decide whether to risk antagonizing their men by adhering to the agreement or to sanction strikes that would halt production. Increases in the cost of living might ultimately nullify wage boosts, but each time workers gained something from a strike pressure built up on other officials to follow suit. Among automobile workers, for example, dissatisfied elements formed a "rank-and-file caucus" which called for scrapping the no-strike pledge, and Chrysler workers who walked off the job booed Walter Reuther when he advised them to return. "These are hard days for Labor men who are trying to keep the wheels rolling," sighed one official.[6]

This diagnosis was in part confirmed by the Michigan CIO's repudiation of the no-strike pledge. In 1942 a resolution asking the national CIO to rescind the agreement had been introduced and, after brief debate, defeated by those who maintained that unions could not afford "the luxury of striking" in wartime. But late in June 1943, even though the arguments on each side had not changed very much, the outcome was reversed. Supporters of the pledge warned that while strikes would enrage the public and provoke an antilabor response in Congress they would not hurt businesses with defense contracts. Opponents replied that Roosevelt had failed to curb living costs, that labor could no longer afford to shackle itself, and that "the corporation that I work for knows only one language and that is the language of strike."[7] One side claimed that strikes would deprive soldiers of weapons, the other that strikes would guarantee servicemen decent conditions upon their return. This time the resolution criticizing the no-strike pledge carried. Even though the CIO did not follow the advice of its Michigan chapter, the debate pointed up the restlessness of many workers.

Maintenance of the no-strike pledge, however, did not mean that strikes would cease. Indeed, during 1943 union members rode roughshod over the agreement. In March machinists in the San Francisco shipyards walked out; in April 55,000 rubber workers in Akron went on strike; in May 28,000 Chrysler employees laid down their tools. "Strikes are spreading at an alarming rate," groaned one member of the War Labor Board, "and unless they are checked immediately, the 'no-strike—no-lockout' agreement will become meaningless."[8] Later in the year stoppages occurred in the aircraft and leather industries, and a nationwide transportation breakdown was averted when the government briefly took over the railroads and allowed a wage hike. These strikes, most of which lasted only a few days, involved a sizeable number of workers: 3.1 million men took part in 1943 compared with fewer than 1 million the year before.

Of course this figure was inflated because 400,000 bituminous coal miners struck on four separate occasions during the year. The coal strikes of 1943 represented the most determined effort by any group of workers to reject regulation. Not only did the strikes have a considerable effect on production—accounting for 63 percent of the time lost through idleness—but they served as a barometer of working class discontent and exposed many of the obstacles to enforcing wage controls. Furthermore, John L. Lewis's decision to take his men out of the pits goaded Congress into enacting, for the first time in the nation's history, legislation expressly designed to curb the political and economic activities of trade unions.

At a conference with the Appalachian operators on March 10, 1943 Lewis listed the miners' grievances. "The coal miners of America are hungry," he declared. "They are ill-fed and undernourished below the standard of their neighbors and other citizens." Wages had averaged only $1715 in 1942, and living costs had skyrocketed in isolated coal towns where price controls were more difficult to enforce than in large cities. Recognizing that miners were not entitled to further increases under the War Labor Board's Little Steel formula, Lewis rejected out of hand the concept of wage controls. "When the mine workers' children cry for bread, they cannot be satisfied with a 'Little Steel formula,' " he asserted. Men with hungry children could not accept a "miserably stupid" formula drawn up by a Board composed of "labor zombies" and headed by a man who wanted to plunge "his long knife" into the "defenseless body" of the United Mine Workers. "If I had a yellow dog I would hate to have his standard of living fixed by this man Davis and the men who are doing his dirty work on the WLB," Lewis snapped. The argument that higher wages would encourage inflation left Lewis cold. "Wars have never been fought without monetary inflation in any country at any time, under any circumstances, in any period of history." The question was not whether inflation would occur, but whether capital or labor would be victimized.[9]

To make certain that the miners did not lose ground, Lewis set forth sweeping demands: a wage increase of $2 a day, double pay for Sunday work, larger vacation benefits, provision of safety equipment at the owners' expense, and portal-to-portal pay. Increasingly the dispute revolved about the latter issue: payment for the time—about one-and-a-half hours—spent travelling from the mine entrance to the place of work and back again. This had not been a source of controversy in the past. In 1940 the operators and union had agreed to exclude travel time, and the matter had not arisen in the 1941 contract negotiations. But in 1943 it seemed to offer an ideal way of skirting the Little Steel formula which fixed hourly wage rates but permitted increases based on stretching out the number of hours worked. Lewis did not intend to calculate the amount of time each miner travelled and pay him accordingly; he favored instead an averaging plan under which all miners would benefit equally. To the charge that this made no more sense than paying automobile workers for the time they spent commuting to the factory, the UMW responded that the descent into the coal pit was infinitely more dangerous and that other branches of mining had accepted the arrangement.

Even though the coal industry was flourishing, the operators saw little reason to meet Lewis half way. They assumed that rulings by the War Labor Board prohibited their doing so and that the Board would consequently decide in their favor. On April 22, a week before the contract expired, bargaining reached an impasse and the dispute went to the Board. But Lewis, viewing the Board as a kangaroo court, refused to recognize its jurisdiction. Instead he master-minded a series of relatively brief shutdowns designed to exact concessions without bringing production to a halt for too long. During May and June the coal miners struck three times. The walkouts, each of which lasted a few days, resulted in the government taking over the mines and placing them under Secretary of the Interior Harold Ickes. Work was resumed only after the President combined appeals to the miners' patriotism with threats to end the draft deferments of those who stayed out, but Lewis made it abundantly clear that each return to work was provisional. Throughout the spring he refused to appear before the War Labor Board, and ignored its directives which accepted the union's demands relating to vacations and safety equipment but rejected those relating to wage increases.

The coal controversy brought to the surface a bitter conflict within the administration over the means of enforcing economic controls. William H. Davis, Wayne Morse and most other members of the War Labor Board saw an essential principle at stake: would pressure groups be permitted to "dictate to the government" by resorting to "economic force?" In their view the coal strikes posed a "serious threat to the maintenance of Government by law and order" for if the UMW defied the government and went scot free then every union with sufficient muscle would take the same path.[10] Unless the government refused to negotiate with strikers and enforced its rulings, the stabilization program would fail. This way of thinking was not confined to the War Labor Board but was fairly widespread in the administration. One member of the Justice Department told Harry Hopkins, "If you don't have a showdown you will have an appeasement which will hit you in the face."[11]

But Harold Ickes and his associates in the Interior Department viewed the dispute differently. They contended that the owners had never sought an honest understanding with the union but had purposely brought on a crisis. Far from being a mischief-maker, Lewis had attempted to keep his men on the job pending acceptance of a suitable contract. The union leader was "probably easier to deal with than would be any of the numerous groups connected with the United Mine Workers that would compete for power if Mr. Lewis should be forced to step aside." The War Labor Board, on the contrary, had acted in an "inconsistent, evasive and illogical" manner in denying the miners' demand for portal-to-portal pay. To refuse to negotiate while a strike was in progress, Ickes thought, would only make a settlement impossible. Unlike Davis, Ickes did not believe that the nation's coal supply should be jeopardized for the sake of a fuzzy principle.[12]

While the President shared many of Davis's misgivings, the logic of events drove him toward Ickes's position. Bad blood had existed between Roosevelt and Lewis ever since 1940 when the union chief, believing that he had been denied enough influence in the making of labor policy, supported Wendell Willkie and attempted to lead the miners into the Republican camp. In November 1941 Roosevelt termed Lewis a "psychopathic" case, and by 1943 remarked venomously that he would be glad to resign as President if only Lewis would commit suicide. At various times during the strike the administration considered arresting union leaders and drafting strikers. It even thought of indicting Lewis for tax evasion but could find no damning evidence. In explaining why the case was stalled Attorney General Biddle commented, "When you shoot at a king you have to hit him."[13]

Wherever he turned Roosevelt met with the same stubborn truth: coal could not be mined without the cooperation of 400,000 miners. "There are not enough jails in the country to hold these men," Ickes reminded the President, "and, if there were, I must point out that a jailed miner produces no more coal than a striking miner." Even personal appeals to the men, which pitted patriotism against loyalty to the union, seemed somewhat risky to Roosevelt. "John thought that they would follow him to the polls in '40, but they didn't; they followed me," Roosevelt told Byrnes. "But Jim, it doesn't necessarily follow that they'll follow me into the mines. Being very thoughtful people, they may think that I know more about politics than John does, and that John knows more about the mines than I do."[14]

His desire not to antagonize organized labor also influenced Roosevelt's response to the coal crisis. Lewis and the CIO were themselves at sword's point. In the fall of 1942 Lewis had taken the miners out of the CIO with the comment that "life is too short for me to answer the yapping of every cur that follows at my heels," and the following spring the CIO accused Lewis of jeopardizing labor's interests by carrying on a "personal vendetta" against the President. Despite these differences, Lewis's boldness placed many labor leaders who opposed wartime strikes but thought the miners had a strong case in an uncomfortable position. As a CIO leader admitted, "Many workers in the plant say to me, 'John Lewis has the right program; he is at least out fighting for the workers and doing something for them.'"[15] Roosevelt, if he were not to forfeit the backing of friendly union leaders, had to draw a sharp line between the coal miners and other workers. "The only successful strategy is to isolate Mr. Lewis and his assistants from other more responsible labor leaders," one official noted.[16] To do this the administration had to avoid any step that might cause labor to close ranks behind the UMW.

If its wish to placate labor pushed the administration in one direction, public opinion pulled it in the other. In June 1943 John L. Lewis was apparently the most hated public figure in the United States. Polls showed that 87 percent of the people had an unfavorable opinion of him, and that of every ten Americans who suspected that some individual might be harmful to the country's future, seven had Lewis in mind. To some extent Lewis served as a whipping boy for those who had always resented trade unions. James Eastland of Mississippi, for one, was disappointed to learn that Lewis could not be charged with treason. But many liberals and friends of labor strongly denounced the coal shutdowns. The

Nation and *New Republic*, while conceding the legitimacy of many of the miners' demands, nevertheless spoke of Lewis's "criminal recklessness" and branded him an "evil influence in the labor movement." The Communist Party, which favored all-out production, could not contain its rage: "Hitler scored one of his biggest victories over the American people when Lewis forced the miners to strike."[17]

These attacks irritated Lewis but did not for a moment alter his course of action or induce the miners to desert him. For coal town residents, to whom governmental authority at all levels often seemed remote or downright hostile, the UMW was a solid rock. "This Union made you free in those coal regions," Lewis once told his followers with evangelical fervor. "This union means life and death to your families in the mining camps of this country. I mean food and shelter and clothing and education and medical treatment." Moreover, at the same time as the public cursed Lewis it expressed considerable sympathy for the miners; 58 percent of those polled, for example, thought that the miners deserved a raise. As the London *Economist* noted, Lewis's constituency loved him for the enemies he had made, "and the violence of the attacks on him reinforces his power not only with the miners but with the submerged everywhere in the United States."[18]

The public outcry, which hardly ruffled Lewis, struck a responsive chord in Congress. Once before the mine workers had nearly caused Congress to curb trade unions. On December 3, 1941, during the captive coal strike, the House had passed the Smith bill which barred new closed shop agreements, denied Wagner Act benefits to unions with communist or Bundist officers, provided for a thirty-day cooling-off period, and prohibited strikes unless approved by majority vote. But the attack on Pearl Harbor caused the Senate to shelve the bill, and the absence of major strikes during 1942 made such legislation seem unnecessary. Then, in the spring, with the nation reeling from the various coal crises and with the public more indignant than ever, the tide again shifted.

Action by state legislatures was one straw in the wind. In 1943 a dozen states passed laws restricting the right to picket, outlawing jurisdictional strikes, banning political contributions by unions and requiring them to file financial reports. By May 1943 it had become plain that, in the words of one observer, "it would be impossible to keep Congress from tieing labor in a knot if the present strike situation continues."[19]

Early that month the Connally bill, which authorized the President to take over strike-bound plants, sailed through the Senate. ("Wouldn't it be wise for the President to just lay off the subject entirely and let us go ahead and do what we please?" Connally had asked James Byrnes, who replied that he "was sure that was [Roosevelt's] attitude.")[20] On June 4 the House adopted an even more stringent measure introduced by Howard Smith of Virginia. The bill won support from nearly three-fourths of the Republican representatives and from more than half of the Democrats, with those from the South most heavily in favor. In final form the Smith-Connally bill extended the power of the President to seize plants useful in the war, made it a crime to encourage strikes in such plants, and mandated their return within sixty days after normal production had been restored. In other establishments union officials had to observe a thirty-day cooling-off period and obtain the approval of a majority of members before calling a strike. The measure also provided a statutory basis for the War Labor Board and outlawed union contributions to political campaigns. Conservatives thus used anti-Lewis sentiment to enact legislation that had long been close to their hearts. By so doing they hoped to drive another nail into the coffin of the New Deal.

For this reason the bill left the President an awkward choice. On the one hand he wanted additional power to deal with strikes; on the other he objected to key provisions, particularly those prohibiting political spending, and knew that organized labor passionately opposed the measure. The men around the President offered sharply conflicting advice.

James Byrnes, Henry Stimson and Frank Knox pushed
hardest for approval; indeed, Stimson imagined that defense workers who left their jobs were no less guilty than
soldiers who deserted their posts. But administrators with
closer ties to labor—including Harold Ickes, Frances Perkins
and Paul McNutt—insisted that the bill would do more harm
than good. Even William Davis concluded that criminal
prosecutions would only drive "responsible and loyal labor
leaders into Lewis's corner."[21] Nor did it seem wise to build
up unrealistic expectations. "The public is under the illusion
that this bill will do two things: a) end the coal strike and b)
throw Lewis in jail," noted Oscar Cox of the Justice Department, "but it is so drafted that you will have a hell of a time
doing anything and even if pressure should result in criminal
procedure he could be out on bail on appeal and if he gets a
reversal then you'll have a boomerang. . . . The people will
say, Jesus Christ, what is this?"[22]

On June 25 the President moved to resolve the dilemma:
he vetoed the bill but at the same time urged Congress to
authorize the government to draft strikers up to the age of
65 as noncombatants. "This will enable us to induct into
military service all persons who engage in strikes or stoppages
or other interruptions of work in plants in the possession of
the United States," he affirmed. Yet even a military draft
left much to be desired. As Stimson put it, "If there should
prove to be a widespread spirit of evasion, passive or active
resistance and of community opposition it would be hard to
overestimate the possible difficulties and delays in the task
and the gravity of the injury to the war effort."[23] The President's solution, however, was never tested for within a few
hours the Senate and House overturned his veto with votes
to spare. Nevertheless, Roosevelt had managed to retain the
good will of most labor leaders who, with the exception of the
mine workers, applauded his veto and paid scant attention to
his alternate prosposal.

The War Labor Disputes Act did not confirm the worst

fears of its opponents. Although the AFL and CIO thundered that it was "the worst anti-labor bill passed by Congress in the last hundred years," and denounced it as "the very essence of Fascism," the Act did not seriously weaken trade unions.[24] Ways were discovered to evade the ban on political contributions and, when necessary, leaders could quietly encourage strikes without saying so in public or exposing themselves to indictment. Since criminal penalties applied only to stoppages in plants taken over by the government, and then only to individuals who fomented strikes rather than those who went on strike, most workers were never in jeopardy. Finally, the government was reluctant to press charges against union officials lest they be made martyrs. In all, 125 persons were indicted under the act; those convicted ordinarily received light fines or suspended jail sentences. For Congress as for the President, denouncing wartime strikes proved simpler than deterring them.

Because the Act rested on a false assumption—that strikes resulted from agitation by a few ruthless labor barons—it failed to effect industrial peace. The belief that strikes were "due to some instigation by agitators who get into the ranks of labor" was as unfounded as it was widely held. Most wartime stoppages reflected rank-and-file pressure; very often they occurred without the approval of union leaders. The mandatory strike vote, which was intended to curb the powers of a John L. Lewis, instead became labor's trump card. Before entering bargaining sessions unions often held a vote to demonstrate their solidarity and raise the sword of government seizure over management's head. Since unions did not have to carry out their threat—of the first 47 voting to strike only 15 actually did so—they had everything to gain and nothing to lose. As a result unions bolstered their position, workers voted to strike as a routine matter, and legislative intent was turned upside down.

The inadequacy of the Smith-Connally Act was also emphasized by its failure to settle the bituminous coal dispute. In June Lewis had called the miners back from their third walkout, but stipulated that they would not work beyond October 31 without an acceptable contract. During the summer, playing the game of divide and conquer to perfection, Lewis worked out a settlement with the Illinois Coal Operators Association that included an across the board raise of $1.25 an hour to cover portal-to-portal pay. When in October the War Labor Board rejected this contract, the union closed the mines for what proved to be the last time that year. Lewis employed a simple ruse to nullify the War Labor Disputes Act: he "ordered" the men to return but left no doubt that his doing so was a pretense. Nothing remained but to find a formula that the mine workers would accept and the War Labor Board could swallow, and this Ickes and Lewis proceeded to do early in November.

The agreement, which gave the miners much of what they wanted, preserved the shell not the substance of wage stabilization. Lewis won a wage hike of $1.50 a day based on a new system of computing working hours. Miners would be paid for 45 minutes of travel time and would cut their lunch period from 30 to 15 minutes; they would, therefore, be paid for an eighth additional hour. "The dyspepsia formula," as it was dubbed, permitted the administration to save face because it did not violate hourly wage ceilings. The public members of the War Labor Board congratulated themselves on having held the line "despite a battering-ram assault," and approved the settlement with one dissenting vote. The union was equally delighted. A UMW spokesman had once remarked, "The true motto of the American labor movement has always been 'put it in the pay envelope,'" and the new contract did precisely that.[25] In 1944 wages in the coal mines reached $2535 and, for the first time in memory, were higher than in most other branches of manufacturing.

Just as anti-trust legislation had once been used against labor unions, so, by an ironic twist, the War Labor Disputes Act was sometimes employed against business. The most celebrated case involved Sewell Avery of Montgomery Ward. In some respects the Ward controversy resembled the coal dispute: both involved challenges to the principle of federal control and the authority of the War Labor Board, both caused the government to resort to plant seizure, and both dragged on for many months. Yet the differences were more revealing: while in one instance the union had been recalcitrant in the other management proved defiant, and while John L. Lewis had been portrayed as a villain Sewell Avery became something of a hero to many Americans. In part because the mail-order concern was clearly less essential to the war than was the coal industry, some of the same congressmen who could not adequately express their hatred for Lewis praised Avery as the most rugged of individualists.

Montgomery Ward, with 600 stores in 47 states, 78,000 employees and gross sales of $634 million, was a huge mail-order merchandising concern. It sold American farmers one-fifth of the manufactured products they bought. The enterprise was run by Sewell L. Avery who sat on the board of directors of half a dozen other corporations including United States Steel. Born during the administration of Ulysses S. Grant, his social values formed in the era of William McKinley, Avery ran his business with an iron hand. "If anybody ventures to disagree with me I throw them out the window," he once remarked. He also believed that modern merchandising could work miracles; in the past, he noted, only the nobility could enjoy great art, but "today, we can take an exquisite Cellini design and reproduce it in full color on a housewife's broom handle." During the 1930s Avery had joined the bitterly anti-Roosevelt Liberty League, and after Pearl Harbor he suspected that the President would use his emergency powers to introduce socialism or worse. In his blunt manner he expressed contempt for the public members of the War Labor Board who were "academics without experience, frequently instructors of law in colleges, and of a pink persuasion." Asked to define pink Avery responded, "I mean pink in the ordinary sense—prolabor might be a better word." Workers at Ward, deleting the periods after Avery's initials, thought it fitting that his name spelled "slavery."[26]

Avery's dispute with the government festered for nearly two years before coming to a head in April 1944. Basically, it involved his refusal to accept the War Labor Board's maintenance of membership formula which he regarded as the equivalent of a closed shop. In June 1942, having rejected a contention that Ward had no direct role in war production, the WLB had assumed jurisdiction over a dispute between the firm and the United Mail Order, Warehouse and Retail Employees Union (CIO). In November Ward ignored a decision granting maintenance of membership privileges. Only after Roosevelt personally ordered him to comply did he do so, but even then Avery protested that he was bowing under duress. The December 1942 agreement remained valid for a year; when it expired the company refused further dealings with the union which, it claimed, did not represent the workers. In January 1944 the War Labor Board ruled that the contract should continue pending a new election but the firm rejected the decision and discontinued the voluntary dues check off. On April 5 Avery rejected an order restoring the old arrangements and a week later his Chicago employees walked out. Since the Board could not very well order strikers back to work for a defiant employer it appealed to the President for help.

By then Roosevelt was armed with the Smith-Connally Act which authorized seizure of strike-bound plants "useful" in the war. But how was the word to be defined, and who would define it? The administration was concerned not with Ward's military usefulness but with its defiance of the War Labor Board. To allow Sewell Avery to disregard a Board ruling would jeopardize the maintenance of membership formula and upset the carefully contrived balance between labor and capital. But to invoke the Smith-Connally Act the administration had to fall back on the dubious assertion that the equipment sold by Montgomery Ward was "clearly useful in connection with the war effort." Lawyers for the firm retorted that this definition robbed words of their meaning, exposed "corner grocery stores, neighborhood drug stores, garages, filling stations" to seizure, and bared Roosevelt's belief that in wartime he was "a military dictator" who could snatch private property from its rightful owner on whim.[27]

The Secretary of War, who was the logical choice to supervise a takeover, held much the same opinion as did Sewell Avery. In April 1944 Henry L. Stimson and his assistant, Robert Patterson, flooded the White House with reasons why the War Department should not be asked to intervene. The Army "had no funds to run a civilian goods business," they complained, and did not belong "in the sphere of social and economic problems." Stimson feared that the Army "would appear ridiculous in the eyes of the public" if it stationed fighting men outside a retail merchandising establishment. But what worried Stimson even more was his conviction that since Montgomery Ward was "devoted entirely to storage, sale and distribution of civilian goods" and had "no relation to the war program or to the war effort," presidential seizure had "a doubtful basis in law." He did not want to use troops to extend "the President's power far wider than I was sure he had or ought to have."[28]

It fell to James F. Byrnes, as head of the Office of War Mobilization, to solve the dilemma. Byrnes was faced with a choice of evils: intervention seemed necessary to back up the War Labor Board and pacify union leaders who were clamoring for action, yet it would almost certainly expose the President to attack. Grasping at straws, Byrnes asked several Chicago industrialists to approach Ward's chairman; they reported that "it was useless to try to influence Avery." Then, still attempting to fend off criticism, Byrnes selected Secretary of Commerce Jesse Jones, the cabinet member with the closest ties to the business world, to take over the company. But Jones thought the seizure an awful idea and turned the chore over to an assistant. To insure that all went smoothly, Francis Biddle flew to Chicago where, on April 27, he met Avery at the offices of Montgomery Ward. Avery refused pointblank to cooperate. "I want none of your damned advice," he told Biddle, "to hell with the government." Biddle directed several soldiers to remove Avery, who, glaring at the Attorney General, spat out: "You New Dealer!"[29]

As the soldiers gingerly carried him out, a photographer snapped a picture that made the front page of literally every newspaper in the country and stirred a groundswell of sympathy for Avery. "Hitler's thugs, in the palmiest days, never did a more efficient job," announced the Denver *Post*. Biddle appeared in cartoons wearing a black executioner's cap and wielding a bloodstained axe. Republicans, milking the affair for all it was worth, asserted that "the whole thing is just a part of the scheme that they have had right along to destroy private business and establish Socialism."[30] To some extent sentiment divided along partisan lines—a House committee investigating the seizure issued a report with the Democrats defending the action and the Republicans denouncing it—but Avery attracted support on many levels. Opinion polls showed that three out of five people supported him. Many Americans resented what seemed an unwarranted display of presidential power, particularly against an individual whose importance to the war had not been shown and whose photograph made him appear frail and grandfatherly. For a moment, Sewell Avery became an object of compassion for all those who were tired of economic controls and disturbed by the elephantine expansion of federal authority.

Avery's expulsion accomplished very little. He continued to direct the business by telephone and as long as Ward's managers followed his orders federal control existed in name only. In May, after the union had won an election for certification as bargaining agent, the government formally relinquished control. Yet Avery proved no more willing than before to observe War Labor Board rulings and so, on December 28,

1944, the government again intervened. This time Roosevelt overrode Stimson's objections and used the Army. It took over the firm's books, changed the combinations on its safes, and discharged managers who refused to cooperate. Even Avery, recognizing the handwriting on the wall, advised compliance. In January 1945 a district judge ruled against the government but permitted it to retain possession pending a Circuit Court decision. By a vote of 2-1, that court held that the War Labor Disputes Act authorized seizure of the mail-order house. Montgomery Ward appealed to the Supreme Court but the government withdrew a day before the case was to be heard. In October 1945 Sewell Avery again assumed control, ripped down posters proclaiming government possession, ended maintenance of membership and prepared once again for battle with the union.

That it should have been Sewell Avery who challenged wartime controls with such bulldog determination was surely paradoxical. Few businesses had benefitted more than his from the revival of mass purchasing power associated with the New Deal and wartime spending. Montgomery Ward, which had gone into the red under Herbert Hoover, never failed to show a profit after Roosevelt took office. Even after wartime taxes Ward's profits in 1944 stood at $21 million. In seizing the concern the administration's objective was not to insure continued operation—as in the coal strike—but to assert the supremacy of federal authority and prove to labor that maintenance of membership would be honored. In this it was ultimately successful, although only after a false start had caused it acute embarrassment. Yet the company, too, had held to its anti-union position and in some respects the government's last-minute unwillingness to submit to a Supreme Court test vindicated Avery's stand.

If in the coal strike the administration had to contend with an intransigent labor leader and in the Ward affair with a cantankerous businessman, in the national service controversy it faced joint opposition from organized labor and the business community. The idea of national service—which would place all citizens, men and women alike, at the government's disposal for assignment to whatever job seemed necessary—was never far from people's minds after Pearl Harbor. Sentiment for the plan ebbed and flowed with the fortunes of war. An unexpected shortage of manpower, a sudden escalation of military requirements, a strike in a particularly vital industry—all were capable of breathing fresh life into the plan. But political opposition was such that the President did not endorse national service until late in the war, when it stood little or no chance of passage, and it did not come before Congress until 1945. Nevertheless, the controversy made crystal clear some of the stumbling blocks to economic regulation. It also showed how ordinarily opposing groups could support a common cause when threatened, for of all wartime proposals none created stranger bedfellows than did national service.

The most ardent advocate of national service was Grenville Clark, a Harvard-trained lawyer who had been a member of former Secretary of War Elihu Root's law firm since 1909. Clark's interest in civilian service went back to World War I when he had played an active part in the preparedness movement and helped found the Military Training Camps Association. World War II rekindled his concern. Clark aided in drafting the Selective Service Act of 1940 and served during the following year as a consultant to his close friend, Henry L. Stimson. By early 1942 Clark strongly advocated some form of civilian conscription. In his view, "half-way voluntary methods simply won't work." Only national service would ensure an efficient use of manpower, bolster morale and serve notice on the enemy that Americans would make any sacrifice for victory. Above all Clark believed that it would "pull the whole country together and keep it united."[31] During 1942 he drafted various versions of a national service bill which he dutifully sent to the President. But Roosevelt, who appeared sympathetic if noncommittal, shuffled the proposal to the War Manpower Commission. Although a WMC sub-committee recommended action, its report was buried in the fall of 1942 because of labor's hostility, the danger of a political backlash and the absence as yet of a severe manpower crisis.

In 1943 two events gave national service a new lease on life. One was the growing manpower deficit, first felt in Pacific Coast aircraft plants, that resulted when draft calls were increased and the supply of unemployed men finally exhausted. The manpower predicament worsened even after the government threatened to draft fathers who did not shift over to war work and virtually called a halt to dependency deferments. A second, more decisive development was the burst of anger at wartime strikes. When John L. Lewis shut down the coal fields, and later when the War Labor Disputes Act proved less than effective, national service came to be seen as a means of disciplining unions. As early as June Secretary of the Navy Frank Knox asked Congressman James Wadsworth, a strong supporter of national service, whether a bill could be drawn that would permit the President to freeze strikers in selected war industries at their jobs. "Wadsworth at once saw the point," Knox informed Roosevelt.[32] Toward the end of the year Stimson decided that national service was "the best solution of the pending troubles with labor" and that with anti-strike sentiment running high the odds in its favor had improved. The prospect of strikes in vital areas, he added, "have furnished a new chance for getting through a National Service Act and I am trying to push it as hard as I can."[33]

Push though he might, Stimson knew that he would not progress without Roosevelt's support. All during the spring, while Congress held hearings on the Austin-Wadsworth national service bill, Roosevelt kept his distance and allowed the measure to be bottled up in committee. Then, in his January 1944 State of the Union message the President surprised most of his advisors by endorsing national service on condition that Congress enact a new tax law, provide for a scaling down of profits on defense contracts, and authorize consumer price ceilings. National service, Roosevelt contended, "will prevent strikes, and, with certain appropriate exceptions, will make available for war production or for any other essential services every able-bodied adult in this Nation." It would help win the war, serve as a "unifying moral force," and prove to the Axis "that we mean business—that we, 130,000,000 Americans, are on the march to Rome, Berlin, and Tokyo."[34]

Why did Roosevelt choose this juncture to endorse the proposal? Undoubtedly he was influenced by a visit to battle zones in Sicily and Tunis on his return from the Teheran Conference in December, and was troubled by how close the nation came to a railroad strike later that month. He also feared that as the war drew to a close people would become dangerously complacent and more likely to leave war jobs for those with a peacetime future. Finally Roosevelt thought that his gesture in behalf of national service would, by testifying to the seriousness of the situation, induce Congress to enact the broad stabilization program he favored. Four days before his speech the President, "with a distinctly melancholy note in his voice, if not a slight tone of bitterness," told his Budget Director that "we would now probably have to have National Service legislation in order to fix all wages and prices firmly."[35]

Even with Roosevelt's support national service made little headway during 1944. James Wadsworth grumbled that the President, by hitching the issue to tax reform and price control, had "muddied the waters" and "pretty nearly killed the bill." Congress gave desultory consideration to the Bailey-Brewster bill which provided merely for drafting men between 18 and 45 who were physically unfit or who had left essential jobs for assignment to war-related work. The administration, meanwhile, appeared willing to compromise. In April Samuel I. Rosenman explained: "What is needed is a measure designed to deal with specific situations as they arise in particular industries in particular localities, much narrower in scope and much more restricted in its powers."[36] By the summer Clark was debating whether or not to go on with his campaign. With the war going well, strikes occurring less often, and a presidential election approaching, most were content to sit back and wait.

Politicians were particularly eager to avoid a showdown because influential pressure groups opposed the plan, and none more fiercely than organized labor. From the time national service was first mentioned until its ghost was laid to rest, labor regarded it as the worst of all possible solutions to the manpower problem. To union leaders national service was a disguised form of "involuntary servitude" that constituted "an open confession that Hitler is right and we are wrong" and would put the United States on "the high road to Fascism."[37] Convinced that most men in the shops would violently resent being told by the government where they must work, labor officials feared that they "would forfeit their leadership if they endorsed it." After talking to William Green and Philip Murray, Congressman Wadsworth grumbled that they were "clinging to the party line—'no forced labor,' " and would fight any measure "which called upon a civilian to do something he did not want to do."[38]

More than this, labor chieftains opposed national service because it suggested that the theory of voluntarism upon which labor relations rested was unsound, because its potential as an anti-strike weapon was all too plain, and because it threatened the closed shop. If the government ordered a worker to leave his job and report elsewhere, advocates of national service never tired of saying, "he must not, upon arrival, be told that he must join a union before he can go to work."[39] Interpreting national service as a frontal assault on union security—even Bernard Baruch conceded that "some employers will try to use the National Service Act to break the unions"—labor did its best to sabotage the plan. In April 1944, seeking a reason for congressional inaction, Stimson noted that "labor has indoctrinated everybody with the idea that national service is . . . slavery."[40]

Were the proposal as dangerous as labor imagined, one

might have expected a certain amount of enthusiasm for it
among businessmen. Yet the National Association of Manufacturers and the Chamber of Commerce opposed civilian
service as solidly as did the AFL and CIO. In a strange way
the interests of the two dovetailed, for management, like
labor, feared a loss of autonomy. Just as workers did not want
to be told where to work, businessmen did not want to be
told whom to hire. With one voice, labor and business cried
that while workers could be led to the assembly line they
could not be forced to produce efficiently. Many executives
also suspected that national service would open a huge can of
worms: if the government drafted workers, would it not inevitably assume responsibility for their housing, transportation, medical care and wages? Even worse, national service
might well increase pressure to limit profits or else eliminate
them entirely for it seemed patently unjust to conscript one
man to work for another's gain. Although business groups did
not invest the same energy in the struggle as did labor unions,
their position was never in doubt. Business leaders, Grenville
Clark remarked in disgust, "are just as blind and obstinate
on this matter as the official leaders of organized labor. There
is no choice between them."[41]

Opponents of national service came from all sides of the
political spectrum. Radicals who thought they detected "one
more indication of the authoritarian character Roosevelt's
war government has assumed" and progressives like Robert M.
La Follette, Jr., who spoke of "nazifying men and women at
home," sounded in some respects very much like right-wingers
who had always followed a rigidly anti-New Deal line and
who saw in national service their worst fears confirmed.[42] None
expressed this better than the head of a women's organization who claimed that the plan, by tearing mothers from their
children, would destroy home and family. "A woman kept on
any job for which there is not inner compulsion, and against
her will, is likely to act like a cat on a leash. Don't forget that
a man may have the strongest *will*, but a woman has the
strongest *won't*."[43]

Conversely, admirers of the measure included, in addition to the War and Navy Departments, the American Legion, which complained that "America has been fighting this war on its fat," and the Communist Party, which would go to any lengths to ensure unimpeded production.[44] Advocates usually couched their arguments in democratic terms. "Equality of obligation along with equality of right is the essence of democracy," said Stimson. The proposal, he went on, was exactly analogous to military service: if one man could be required to shoulder a gun surely another could be required to manufacture it. Furthermore, compulsion would probably be unnecessary because the existence of a clearly defined obligation would inspire voluntary compliance. Great Britain was used as proof, if more were needed, that national service was consistent with democratic practice. These examples, however, had to be selected with some care. As one partisan warned James Forrestal, "the assertion that we must accept universal service because Germany and Japan have it is very bad propaganda. It will be used against us. I think it should be deleted."[45]

In December 1944 the one event that could revive hopes for national service—a sudden military reversal—occurred when German troops broke through Allied lines in the Ardennes, overran 700 square miles of Belgium and Luxembourg, and touched off the Battle of the Bulge. Spurred by the emergency and fears of a drawn-out conflict, the House passed a diluted national service bill that required every male registrant between 18 and 45 to work at an essential job if so ordered. Unlike the legislation considered during 1944, the measure provided for the use of civil sanctions rather than the draft in case of noncompliance. The Army, although it thought the bill too weak, realized that it was the best that could be gotten. "If [you] can't ride a horse," Stimson commented, "ride a mule." Although it passed in the House by the comfortable margin of 246-167, by the time it reached the Senate in March the German counteroffensive had been turned back and victory in Europe was in sight. The Senate proceeded to tear the bill to shreds, substituting one which in Wadsworth's judgment "isn't worth the paper it is written on." Then the Senate overwhelmingly rejected a conference report that tried to reconcile the two versions, and the national service controversy sputtered to an end.[46]

Frustrated in its fight for national service the administration cast about for other ways to gain firmer control over manpower. In December 1944 Byrnes issued a "work-or-fight" order which provided for drafting men under 38 who were not working at essential jobs and assigning them to industry. The Army, however, balked at using the draft as a manpower sanction—Stimson thought it turned military service from an honor into a disgrace—and the 12,000 men ultimately drafted under Byrnes's directive never were released to industry. In June 1945, when the order was restricted to men who met the Army's usual qualifications for induction, it became a dead letter. Nor did efforts to end agricultural deferments prove successful. Early in 1945, at a time when three farmers were deferred for every industrial worker and farmers constituted the lone source of draftable men under 26, Byrnes told local boards that farmers could no longer be exempt. But that spring the House and Senate passed a joint resolution protecting most farmers from the draft no matter how desperate the need. Despite a presidential veto the combined resistance of selective service, Congress and local draft boards could not be overcome.

In seeking national service legislation the President had greater difficulty than in trying to stop the coal strike or bring Montgomery Ward into line for he was requesting new, far-reaching authority rather than endeavoring to use powers he already had. Also, he faced opposition from both business and labor rather than from one or the other. Whether or not he had public support, as measured by opinion polls, was not always decisive: the public favored action against John L. Lewis, opposed action against Sewell Avery, and split nearly down the middle over national service. Yet in all three instances Roosevelt was boxed in by similar forces—political considerations, pressure from groups he could not afford to alienate, the difficulty of applying sanctions even when authorized by law, and the waning sense of urgency as the war drew to a close. In his contest with Lewis and Avery the President had battled to something of a standoff. Only in his belated campaign for national service did Roosevelt suffer an unmixed defeat, but even so, the collapse of Germany just as the manpower crisis approached a climax removed much of the sting.

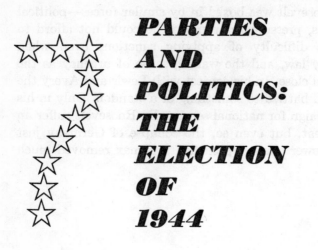

PARTIES AND POLITICS: THE ELECTION OF 1944

WORLD WAR II BROUGHT about far-reaching changes in the American political system. The war set in motion an interstate migration of millions of workers, many of whom carried their party loyalties with them, and it introduced issues of domestic as well as foreign policy that disrupted existing electoral coalitions, strengthening some and weakening others. Furthermore, political developments that first appeared during the 1930s crystallized during the war: Republicans and Southern Democrats consummated their alliance in Congress, the federal bureaucracy expanded its power, Democrats consolidated their support in the big cities, labor unions took a more energetic part in national elections, Republican leaders accepted the main features of the welfare state, and politicians attached increasing importance to public opinion polls in calculating their chances and defining their strategies.

Shortly after Pearl Harbor the Democratic and Republican

national chairmen pledged to keep politics out of the war. Even so, efforts to arrange a truce, whether in the broad sense of suspending all political activity and establishing a coalition government or in the much narrower sense of agreeing not to exploit issues connected with the war for partisan advantage, were highly unsuccessful. Unlike England, where elections could be suspended by an act of Parliament, the United States in the absence of a constitutional amendment had to conduct regular elections. Even at the state level proposals to bypass politics made no headway. In Wyoming, for example, where Republicans controlled the state house and Democrats the congressional delegation, a suggestion that both parties agree to return incumbents to office without an election was flatly turned down. Political leaders agreed that it would be unwise, impractical and unconstitutional.

In addition, politicians rejected a nonpartisan approach because the stakes were so high. Many Republicans continued to believe, as they had throughout the 1930s, that Roosevelt and his advisors would not think twice before snuffing out traditional liberties. The President's motto, said one county chairman, might well be "me and my labor friends come first, to hell with how the war comes out—I want a 4th term."[1] Republicans, therefore, became adept at clothing partisanship in the garb of patriotism. There was a great difference, they claimed, between national unity and political unity. Criticism of public officials, as long as it did not reveal valuable information to the enemy, tended to preserve liberty, for if the minority remained silent the majority would use the emergency to entrench itself in power. As Robert Taft put it, "the New Dealers are determined to make the country over under the cover of war if they can." By the summer of 1942 one Republican who had just won a primary contest could boast, "There was no pulling of punches on my part, and I went after the Roosevelt foreign policy with just as much vigor and venom as though there were no war."[2]

Conversely, Democrats sought to gain a political advantage

from the widely-felt impulse toward national unity. Some
called for a political truce, others for a moratorium on criticism of the administration, and nearly all for the election of
Democratic candidates. One member of the Democratic
national committee noted that the American system operated
most effectively when the President could work with a majority of his own party in Congress; since "fate decreed" that
a Democrat would be in the White House when Japan
attacked, voters should do the patriotic thing by supporting
Democratic candidates. (Had fate decreed otherwise, he
added, he, for one, would gladly have voted Republican.)
Ed Flynn, the Democratic national chairman, asserted that
"the only beneficiaries of the Republican policy of criticism
are in Tokyo, . . . in Rome, in Berlin, and in other Axis
centers." When Flynn added that a Republican triumph in
1942 would be the worst blow America could suffer short of a
military disaster,[3] Roosevelt quickly disavowed the remark
and called instead for the election of congressmen, regardless
of party, who would "back up" the government. In this
instance an appearance of standing above the battle was the
very best kind of politics.

As Flynn's statement suggests, the war, far from effecting
a suspension of partisan activity, actually heightened its
emotional intensity. Few could resist the temptation, at one
time or another, to regard a political enemy as an enemy of
the nation, or to claim that an opponent's victory would aid
the Axis. Although the American political system normally
blurs sharp lines of conflict and encourages losers to accept
defeat gracefully, the life-and-death character of war often
gave a raw edge to partisan debate. Harold Ickes, who had
voted Republican before joining Roosevelt's cabinet, said
early in 1942 that the men formerly termed economic royalists
"might now be called American Fascists and that is how I
classify them." Roosevelt should prepare "to meet the enemy
at the polls" by seeking the support of those who believed
in democratic principles "with the copper-heads separated

out so that we could see them and know them for what they are." "Whenever a viper's head appears," Ickes concluded, "a club should be taken to it."[4]

The controversy that raged around the Office of Civilian Defense early in 1942 showed how easily wartime problems could become grist for partisan mills and how enduring were conservative suspicions of the Roosevelt administration. The OCD was supposed to bolster morale and protect civilians from enemy attack by training first-aid workers and air-raid wardens. The agency was headed by Fiorello La Guardia and included a Volunteer Participation Committee, under the direction of Eleanor Roosevelt, which conducted physical fitness clinics. When Mrs. Roosevelt placed actor Melvyn Douglas and dancer Mayris Chaney on the committee payroll Republicans in Congress flew into a rage. They claimed that the OCD was a New Deal wolf disguised in the clothing of national defense, that Douglas was a fellow traveler, and that the President's wife had appointed "her communist friends" to the agency. "This is just another sample of the way the New Deal operates," said John Taber. "Under the direction of Mrs. Roosevelt, and certainly with the approval of the President himself, they have taken the old WPA crowd, plus some 'red' recruits and promoted them into the OCD office."[5] Democrats complained of a "Republican blitzkrieg," but within weeks La Guardia, Mrs. Roosevelt, and her aides resigned and the physical fitness program was transferred elsewhere.

Squabbles over civilian defense, however, provided a mere taste of what was to come in the political campaigns later in 1942. The elections saw the Republicans make heavy gains, capturing 44 additional seats in the House and 9 in the Senate, and turning Democratic governors out of office in New York, Michigan and California. Some of the most prominent liberals in Congress—such as George Norris of Nebraska and Josh Lee of Oklahoma—went down to defeat, and many Republicans with the most conservative and isolationist records—

including Stephen A. Day of Illinois, Clare E. Hoffman of Michigan, and Hamilton Fish of New York—were returned. In 1942 the emergence of new issues and the drastic population shifts caused by war altered the balance of political forces and permitted conservatives to tighten their hold on Congress.

The coalition that had carried Franklin Roosevelt and the Democrats to victory during the 1930s had been built around bread-and-butter concerns. By 1942, however, with unemployment disappearing and the number of people on relief dwindling, the issue of economic security had lost much of its appeal. What grievances there were often hurt the Democrats and helped the Republicans. Workers who believed that wage controls were too strict and price controls not strict enough, farmers who thought that labor costs were too high and price supports too low, white collar workers whose salaries had not kept pace with inflation—these were not voters whose allegiance the Democrats could take for granted. "I'll bet half the people who were on W.P.A. wouldn't admit that fact if they were asked," one Democrat noted despairingly. "Actually, they think it was somebody else who was starving back in 1933."[6]

Democrats believed, with some justice, that as traditional economic concerns were brushed aside their party paid a heavy price. When asked to account for their poor showing they cited a number of reasons: the general resentment at shortages, gasoline rationing and bureaucratic red tape; the hostility of German-, Irish- and Italian-Americans toward the war; southern fears that the administration was buckling under to demands of militant Negroes ("there was in certain letters from the South a hint of the breaking of the 'Solid South,'" reported one party leader with mixed panic and disbelief.) Democrats also complained that an act lowering the draft age from twenty to eighteen had cost them votes. Although it had received bipartisan support, the measure, they argued, exposed incumbents to the charge of cradle-robbing. "When the eighteen-nineteen year draft law was passed, immediately before the election, this charge then became a swelling chorus that carried conviction to the Democratic mothers whose very babes (for all children remain babies to all mothers) were being sent out by Roosevelt to be killed in HIS war," said a former congressman. "And they voted that conviction."[7]

But the Democrats suffered more in 1942 from an astonishingly low turnout than from anything else. Only 28 million people voted, 8 million fewer than in 1938 and nearly 22 million fewer than in 1940. Although this was partly a result of the waning interest in economic issues, to an even greater extent it reflected wartime social upheaval: young men in the armed forces lacked the opportunity or incentive to cast absentee ballots, and war workers who had recently taken jobs in different states could not meet residency requirements. At the time, five states demanded two years' residence and thirty-two others insisted on at least one year. Even when workers met these requirements they were often reluctant to forfeit wages by taking time off, and those working night shifts or overtime found voting an inconvenience. "Defense plants ruined the Democrats," claimed an unsuccessful candidate in Illinois, "workers wouldn't give up a day's pay to vote and their normal hours wouldn't permit their getting to the polls."[8] Since many war plants were built on the outskirts of cities, commuting back and forth to the polling booths was more time-consuming than before.

Ordinarily a decline in turnout does not hurt one party more than another, but in 1942 it worked a disproportionate hardship on the Democrats who relied heavily upon draft-age voters and the working classes. In district after district the Republican vote fell slightly or remained stable, but the Democratic vote dropped precipitously. Ohio, where the Republicans won eight new House seats, graphically illustrated the pattern. One district, which included the city of Akron, had voted safely Democratic for a decade, but in 1942 it went Republican. While the Republican vote dipped from 76,000 in 1938 to 60,000 in 1942, the Democratic vote plunged from 87,000 to 57,000. Consequently, even where voters faithfully followed party lines the Democrats faced difficulty. "The Republicans won their seats," observed a student of electoral behavior, "simply because more traditional Republicans went to the polls."[9]

The relative unimportance of economic issues and the tendency of low-income voters to stay at home had disastrous consequences for the Democratic party in New York, where big city majorities were necessary to offset Republican strength upstate. After a fierce internal struggle the Democrats selected John J. Bennett to face Thomas E. Dewey in the gubernatorial race. Bennett's nomination had been engineered by James A. Farley, who had once been Roosevelt's chief political strategist but had broken with him over the third-term issue. The President had opposed the choice in the belief that Bennett, a Tammany politician, would do poorly upstate and would not receive American Labor Party endorsement. Events confirmed Roosevelt's judgment: Dewey received 2.1 million votes, Bennett 1.5 million and the ALP candidate 400,000. Far fewer people voted than had in the last gubernatorial election, but the sharpest reduction occurred in traditional Democratic strongholds: from 1938 to 1942 the Republican vote in New York City fell by 40,000, the American Labor Party vote remained constant, and the Democratic vote dropped by 300,000. After twenty years of rule by Al Smith, Franklin Roosevelt and Herbert Lehman, Democrats ruefully acknowledged "the temporary passing of our era of State Government."[10]

Democrats met with a still more embarrassing reversal in their effort to unseat Hamilton Fish, who had represented the congressional district embracing Roosevelt's own Hyde Park since 1921. As ranking minority member of both the Foreign Affairs and Rules committees, Fish was perhaps the most notorious isolationist in Congress. Many Republicans, particularly those associated with Wendell Willkie, regarded him as an albatross around the party's neck and threw their support to Augustus Bennet in the primary. When Fish easily disposed of this challenge, internationalists in both parties warily explored the possibility of cooperating in November. Bennet hoped to win Democratic endorsement but knew that they would not "overlook their distaste for me as a regular Republican and support me" as long as they had hopes of electing one of their own. Democrats, however, advised Republicans to put principle before party loyalty by backing their candidate, Judge Ferdinand Hoyt. Roosevelt, who was keenly interested in the race, noted that "it is up to the anti-Fish Republicans to play ball with Judge Hoyt," who was an "independent Democrat" and not "a violent Party man."[11] In the end, Dewey, Willkie and other prominent Republicans refused to support Fish but he nevertheless won reelection by a reduced margin. Democratic chieftains found a partial explanation in the low turnout in Poughkeepsie's Irish and Italian wards. Many immigrants, they concluded, "were just not voting this year."[12]

Nothing better illustrated the Republicans' ability to combat charges of isolationism, exploit tensions within the Democratic party, and profit from poor turnout than the senatorial race in Illinois. There, Republican C. Wayland Brooks, who had opposed most collective security measures and had appeared frequently at America First rallies, faced Raymond McKeough. Just as liberal Democrats in New York were dismayed at James Farley's influence, so in Illinois they condemned Chicago Mayor Edward Kelly's grip on McKeough, charging "Kelly-Nash men behave like Hitler storm troopers. The machine is entirely like Hitler in its methods." In the campaign Brooks called attention to his combat record in World War I and warned that the Chicago machine was seeking to spread its octopus-like tentacles over the state. Democrats countered that if Illinois repudiated Roosevelt's leadership by choosing an arch-isolationist "then there will be rejoicing in Berlin and Rome and Hirohito and his hordes will rejoice as well." But the attempt to tar Brooks with an isolationist brush failed. The Democratic vote fell substantially below expected levels and Brooks piled up large enough majorities in rural areas to win.[13]

The defeat of Democrats in the North and Midwest measurably enhanced the influence of southern Democrats in Congress. This resurgence, moreover, coincided with a growing fear that the Roosevelt administration was betraying white supremacy. The obsession with race had affected Democratic primaries throughout the region. In South Carolina one candidate attacked racial policies in the District of Columbia where "white ladies are ordered to call Negro officials Mister." In Georgia the "liberal" Ellis G. Arnall running against incumbent Governor Eugene Talmadge (who had cost the state university its accreditation by ousting faculty members who allegedly tried to impose integrated coeducation) found it expedient to announce that "if a nigger ever tried to get into a white school in my part of the state, the sun would never set on his head."[14] When Congress convened in 1943 resentful southerners talked openly of bolting the Democratic party. But they did no more than talk, for as overall Democratic strength shrunk the relative strength of the South grew: representatives of 15 southern and border states held 120 of 222 Democratic seats in the House, 29 of 57 in the Senate, and they continued to rule most important committees.

The changed complexion of Congress enabled southern Democrats to solidify their alliance with Republicans. This coalition had originated in the late 1930s when conservatives in both parties combined to thwart efforts to broaden the New Deal. Yet it had remained inchoate before the war, in part because the President's foreign policy and domestic program still commanded considerable support in the South. After the elections of 1942 the coalition became at once more powerful and cohesive. Since southerners filled more than half of all the Democratic seats in Congress and Republican strength had increased to 208 in the House and 38 in the Senate, the two groups could make or break legislation more frequently than in the past. In 1943 they tasted blood by liquidating the National Youth Administration and the National Resources Planning Board, cutting the budget of the Farm Security Administration, and passing the Smith-Connally Act, but collaboration reached a wartime peak in 1944 when the coalition operated on four of every ten closely contested votes in the Senate.[15]

The cement that held the coalition together was provided not only by a mutual desire to protect states' rights, regulate labor unions and curb welfare spending, but also by a shared resentment over the mammoth wartime expansion of executive authority and the corresponding erosion of legislative influence. As the federal bureaucracy grew by leaps and bounds (by January 1943 emergency war agencies employed 172,736 civilians), as administrators exerted unprecedented control over people's lives, and as the war riveted public attention on the Commander-in-Chief, many congressmen—but particularly those who lacked confidence in Roosevelt to begin with—looked for ways to reassert their prerogatives. If they could not prevent the drift of power from Capitol Hill to war agencies and the White House, they could at least check up on how it was being used. Special committees were therefore created to investigate the defense program, the effect of the war on small business, the gasoline and fuel shortages, the seizure of Montgomery Ward and, under Howard Smith of Virginia, the "Acts of Executive Agencies Beyond the Scope of their Authority." Similarly, congressmen bristled when they were accused of rubber-stamping administrative decisions. Responding to one such charge in July 1943 a Republican exploded, "Great God, have you been watching what the Congress has been doing in the last three or four weeks despite the protests of the President and the whole New Deal administration?"[16]

Hostility toward the federal establishment flashed into the

open in February 1943 when Martin Dies of Texas who, as chairman of the House Committee on Un-American Activities had been skirmishing with the administration for years, attacked "crackpot" bureaucrats who had worked their way into government service. Pricking the wounded pride of his colleagues, Dies stressed the need to "guard jealously and zealously the rights and the prerogatives of this body," and painted a grim picture of a future in which "the real power and function of government will not be exercised in this Chamber, but . . . by bureaucracy." Then, after dutifully praising "the heroism and the courage of the Russian people," he linked the rather generalized resentment of bureaucracy with the more specific fear of communist infiltration. Dies named some forty officials who had allegedly supported left-wing causes, expressed radical opinions, or held other unortho-dox views. One employee, he noted darkly, had "advocated the practice of universal nudism in office and factory."[17]

Roosevelt had once ridiculed Dies's allegations by telling newsmen "we have discovered that in the House of Repre-sentatives itself, we have got something far worse than a nudist—we have got an exhibitionist!" But if Dies's charges were, to some extent, old hat, in 1943 they provoked a startling response. The House authorized a hearing into the loyalty of a number of employees including Goodwin B. Watson and William E. Dodd, Jr. of the FCC, and Robert Morss Lovett, government secretary of the Virgin Islands. The three men, all of whom had at one time been university professors, were grilled not on their activities since assuming government posts but rather on what they had said, what organizations they had joined, and who they had known during the 1930s. Even professions of doctrinal purity—"Do you believe in a system of private enterprise?" Dodd was asked. "I do." "You believe in the capitalist system?" "Yes, sir."—failed to satisfy the inquisitors who found the three guilty of having harbored subversive views and recommended their dismissal.[18] The House, with the reluctant approval of the Senate, then

attached a rider to a deficiency appropriation bill providing
that Watson, Dodd and Lovett would be dropped within
four months unless reappointed by the President and confirmed by the Senate. Roosevelt, who could not risk vetoing
a critical appropriation bill, signed it under protest. Not until
three years later did the Supreme Court rule that Congress,
by punishing individuals without a trial, had violated the
constitutional ban on bills of attainder.

Considerably more was at stake in the congressional battle
over the soldier vote than in these antibureaucratic and anti-
radical rumblings. In 1944 there were over nine million
servicemen, nearly five million of whom were stationed
abroad, and their votes might well determine the outcome of
the election. Since everyone assumed, and the polls justified
the assumption, that they would lean heavily toward the
Democrats, the administration wanted to make it as easy as
possible for the largest number of men in uniform to vote. As
Ed Flynn admitted, "the most important problem that we
have in this election is the vote in the Armed Forces."[19]
Republicans, of course, knew that the larger this turnout the
poorer their own chances, and they found allies in southern
Democrats who feared any proposal that might undermine
state control of voting and enfranchise Negro servicemen. In
the legislative scuffling over the soldier vote early in 1944
the conservative coalition began to mature.

The administration's plan for soldier voting was embodied
in the Green-Lucas bill. When first introduced in June 1943
the measure ran into opposition from Secretary of War Henry
Stimson who feared that transmitting ballots and lists of
candidates might interfere with military communications.
But early in the fall, after Roosevelt had asked James Byrnes
to "lay down the law," these differences were overcome. The
bill greatly simplified the process of absentee voting: rather
than requiring each soldier to apply for a ballot, wait to receive it, and execute it weeks later, all servicemen would receive ballots in advance of federal elections and could mark

them at an appropriate time. Civilian employees of the government living overseas and the merchant marine also received the same privilege. To supervise the procedure the bill contemplated a bipartisan War Ballot Commission composed of four members; in the event of an impasse a fifth vote would be cast by a Supreme Court justice. The administration believed, in the words of Samuel Rosenman, that "only a bill such as the Green-Lucas bill which asserts Federal supremacy over State law and State constitutions, based upon the war powers of the Congress, could overcome the difficulties."[20]

This challenge to states' rights provided a rallying point for opponents of the measure. John Rankin of Mississippi claimed that it would create a "super-bureaucracy" and "wipe out State laws and State qualifications for the electors in violation of the Constitution." The sponsors, he added, had a "wild desire to concentrate into the hands of the Federal Government all power over elections." Republicans dwelt on many of the same themes but added several new twists. They revived memories of the disputed Hayes-Tilden election of 1876 when the deciding vote on contested ballots had been cast by a member of the Supreme Court along straight party lines. They argued that the Green-Lucas bill lacked safeguards "against the young men and women of our armed forces being intimidated to vote for their Commander-in-Chief," and pointed out that the bipartisan character of the War Ballot Commission meant little as long as the President could appoint Republicans with "pink tendencies, New Deal tendencies."[21] But always the argument reverted to states' rights: "If an out and out Federal war ballot act is adopted, it will forthwith make the Federal government the outstanding governmental interest of our voters and indeed relegate the states to an extremely minor position."[22]

In place of the federal ballot, Senators James Eastland of Mississippi, John McClellan of Arkansas and Kenneth McKellar of Tennessee proposed a "state control" bill. Under

its terms Congress would recommend to the states the enactment of legislation enabling soldiers to cast absentee ballots
"wherever practicable, and compatible with military operations." This measure, which left the states in full control,
passed the Senate in December 1943 by a vote of 42-37 with
the support of every southern Democrat except Claude Pepper
of Florida. Then, early in February, the House rejected a
motion to replace the Senate version with the federal ballot
by a vote of 168-224. Southern Democrats were less united
in the House than in the Senate: while representatives from
Florida, Maryland, North Carolina, Tennessee, Texas and
Virginia voted 47-12 for the federal ballot, those from the
deep South—Alabama, Georgia, Louisiana, Mississippi and
South Carolina—voted 25-1 against it. Even though a majority of southerners backed the federal ballot, enough of
them worked with Republicans to kill the plan.

When the War and Navy departments insisted that the
bill was unworkable the Senate subsequently authorized
those soldiers who were beyond the reach of absentee voting
procedures to use a federal ballot, but the measure that
emerged from conference in March 1944 did not give Roosevelt what he had wanted. It provided for a federal ballot
only when a state expressly approved its use, and when a
soldier had applied for and failed to receive an absentee
ballot. Roosevelt, who bitterly denounced "that fool bill,"
saw no alternative but to let it become law without his
signature.[23] For all its shortcomings the measure did prompt
most states to reform their absentee voting procedures so as
to enfranchise servicemen. While only twenty states ever accepted the federal ballot (111,773 were cast in 1944), more
than four million soldiers mailed in absentee ballots. In a
roundabout way, then, the administration had achieved its
purpose.

If the struggle over the soldier vote exposed some of the
forces with which Roosevelt had to contend in Congress, the
dispute over taxation illustrated how the conservative coali-

tion could exploit cleavages within the Democratic party and between the President and Congress. The controversy was rooted in a 1943 Treasury request for $10.5 billion in additional revenue, of which $6.5 billion was to come from personal income taxes, $1 billion from corporate taxes, $2.5 billion from excises, and the remainder from estate and gift taxes. The House Ways and Means Committee rejected these proposals and substituted a measure, passed by the House in November 1943, which would have brought in some $2 billion. In January 1944 the Senate, which was equally reluctant to impose stiff levies in an election year, passed a similar measure and after discrepancies were adjusted in conference the bill went to the White House. But Roosevelt, who had grown more and more resentful of foot-dragging in Congress, was inclined to listen to those advisors who advocated a veto. Samuel Rosenman, for one, complained that the bill "contains so many special interest provisions inserted through the influence of selfish lobbies that it is really a vicious piece of legislation."[24]

On February 22, 1944 the President sent down a stinging veto message which touched off a revolt among the Democratic leadership. Roosevelt accused Congress of providing relief "not for the needy but for the greedy" by permitting depletion allowances for minerals, exempting natural gas pipe lines from the excess profits tax, and allowing lumbermen to treat income from timber cutting as a capital gain. Within hours Alben Barkley of Kentucky announced his intention to resign as Senate majority leader and even permitted personal remarks to creep into his speech. (The President prided himself on his knowledge of forestry, but Barkley noted that this experience had been confined to selling Christmas trees at Hyde Park; "to compare these little pine bushes with a sturdy oak . . . would be like comparing a cricket with a stallion!") Although White House emissaries begged him to reconsider—"If men like you and I desert the President, he is sunk," James Byrnes remarked—Barkley went ahead with his resignation only to be unanimously reelected by the

Democratic caucus. The House then proceeded to override the veto by a margin of 299-95; the Senate vote was 72-14. For the first time in the nation's history Congress had passed a revenue law over a presidential veto.[25]

In the scuffle over the tax bill Republicans and southern Democrats attempted with considerable success to divert attention from tax rates, profits and exemptions and focus it on congressional pride, dignity and self-respect. Furthermore, the coalition in the House exhibited a far greater degree of cohesion than it had earlier that month in the soldier vote controversy. Of the 95 congressmen who voted to sustain the President's veto, 93 had supported his plan for soldier voting, but 40 southerners who had backed the federal ballot now joined Democrats from the deep South and Republicans in overriding the veto. The troubles that Roosevelt encountered on the Hill convinced him that the coalition was virtually unstoppable. According to Harold Smith, Roosevelt commented "that he had made up his mind that it is impossible to get along with the present Congress; and that he is losing no sleep over the matter . . . . He continued that for all practical purposes we have a Republican Congress now."[26]

The controversies over taxation and the soldier vote not only emphasized the success of conservatives in Congress, but also had a direct bearing on preparations for the presidential election. Certainly Roosevelt interpreted them as the opening volleys in the 1944 campaign. "The Republicans are in the midst of a campaign to sow discord among us," he told one Congressman in March, and he went on to blast "a very small number of people who would rather nail my hide to the barn door than win the war."[27] Although the war witnessed an unusual amount of collaboration by Republican and Democratic conservatives in Congress, as spring gave way to summer and the conventions drew near, traditional loyalties reasserted themselves and habitual rivalries reappeared. Both conventions demonstrated the strength of party regulars and their ability to dispose of challenges from mavericks.

In the spring of 1944 the chief contenders for the Republican nomination were Wendell Willkie and Thomas E. Dewey. As in 1940 Willkie inspired considerable enthusiasm among the public at large but little or none among professional politicians. Not only did his Democratic background trouble party leaders, but by 1944 Willkie had moved far to the left of most Republicans, few of whom could feel entirely comfortable with a candidate who defended immigrant radicals against deportation, told an NAACP convention that "we have practiced within our own boundaries something that amounts to race imperialism," or suggested that the government recognize its "duty toward every citizen in this land to protect him or her . . . against the hazards of unemployment, old age, accident or ill health." Even more than his position on civil liberties, civil rights and economic security, Willkie's advocacy of internationalism and attempt to weed isolationist influence out of the GOP cost him support, particularly among Republican congressmen. Too often Willkie appeared to lack the politician's touch. "I don't know whether you're going to support me or not," he told a group of St. Louis businessmen and party leaders in October 1943, "and I don't give a damn. You're a bunch of political liabilities anyway."[28]

Given this lack of support at the top, Willkie needed a smashing primary victory to make his candidacy credible. The battleground he chose was Wisconsin, the only state other than Indiana in which he had run ahead of Republican gubernatorial and senatorial candidates in 1940. Yet despite a whirlwind campaign in which he traveled 1400 miles and made 40 speeches, Willkie's brand of liberal internationalism left most Wisconsin Republicans cold. His greatest appeal had never been to the rock-ribbed party members who were most likely to vote in a primary, and the strong isolationist tradition in Wisconsin, especially among German-Americans, also worked to his disadvantage. As one observer put it, "the ghost of old Bob La Follette still stands beside the polling booths in the Wisconsin hinterlands."[29] Willkie received only 16 percent of the vote and trailed Thomas E. Dewey (who did not bother to campaign), Harold Stassen and Douglas MacArthur; not one delegate pledged to Willkie was elected. The disastrous showing crushed Willkie's political hopes.

As Willkie's star faded, Dewey's seemed to shine more brightly than ever. Both men represented the party's eastern wing, yet they could hardly have been less alike. Where Willkie's party orthodoxy was suspect, Dewey was a Republican to the core (indeed, his grandfather had helped found the party in Michigan before the Civil War.) Willkie had never held public office, but Dewey—after prosecuting such underworld characters as Waxey Gordon, Legs Diamond and Lucky Luciano—had become District Attorney in New York City, had narrowly missed defeating Herbert Lehman in 1938, and had then been elected governor in 1942. Although Willkie's domestic program verged on heresy, Dewey's was quite conventional ("it is absolutely necessary that we get rid of the New Deal to save the country," he remarked in 1940.) Willkie fought isolationism from the start, but Dewey sat on the fence for a rather long time (in April 1941 he said, "it is an intolerable situation if we stay out and Germany wins and it is an impossible situation if we do go in.").[30] Dewey also lacked Willkie's knack for establishing rapport with large crowds. Some said that when a photographer called out, "Smile, Governor," Dewey replied, "I thought I was."

As governor of New York, Dewey had taken giant strides toward the nomination. He built an impressive record by modernizing the state's fiscal system, providing subsidies for low-income housing, overhauling the workmen's compensation system, and pushing through a plan of legislative reapportionment which, to the dismay of some Republicans, increased New York City's representation. Dewey healed the bitter divisions between upstate conservatives and a more liberal faction centered in New York City which had crippled the party for a decade. Unlike 1940, when the state's delegation was hopelessly split, Dewey came to the Chicago convention in July 1944 with a solid base of support. By the time the convention opened Willkie had withdrawn, the MacArthur boomlet had collapsed, most favorite sons had stepped aside, and Dewey had clinched the nomination. His managers— Herbert Brownell, J. Russell Sprague and Edwin Jaeckle— ran the proceedings with cool efficiency: Earl Warren's key-note speech was submitted in advance for Dewey's approval; the platform, tailored to Dewey's liking, was adopted in twenty seconds; the delegates selected Dewey on the first ballot with but one dissenting vote, and chose John Bricker of Ohio as his running mate to provide the ticket with proper geographical balance.

When the Democrats met in Chicago a few weeks later Roosevelt's renomination was never in doubt. Nevertheless, a struggle took place over the second spot on the ballot, a struggle made all the more macabre by the belief that Roosevelt had grown too weak to survive another four-year term and that much more might be at stake than the choice of a vice president. The two leading candidates, Henry A. Wallace and James F. Byrnes, represented the major groups that were by 1944 jostling one another uneasily within the party, and for that reason each man had as many enemies as he did friends. Byrnes, the candidate of the South, was anathema to the CIO, Negroes, and, because he had broken with the church, to some Catholics; Wallace, the darling of labor and the liberals, was unacceptable to the South and the city bosses. Most Democratic leaders recognized that neither Wallace nor Byrnes would attract independent voters, and that either might repel voters who would otherwise support the party. At a meeting with national chairman Robert Hannegan and other party officials, Roosevelt, too, accepted this assessment. He settled on Harry S. Truman of Missouri as a suitable compromise, but could not bring himself to inform the other hopefuls of his choice.

With each faction in the party operating as a veto group,

the convention, following Roosevelt's lead, nominated Truman on the second ballot. As a border state Senator whose parents had identified with the Confederate cause Truman appealed to the South, yet his civil rights credentials were respectable enough to woo Negro voters in Detroit, Chicago and New York. As a product of Tom Pendergast's Kansas City machine Truman spoke the same language as the other city bosses, yet his loyal support for New Deal social legislation satisfied labor and the liberals. Truman had also acquired a national reputation with his investigation into the defense program, yet had earned Roosevelt's gratitude by scrupulously refusing to second-guess the military conduct of the war. Although conservatives claimed to be outraged that the CIO could have blackballed Byrnes, and the liberals professed anger that the machine politicians could have dumped Wallace ("I wouldn't have been for the Angel Gabriel himself as the 'take it or leave it' candidate of Hannegan, Kelly, Flynn and Hague," asserted Harold Ickes), the "Missouri compromise of 1944" permitted the Democrats to enter the campaign less divided than they might otherwise have been.[31]

Roosevelt's hopes rested chiefly on a heavy working class turnout. At a time when two out of three union members considered themselves Democrats, a light vote, such as had occurred in 1942, might allow Dewey to win by default. Throughout the fall the President tried to drum up labor's interest by emphasizing economic themes. The Republicans, he reminded audiences, were the party of Hoovervilles and breadlines; the Democrats, as the party of collective bargaining and social security, could alone guarantee jobs for everyone when the war was over. But ideological appeals would not bring workers into the voting booths in the absence of grass-roots registration and voting drives, and these tasks fell to the CIO's Political Action Committee. Although trade unions had taken part in past campaigns, the 1944 contest drew labor into politics on an unprecedented scale and its involvement did much to influence the outcome.

The Political Action Committee, the brainchild of Sidney

Hillman and Philip Murray, had been formed in July 1943 and, paradoxically, reflected both the CIO's awareness of its newly-acquired strength and its apprehension at rising antilabor sentiment. Conceived as a response to the Smith-Connally Act, which Congress had passed during the coal strike in an attempt to stifle union activity, PAC represented more than a sharp retort to what labor regarded as vindictive legislation. Hillman and Murray recognized that the wartime growth in union membership had vastly increased labor's potential influence, that labor's failure to vote in 1942 had bolstered conservative forces in Congress, and that politics had acquired added importance as the government assumed responsibility for regulating wages and working conditions. Finally, Roosevelt's friends in the labor movement, disturbed by rumblings of third party activity in Michigan, sought to steer labor's political energy into safe channels. Hillman assured Roosevelt that PAC aimed "to unite the forces of labor and mobilize them for active and effective participation in the political campaigns" by helping candidates who supported the President.[32]

To mobilize labor for political action required surmounting legal obstacles, overcoming organizational inadequacies, and resolving factional disputes. The Smith-Connally Act prohibited the use of union funds for political purposes, but PAC discovered convenient loopholes: money spent prior to the conventions was not restricted, and afterwards PAC did not draw on union treasuries or donate money directly to candidates but instead solicited "voluntary" contributions and put out its own material. In addition, it created a National Citizens-PAC (composed of representatives of farm, civil rights and professional organizations) which, although it was a satellite of Hillman's group, had no official ties to the CIO. PAC also undertook the huge task of reclassifying union membership lists, which were arranged by shop rather than by ward or precinct, so that registration drives could be conducted and tabs kept on voter turnout. Then too, PAC made a valiant if not entirely successful attempt to smooth over divisions in the labor movement by seeking support from the AFL and the Railway Brotherhoods. United labor committees were established in such cities as St. Louis, Buffalo, St. Paul, Cleveland and Philadelphia, although the AFL at the national level always held PAC at arm's length.

The activities of PAC implied a fundamental reordering of labor's priorities. "We are going to have to overcome outmoded attitudes about political action within the labor movement itself," Hillman and Murray reported in April 1944. "We are going to have to develop new, politically-conscious attitudes among the leadership and rank and file of labor." They asked union chiefs to make political action "a primary concern for 1944, around which your normal trade union activities revolve."[33] Although it was easy to say that the worker's standard of living, the prospects for union growth and the future of collective bargaining all depended upon electing the right men, it was more difficult to convey this to local union officials, many of whom were occupied with a thousand and one details of plant routine. One PAC regional director complained: "Their time is so taken up with organizing and industrial problems that they seem to have very little or no time for political action."[34] Given the pull of more traditional concerns, PAC achieved a surprising amount of success in directing labor's attention to politics.

Although opponents did their best to pin a radical label on PAC, its program was liberal, nationalistic and pragmatic. It believed that the government should offer protection against unemployment, sickness, hunger and the hazards of old age, and should do so through national planning. But PAC envisioned a cooperative effort by labor, industry and agriculture "working together with and assisted by the Government," saw no conflict between "planned utilization of our national resources and genuine free enterprise," and stressed the mutuality of class interest.[35] PAC's spread-eagle brand of nationalism did no more than its economic program to dispel

the radical bugaboo. PAC literature could hardly have taken
a more didactic form: " 'I am an American.' You are proud
when you say that. We are all proud when we say that. We
have a right to be proud. It is good to be an American. We
love America." PAC also blended a faith in the wisdom (or,
to be more precise, the Democratic leanings) of the common
man with a frank acceptance of political reality. One pamphlet aimed at Negro voters conceded that Mississippi's John
Rankin and Theodore Bilbo were a "stench in our nostrils,"
and added: "But let not their presence in the Democratic
Party drive you to support the Deweys and the Brickers and
their followers—for they are against us and against you."[36]

Not only did PAC work for the election of Democratic
candidates, but it also served as a liberalizing force within
the party and in some areas acquired considerable influence in
party councils. Labor's role varied inversely with the strength
of local Democratic organizations: in cities like Chicago,
where the machine remained strong, PAC functioned as its
adjunct; in Michigan and Ohio, where, according to Hillman,
the Democratic organization had "just about withered away,"
PAC won a larger voice in setting policy and selecting candidates. On a tour of the Pacific Coast Hillman found that
labor "can play a powerful role within the Democratic party
of Washington," and that "the party in California is looking
primarily to our movement to solidify its own ranks and give
it new organizational strength."[37] If, as Hillman believed, a
national third party was impractical, PAC could at least
offset conservative influence within the Democratic party
and, by helping to elect liberals, make it more responsive to
labor's interests.

Only in New York state, where he had helped found the
American Labor Party as a haven for anti-Tammany liberals,
radicals and trade unionists, did Hillman choose to work
outside the Democratic party. In 1940 the ALP had provided
the margin by which Roosevelt carried the state, but with
each year that passed the party had become more badly split

between a "right-wing" faction headed by ILGWU leader David Dubinsky and a radical group led by East Harlem Congressman Vito Marcantonio. Nevertheless, in 1943 Hillman viewed the ALP as the most suitable vehicle for political activity in New York. He returned to the party (which he had bolted in 1942 to support the Democratic nominee for governor) with a proposal that it give trade unions a larger voice in its affairs, a suggestion that delighted Marcantonio but horrified Dubinsky who feared that it would throw the party into the hands of communist-dominated CIO affiiliates. Hillman replied that his plan would strengthen the party by broadening its base and even agreed to a proposition barring communists from the state committee. In March 1944 after Dubinsky rejected Mayor La Guardia's attempt to mend the differences, Hillman's supporters triumphed in state-wide party elections. Dubinsky and his followers quit, founded the rival Liberal Party, and assailed Hillman as a communist stooge. Hillman, though, had captured the party as a PAC outpost in the campaign and, as Attorney General Biddle noted, it "hold[s] the balance of power in New York State."[38]

Labor contributed to the Roosevelt campaign in numerous ways. It undertook registration drives that brought impressive results: 1,000 canvassers were set to work in the Detroit area, and as many as 36,000 voters signed up in one day in St. Louis. Officials in Los Angeles cooperated by setting up registration booths inside the factory gates. PAC distributed 85 million pieces of campaign literature, and sent out canvassers with instructions on how to make themselves welcome in the homes they visited. ("Canvassing is like love. There is no substitute for love. There is no substitute for doorbell-ringing.") On election day PAC made telephone calls to CIO members, provided babysitters for housewives, and transported voters to the polls. The CIO eventually spent $1.57 million in 1944, and labor's total contribution—over $2 million—comprised 30 percent of all Democratic expenditures. The policy of rewarding labor's friends and punishing its enemies was rooted in the past, but the scale on which PAC operated and the degree to which it collaborated with the Democrats represented a new departure.

The more active PAC became, the more Republicans condemned its involvement in the campaign and sought to make an issue of Sidney Hillman's influence in the Democratic party. Republicans charged that Roosevelt had told his henchmen to "clear everything with Sidney" at the Chicago convention and, much as Al Smith's enemies had once warned of a Papal conspiracy, pleaded with voters to "Keep Sidney Hillman Out of the White House." By making Hillman a whipping boy Republicans not only exploited a rather widespread resentment over the growing strength of organized labor, but also played on fears of communist infiltration ("YOU don't have to 'Clear Everything with Sidney.' Vote Republican and keep the Communists, Hillman and Browder, from running your country and your life"), nativist bias ("If my head is to roll in a basket," said Republican congresswoman Clare Booth Luce, "at least it's a more American head than Sidney Hillman's"), and a thinly-disguised anti-Semitism (Hillman, it was noted, was a "Lithuanian pants presser" who had received an "early rabbinical training.")[39]

Red-baiting was an old tactic in presidential campaigns and Thomas Dewey eventually succumbed to its use. Early in October he pointed out that Roosevelt had the support of Earl Browder, "the same Earl Browder . . . who was convicted as a draft dodger . . . convicted again as a perjurer and pardoned by Franklin Roosevelt in time to organize the campaign for his fourth term." Dewey grew more shrill as the campaign entered its final days, asserting that Roosevelt had "so weakened and corrupted the Democratic Party that it is subject to capture, and the forces of Communism are, in fact, now capturing it."[40] Polls showed that three out of ten voters believed that Roosevelt's election would give communists an unhealthy amount of influence in the government, and Biddle, after talking to party bosses, reported: "I got the feeling that the 'Communist' issue was doing us a good deal of harm in certain sections in New York."[41] Disturbed by the impression Dewey's charges might make, particularly on Catholic voters, Roosevelt did his best to ridicule the allegations. Even in 1944, at a time when Soviet-American relations were their most cordial, communism was a highly charged political issue.

If in one breath Dewey accused Roosevelt of auctioning his administration off to subversive bidders, in the next he endorsed virtually the entire reform program of the New Deal. Dewey supported social security, unemployment insurance, relief for the needy, farm price supports, and collective bargaining. Since the Democrats had failed to restore prosperity —"It took a world war to get jobs for the American people" —voters should replace a "tired, exhausted, quarreling and bickering administration" with a fresh and vigorous one. Dewey pledged to keep the welfare state but to administer it more efficiently, and while he was not the first Republican to do so he, unlike Willkie, spoke for the mainstream of his party. By accepting the essentials of the New Deal, Dewey helped place the welfare state beyond the range of partisan dispute. One Democrat even dubbed him "Little Sir Echo."[42] No matter how liberal Dewey sounded he never ran much risk of losing the votes of die-hard Republicans, to whom his speeches may have represented little more than clever campaign rhetoric. One liberal Republican, who voted for Roosevelt, thought that Dewey "is obviously entirely willing to send cold shivers down the spines of reactionaries on the basis of being sure of their votes no matter what he says."[43]

Having accepted the broad outlines of the welfare state, Dewey further departed from past controversies by refusing to stir up dormant isolationist feeling. He resisted the temptation to criticize the lack of preparedness at Pearl Harbor, did not divulge that the United States had broken the Japanese code, and had one of his advisors, John Foster Dulles, confer with Secretary of State Cordell Hull in an effort to prevent foreign policy from becoming a partisan issue. Although he asserted that the United States could not avoid postwar responsibilities, Dewey had no desire to open old wounds in his party and took a low-key approach. As Arthur Vandenberg of Michigan warned, "my Republican Mid-West" would sanction international cooperation so long as it knew "that we aren't going to be international 'saps' in 'giving America away.' But it demands this constant reassurance."[44] Recognizing also that Roosevelt's strongest suit was his experience in the conduct of foreign affairs, Dewey centered most of his fire on domestic matters.

The campaign, which put a bipartisan stamp on many of Roosevelt's policies, produced claims that the Democrats had sold out to communism, and witnessed the broad involvement of organized labor, also enhanced the prestige of public opinion polls. Faith in polls had always marked Dewey's political career. In 1940 he confided, "never argue with the Gallup Poll. It has never been wrong and I very much doubt whether it will be, so long as George Gallup runs it." In 1942 he hired the Psychological Corporation of New York to measure voter response to different issues. In 1944 he demonstrated his confidence in Gallup by putting little effort into those states which the polls predicted were safely Republican, and by scheduling special trips to others—New York, Missouri, Massachusetts, Maryland—which, according to the polls, were undecided. Surveys conducted for Republican candidates also identified the issues likely to have the greatest appeal: "Roosevelt must try to keep a united labor front; Dewey must try to split this front insofar as possible. The primary Democrats' move, as with the CIO Political Action Committee, is to get the labor vote out. The primary Republican move is . . . to castigate the Hillman group as extremists and radicals."[45]

Dewey's reliance on Gallup was matched by that of Roosevelt on Hadley Cantril who, as head of the Office of Public Opinion Research at Princeton University, had been feeding information to the White House for several years. By 1944 Cantril was applying sophisticated techniques to opinion sampling. He informed Democratic leaders that if a secret ballot were used rather than personal interviews the "no-opinion" vote dropped sharply and did not divide evenly. Prestige was bound up with stating party preference: on secret ballots, upper-income voters were 3 to 4 percent more pro-Roosevelt and lower income voters 6 to 10 percent more pro-Dewey. "This is *doubly bad*—this shift is larger, there are so many more low income." Cantril found that poorer people "now feel more secure economically, are disturbed by the taxes they are paying for the first time, don't want to admit in personal interviews that they're going back on the Commander-in-Chief." Also, "what apparently happens is that the anti-Roosevelt sentiment of the Irish Catholics, Italians and Germans in New York City is brought out." Cantril offered a straightforward solution: since the number who voted on the basis of issues was small compared with those who voted "because 'they are Democrats or Republicans,'" the President must attract a large turnout, and since "people think of Roosevelt as the man we need if there is a crisis ahead, convey the impression that the years ahead *are* critical." "Neither Gallup nor I would as yet put any money on Dewey," Cantril remarked, "although I'm sure Gallup wishes he could do so safely."[46]

The use of more advanced methods—such as secret ballots and election district sampling—and the greater weight assigned to the polls, were to some extent an offshoot of the war itself. During the late 1930s Gallup, Cantril and Elmo Roper had perfected their surveys and businessmen had become increasingly aware of the profitable uses to which polls could be put. Then the war provided new incentives for taking the public's pulse. It became vitally important for the government to have answers in advance to all kinds of questions—how consumers would react to rationing, how Catholic morale would be affected by the bombing of Rome, how farmers felt about agricultural subsidies, what kind of propaganda would be most effective in reaching people in Axis countries. Some agencies, such as the Office of War Information, undertook their own surveys; others, such as the State Department's Office of Public Affairs, employed outside experts. The added expertise gained during the war paid off handsomely in the election of 1944 (which, unlike that four years later, did not see a widespread shift in preference in the weeks between the final poll and election day.) In predicting Roosevelt's share of the popular vote, Roper erred by one-fifth of one percent, Cantril by one-half of one percent, and Gallup by less than two percent.

Roosevelt, although he carried 36 states and received 432 electoral votes to Dewey's 99, won his most slender victory. The President obtained 53.4 percent of the popular vote compared with 54.7 percent in 1940, and had a margin of 3.6 million votes as against 5 million in 1940. Although Dewey's youthfulness and physical appearance made him the butt of endless jokes (people said that he looked like the bridegroom on a wedding cake, that he rode a great dane to work, that he spent election eve pacing back and forth beneath the bed), and although he supposedly projected too slick and icy an image, he nevertheless received proportionately more votes than Willkie had four years before. But Roosevelt simply had too many advantages: his show of vigor late in the campaign helped dispel doubts about his health, widespread concern about the possibility of a postwar slump worked in his favor, and PAC helped ensure a respectable labor turnout. Above all, Roosevelt exploited his prestige as Commander-in-Chief and architect of the D-Day invasion. As Robert Taft later admitted, "I believe we underestimated the difficulty of changing a President at the very height of a victorious war."[47]

The key to Roosevelt's victory was the urban vote. Indeed, throughout the war economic class somewhat diminished and place of residence took on new importance as a determinant of voting behavior. In cities with a population over 100,000

Roosevelt garnered 60.7 percent of the vote. Pittsburgh, Philadelphia, Baltimore, St. Louis, Boston and San Francisco contributed a higher proportion of votes to state Democratic pluralities than in 1940. In seven states with enough electoral college strength to have reversed the outcome—New York, Illinois, Pennsylvania, Michigan, Missouri, Maryland and New Jersey—Roosevelt's plurality in the largest city overcame a Republican majority in the rest of the state. To carry Ohio and Wisconsin, on the other hand, Dewey had to offset large Democratic pluralities in Cleveland and Milwaukee. As the Democratic vote became urbanized it also contracted: in Illinois, Roosevelt carried 71 counties in 1936, 29 in 1940 and 17 in 1944, but the state remained securely in his column. Of course Roosevelt had always run well, if not quite as well, in urban areas; but in 1944, as Democratic support trailed off elsewhere, the urban vote proved decisive. "In a sense," remarked one election analyst, "the victory of the Democrats was a victory of the city over the country."[48]

The party's urban cast was even more pronounced in Congress where, outside the South, the overwhelming majority of Democratic representatives were elected from urban constituencies. Of the House seats regained from Republicans, fully two-thirds were in districts with a city of 100,000, and one-third were in districts with a city of 500,000. Unlike 1942, when migration and a correspondingly low turnout had hurt the Democrats, in 1944, as more war workers registered and could meet residency qualifications, safe Republican districts were suddenly thrown up for grabs. This was particularly true in cities in the Midwest and on the Pacific Coast which had received a large influx of workers from the South. "I was beaten by the votes of several thousand war-workers who had recently come into my district," explained a Republican in Washington; in Illinois another candidate ascribed his downfall to "registration of all voters, thousands of whom had migrated from Southern States during the past two years to seek employment in steel mills and defense plants."[49]

In all, the Democrats picked up 22 seats in the House and

lost 1 in the Senate. Among the casualties were such conservative Democrats as David I. Walsh of Massachusetts, Bennett Clark of Missouri and Guy Gillette of Iowa, and such Republican isolationists as Gerald Nye of North Dakota, Hamilton Fish of New York and Stephen A. Day of Illinois (who complained, "Dewey approved F.D.R. foreign policy *in toto*. This cramped my style and served as a stymie in a Nationalist State.")[50] Conversely, the election, although leaving the alliance of Republicans and southern Democrats intact, brought to prominence many who would play an important part in postwar politics, including Wayne Morse, J. William Fulbright, and Adam Clayton Powell. More important than new faces, however, were new political forces uncovered by the election, among which were a bipartisan accord on major aspects of Roosevelt's program, organized labor's coming-of-political-age, a greater emphasis on public opinion polls, and a consolidation of Democratic strength in urban areas.

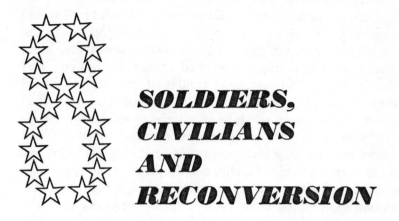

SOLDIERS, CIVILIANS AND RECONVERSION

OF THE MANY CONFLICTS arising during World War II few had greater significance than that between civilians and the military over economic mobilization. Military officials believed that the civilians responsible for war production were moving at a snail's pace, that they were overly solicitous of home front needs and not nearly sensitive enough to military requirements. Many civilians, on the other hand, were equally certain that the military was attempting to dominate the economy in order to gain the lion's share of production. Chairman Donald Nelson of the War Production Board asserted that the Army did its best "to make an errand boy of W.P.B.," and one official complained that Nelson himself offered only halfhearted resistance to the attempt: "One of these War Department generals will stick a knife into Nelson and all Nelson does is pull the knife out and hand it back and say, 'General, I believe you dropped something.' And the general will say, 'Why, Don, thanks, I believe I did'—and right away he sticks it back in again."[1]

In truth the situation was a good deal more complex than a neat categorization into "civilians" and "the military" would suggest. Seldom did a dispute over economic policy find the line between civilians and soldiers drawn so decisively. More often than not civilians disagreed among themselves, and even the Army and Navy had trouble in presenting a united front. Moreover, the civilian-military distinction was itself usually hazy. Many of those in charge of military procurement weré not professional soldiers but recently-commissioned reserve officers; they had been trained not at West Point but in the business world. Finally, what seemed at the time to be an attempt by the military to gain a strangle-hold over production was nothing more than an aggressive assertion of the military claim to scarce materials. "I have never seen any effort on the part of the military to control the American economy," said Bernard Baruch late in 1942, "but I have seen them fight to get the things they want when they want them."[2]

If the line between civilians and the military was difficult to draw and was often crossed, two points of view broadly reflecting civilian and military interests nevertheless existed. That these points of view collided was perhaps unavoidable given competing demands for economic resources, and the mutual suspicion between Nelson and the military leaders. There were also critical questions at stake: where would defense plants be built? which companies would receive contracts and on what terms? which workers would get jobs and of what kind? what proportion of industrial output would be earmarked for military rather than civilian use? Above all, who would make these decisions, what criteria would be used in making them, and what social interests would be taken into account?

The conflict over economic mobilization, however, was the exception not the rule. As Samuel Huntington has pointed out, in the area of foreign policy and wartime strategy the Joint Chiefs of Staff moved with the prevailing political winds and were in essential accord with civilians in the Roosevelt administration. Only with respect to economic policy did the armed services place the narrow military interest first. Moreover, in their contest with civilians in the War Production Board, military spokesmen enjoyed unmatched advantages: they alone were privy to the strategic plans upon which production had to be based, and they commanded the deference always shown to men in uniform in wartime. After the lean years of the 1930s, when every military request had been gone over with a fine tooth comb, Army and Navy officers exploited to the utmost their newly acquired prestige. "Many a priority argument was closed by junior officers with hints of strategy considerations which could not be disclosed," recalled one civilian.[3]

The central concern of the armed forces was to retain control of procurement. In the past when the military had drafted plans for industrial mobilization to be used in the event of war, it had assumed civilian control of production, labor, prices and finance, but had believed that the Army and Navy would determine their own requirements, award contracts to industrialists, schedule deliveries, and inspect finished products. Occasionally during the war Army officers advanced an elaborate justification for this position. Military operations, they said, could not be divorced from supply for both were parts of an integral process. Only military men, they argued, had sufficient expertise to carry out the task. To scrap an efficient system in favor of an "untried, unproven, experiment" would be an enormous blunder.[4]

Nelson supported the military not because he agreed that logistics and strategy were inseparable but because he had no real alternative. He lacked the time to build up a civilian procurement agency, feared that if civilians let military contracts they would be open to the charge of favoritism, and shared Roosevelt's common-sense view that "the final determination of the character of Army and Navy material has to be made by the people who know best about it."[5] In the spring of 1942 Nelson, Undersecretary of War Robert Patterson and Assistant Secretary of the Navy James V. Forrestal reached an understanding: the military would continue to place contracts and the War Production Board would supervise the planning and scheduling of production. Procurement throughout the war was handled by the Army Service Forces, the Army Air Forces, the U.S. Maritime Commission (which contracted for cargo vessels), and several Navy bureaus under the Office of Procurement and Material. The Army awarded some $75 billion in contracts, and the Navy spent $20 billion on ships alone.

Procurement officers were granted unusual discretion. The services suspended the peacetime practice of competitive bidding in favor of negotiated contracts because a low bidder might be unable to deliver in the shortest time, or might be located either in an area where labor was scarce or in one considered vulnerable to enemy attack. Moreover, soliciting bids from manufacturers who were already working around the clock made little sense. The Army and Navy also gained a substantial if not absolute exemption from price controls in purchasing military hardware. In the fall of 1942 they reached an agreement with Leon Henderson of the Office of Price Administration which prevented the extension of maximum price controls over "strictly military goods" (although not over materials at a stage below their emergence as military end-items) provided the services tried to hold down prices and profits. Under this arrangement about two-thirds of the value of War Department prime contracts was exempted from OPA controls.

Entrusting the power of procurement to the armed forces had broad repercussions. For the most part the Army and Navy preferred to deal with large manufacturers whom they knew to be dependable and who could produce munitions swiftly and in large quantities. Working with relatively few firms, and permitting them to handle any necessary subcontracting, was also an administrative convenience. Despite

complaints from spokesmen for small business, most officers
believed that their task was to obtain tanks and ships "and
not to 'spread the work' for the sole purpose of spreading it."
Consequently, two-thirds of all military contracts went to
one hundred firms; nearly one-half went to three dozen
corporate giants. In 1943 firms employing fewer than 100
people obtained just 3.5 percent of Army contracts, those employing fewer than 500 received 12.6 percent, and half a
million fewer small businesses existed than in 1941. Robert
Patterson once remarked that "we had to take industrial
America as we found it;" he might have added that they by
no means left industrial America as they found it.[6]

Close ties often developed between procurement officers and
the businessmen with whom they dealt. Career officers and
corporation executives found they had more in common than
either had realized, and new organizations developed from
their mutual concerns. In 1944 James Forrestal founded the
National Security Industrial Association to assure that
"American business will remain close to the Services." The
Quartermaster Association, whose membership had been
confined to Army and Navy officers, first invited industrialists
to become associate members and then, in "recognition of
the close relationship which has existed between the Quartermaster Corps and industry during the war emergency,"
extended full membership to "key men in business." There
were also ideological points of contact. The Army Chief of
Ordnance considered it his task to "clear a vast accumulation
of ideological debris out of Industry's path and to prevent
dictatorial minded bureaucrats from bludgeoning Industry
with decrees or suffocating Industry with wads of red tape."[7]

Although Nelson did not at the outset challenge military
control of procurement, he found himself engaged in a con-
tinuous struggle with the men who headed the services.
Secretary of War Henry L. Stimson and Undersecretary
Robert Patterson, while themselves civilians, strongly identified with the military outlook. Stimson wrote that "I am

the one man—or rather the highest man—in the Government whose duty it is to see that the United States Army is equipped." According to one biographer, Stimson "grew almost tearfully sentimental whenever he joined with veteran artillerymen to sing 'As the caissons go rolling along.' "[8] "Judge" Patterson, who had served as an officer in World War I and come to the War Department from the Circuit Court of Appeals, liked to wear a belt taken from a German soldier killed in 1918. Lieutenant General Brehon B. Somervell, chief of the Army Service Forces, was hard-driving and at times arrogant. Trained as an engineer, he had joined General John J. Pershing's expedition against Pancho Villa, and from 1936 to 1940 served as administrator of the WPA in New York City. He later concluded that civilian war agencies were part of an attempt by "Henry Wallace and the leftists to take over the country."[9]

Not surprisingly, Stimson, Patterson and Somervell considered Nelson a weakling who failed to understand that "there must be more sacrifices from civilian purposes to war purposes." Civilians in the War Production Board, for their part, believed that the military cared only for its own needs and wanted to make "the basic determination as to what gets produced."[10] The extent of the disagreement was revealed in May 1942 when Somervell proposed that control over basic industrial materials be given to a Combined Resources Board which, while it would have a civilian chairman, would be responsible to the combined American and British Chiefs of Staff. Nelson snapped that Somervell was "basically in error" because the success of industrial mobilization "rested not with the Chiefs of Staff, but with the chiefs of production."[11]

But it was the controversy over a feasible military supply program that, more than anything else, soured relations between the two sides in 1942. To some extent the dispute originated in the "Victory Program" announced by Roosevelt in January. Influenced by his military chiefs, by the advice of civilians like Harry Hopkins, by Lord Beaverbrook's assertion that Allied hopes rested on "the immense possibilities of American industry," and by his own belief that it was better to aim too high than too low, Roosevelt announced spectacular goals for 1942: 60,000 airplanes, 45,000 tanks, 20,000 anti-aircraft guns, and 8,000,000 tons of merchant shipping.[12] The United States had spent $18.5 billion on defense in 1941 and had planned to spend $27 billion in 1942; Roosevelt now called for an outlay of $52–55 billion, or half the nation's total output. Goals for 1943 were pegged still higher: 125,000 airplanes, 75,000 tanks, 35,000 anti-aircraft guns, and 10,000,000 tons of merchant shipping. Taking their cue from the President, the armed services supported an even more gargantuan supply program.

Opposition came when economists associated with the War Production Board's Planning Committee—including Robert Nathan, Simon Kuznets and Stacy May—decided that production goals, if set unrealistically high, would do more harm than good. Granting the psychological benefit of aiming at a difficult target, they nevertheless foresaw economic chaos in aiming at an impossible target. What was the good, they asked, of building factories, ships or trucks if there would be no raw materials, engines or tires for them? Overly ambitious goals would mean the allocation of resources without rhyme or reason. The result would be a piling-up of partially finished and therefore wholly useless items. Feasible goals, they concluded, could be exactly determined by analyzing the supply of labor, raw materials and industrial facilities available. In March Nathan informed Donald Nelson that the armed services' demands were "completely out of line" and "wholly impossible" to meet.[13]

Nelson believed the Planning Committee correct, but in the spring of 1942 he had little success in trimming the military program. The concept of feasibility, running as it did against the grain of American optimism, met resistance not only from the military but also from civilians in the War Production Board who believed in "incentive scheduling." Moreover,

Nelson, as a pre-Pearl Harbor advocate of an increased defense program, found it awkward to do an about-face and press the services to cut their requests. Nelson also feared that a call for a cutback might be construed as a confession of his own inadequacy. On February 11 Roosevelt (in a letter drafted by Harry Hopkins) told Nelson to inform him if military needs could not be met so that he could ask the Joint Chiefs which items might be delayed. "Needless to say," Roosevelt added, "I believe you will not ask me to do this."[14] In the spring Nelson persuaded the services to modify their program slightly but it remained well above what Nathan and the others considered feasible.

Before long the issue of feasibility came to take on broader dimensions. During the summer Kuznets prepared, and the Planning Committee accepted, a study which claimed that 1942 output would fall $15 billion short of the Army's expectations, and that the 1943 goal, if it were to bear any relationship to actual capacity, should not exceed $75-80 billion. At the same time the Committee made another proposal, related to but distinct from the notion of feasibility, that caused a crisis. To ensure a fusion of "strategic, production and social considerations," Nathan's group recommended the creation of a supreme war production council composed both of soldiers and civilians. Under this plan military strategy would no longer be left exclusively to the generals. The committee concluded: "The idea that war strategy is so secret, and so exclusively military that it must be hush-hush insofar as civilians are concerned, is untenable."[15]

In September the Planning Committee sent its proposals to Somervell who responded with fury. The report, he said, was "an inchoate mass of words" that should "be carefully hidden from the eyes of thoughtful men." He suspected that the very idea of feasibility was a cover-up for civilian inefficiency; the prospect of civilians with "social or political" concerns sitting on a strategy board appalled him. Somervell seemed unable to decide whether this meant that representatives of the Joint Chiefs would have to meet with backroom party bosses or with long-haired social visionaries, but in any case the military wanted none of it. In some ways the Planning Committee's position was a mirror image of the War Department's. Each agreed that production and strategy were closely related, but the Army believed that generals, as the ones who made strategy, should have a greater say over economic policy while the Planning Committee assumed that civilians, as the ones responsible for economic policy, should have more to do with setting strategy.

These antithetical views clashed when the War Production Board met on October 6, 1942 to vote on a military supply program for the coming year. Somervell and Patterson insisted that their projected program, which added up to $115 billion for supplies and construction, had been computed "realistically, not theoretically." Furthermore, they "failed to see what benefit would be derived from a board composed of an economist, a politician, and a soldier who does not know production." Civilian officials, exhibiting a rare amount of unanimity, lashed out at the Army for padding its supply needs. Remarking that the military program would require a cut in consumer expenditures to a level 40 percent below that of 1932, Henry Wallace asked whether "the public could be brought to accept such a reduction." Leon Henderson, in the course of a brutal denunciation of Somervell, claimed that the War Production Board's estimate of a feasible program represented an enormous outlay. He added that if the Army could not fight a war on that amount, maybe "we ought to get rid of our present Joint Chiefs, and find some who can."[17]

Behind Henderson's statement was the conviction that the civilian economy was being sliced to the bone while the military program was larded with fat. If the debate over feasibility concerned what could be allotted to the military, it just as surely concerned what could be denied to civilians. It also involved the question of the armed forces own manpower requirements. At the same time as Nelson and Somervell feuded over the supply of munitions, they disagreed about the size of the Army. Somervell wanted to provide training for "all the men the Army can induct," and the Joint Chiefs, following the same reasoning, sought to have 10.8 million men in uniform by the end of 1943.[18] Civilian officials considered this figure far too high, claiming that the number of soldiers who could be sent to combat zones was restricted by the shortage of transportation and that many men would be more valuable on the assembly lines than in boot camp. Eventually the military view prevailed. To many civilians, the Army's desire to increase troop levels, its opposition to the concept of feasibility, and its failure to appreciate needs other than its own were all related.

The feasibility dispute ended in a compromise shortly after the October meeting of the War Production Board. The Board gained several concessions: the services recognized in principle that their objectives "ought not to be far in front of estimated maximum production," and the Joint Chiefs proceeded to trim their 1943 munitions schedule from $93 to 80 billion, mainly by extending delivery dates into the following year.[19] This method, since it did not require the cancellation of any contracts, allowed the Army to save face. Yet the compromise worked both ways: the Army won a major victory when the proposal for a joint board to blend strategy and production—what Somervell had tagged the "grand super super board"—was dropped. From the military standpoint this was the key to everything.

No sooner had Nelson resolved one disagreement with the services than he was engaged in another. Troubled by a slackening rate of industrial expansion in the fall of 1942, and disturbed at what he considered a growing military influence, Nelson invited Charles E. Wilson, the president of General Electric, to join the WPB as a vice chairman and head of a newly-formed Production Executive Committee. In November, Wilson, with Nelson's approval, proposed that military agencies clear their procurement plans with the Production Executive Committee to ensure that they were consistent, balanced and integrated. This would not deprive Army and Navy officers of the power to let contracts, but it would force them to win advance approval for their production schedules. Nelson regarded the distinction as crucial. He spoke of his "life-or-death fight with the Army" to Roosevelt, who appeared sympathetic and remarked, "Well, if you need me come to Poppa."[20]

The military responded to Wilson's initiative in a wholly predictable way. Indeed, the debate began to sound annoyingly like a broken record: Somervell accused civilians of trying to usurp military prerogatives and "dictate whether we [make] cannon, tanks, airplanes, battleships or other war materials;" Wilson, disclaiming any such intention, replied that scheduling required central coordination. In the end Roosevelt ordered Nelson, Stimson and Frank Knox to compose their differences and early in December 1942 they found a formula which left the balance between the War Production Board and the services essentially unchanged. Nelson authorized the Production Executive Committee to "direct the scheduling of the various [military] production programs" but provided that any cuts would be made by the Joint Chiefs and that the services would continue to establish end-item schedules.[21]

The controversies over feasibility and production scheduling, however, were not all sound and fury. By 1943 military leaders had decided that they could no longer live with Donald Nelson and, with the backing of Economic Stabilization Director James F. Byrnes, they urged Roosevelt to appoint Bernard Baruch. As always Roosevelt had mixed feelings about Baruch, recognizing that although his reputation could be of use it could also prove embarrassing if he criticized administration policy. Nevertheless in February 1943, Roosevelt approved the appointment. Byrnes drafted the necessary letter and delivered it in person. But Baruch returned to New York the next day, became sick, and delayed his response. When he finally appeared at the White House to announce that he was reporting for duty Roosevelt had changed his mind and turned the conversation to unrelated matters. "Let me tell you about Ibn Saud, Bernie," he began. Not once did the President mention the WPB position and Baruch could not raise it himself.[22]

Roosevelt had considered axing Nelson not only because of his bad relations with the services (news of which often leaked to the press) but also because of his inability to give unified direction to the War Production Board itself. The winter of 1942–1943 witnessed a fierce struggle between Nelson's top aides, Charles E. Wilson and Ferdinand E. Eberstadt. Wilson supervised production while Eberstadt, who had formerly headed the Army-Navy Munitions Board and was considered a proponent of the military point of view, controlled raw materials. The conflict between "two strong personalities lacking in mutual confidence," Roosevelt learned, resulted in a "lack of unity, vigor, and definite policy by WPB as a whole."[23] Gradually, the scales tipped in Wilson's favor; his jurisdiction expanded while Eberstadt's shrunk. At the last minute, when Nelson learned of the plan to appoint Baruch, he forced Eberstadt out and elevated Wilson to the position of Executive Vice President with broad authority over Board operations. Announcing these decisions, Nelson figured, would make it difficult for Roosevelt to replace him. Doing so might give the impression that war production was a game of musical chairs.

Nelson thus gained a temporary reprieve, but in the spring of 1943 the ground rules governing his contest with the armed services were changing. First, influence in the War Production Board gradually shifted from Nelson, who now limited himself to formulating over-all policy, to Wilson, who took charge of actual day-to-day operations and to whom most Board officials consequently gave their loyalty. Second, the locus of power moved from the Board itself to Wilson's Production

Executive Committee which, consisting as it did of people responsible for procurement, was heavily military in composition. Its Committee on Production Scheduling, for example, included three civilians, a major general, a brigadier general and two rear admirals. Third, Roosevelt's disenchantment with the Board led him in May 1943 to create the Office of War Mobilization under James F. Byrnes. The OWM did not absorb the operating functions of the WPB but did assume much of the policymaking role originally envisaged for Nelson. The OWM came to constitute a court of last appeal, a body that adjudicated disputes between the military and civilians or between competing civilian interests.

This was the institutional framework within which the Board's dispute with the services over reconversion took place. The clash over resuming civilian production while the war continued was so intense and dragged on for so long—from mid-1943 to 1945—that it came to be known as "the war within a war." The dispute resembled earlier ones over feasibility and production scheduling in that it concerned the balance between civilian and military needs, but it differed in important respects: there was substantially less unity among civilians than before, and the nature of the post-war economy was more directly at issue. The controversy hinged on measuring such imponderables as the psychological impact that a return to normal production would have on the morale of workers and employers, or the probable supply needs of the military after the war in Europe had ended but before Japan surrendered. Both sides agreed that "essential" military needs should take precedence over everything else. But "essentiality," it turned out, was the most difficult of all concepts to define with precision.

As early as April 1943 Nelson had begun to wonder how to cushion the shock that would come when the government cut back military production and threw workers out of defense jobs. Yet while he authorized a preliminary study of the matter, not until the fall did a general interest in reconversion develop. In September the WPB undertook a more thorough investigation. Two months later the OWM asked Bernard Baruch and his long-time associate John M. Hancock (who had directed Navy purchasing in World War I), to submit a reconversion program, and committees of both the House and Senate urged the administration to prepare for putting the economy back on a peacetime footing. By then it seemed almost certain that the annual rate of munitions production— $74 billion—could be cut in 1944 and sliced by more than half in 1945. To take up the anticipated slack Nelson, on the last day of November, announced a new policy: the WPB would authorize additional civilian production which would not jeopardize the military program.

This, however, proved to be no more than a trial balloon and it was soon punctured. The Army and Navy first asked that reconversion be assigned to the Production Executive Committee—an idea that appealed to Wilson but not to Nelson—and then claimed that it would be too risky to proceed at all before the invasion of Europe, which was expected in the spring of 1944, had succeeded. In January Nelson retreated. Admitting that the war had "not yet entered its most violent stage," he told the press that plans to resume civilian production were premature. Nelson apparently reasoned that there was no immediate prospect of releasing a substantial number of men or machines from military purposes, and that he could, if necessary, interpret existing regulations more liberally in isolated instances. Nor was he sure that the OWM would side with him. Above all, Nelson and other civilian officials withdrew before the argument that no letdown should occur before D-Day. As Forrestal later said, "The only thing that won us our battle was the convincing argument that we ought to at least wait until the outcome of the Normandy invasion."[24]

During the early part of 1944 Nelson's determination to begin reconversion as soon as possible was hardening. In his view, the American economy was "delicately balanced be-

tween military and non-military segments" and any decline
in one should be offset by an increase in the other. Making
more goods and services available to civilians, especially
in congested areas, would produce a more efficient labor
force. Allowing workers who were laid off in defense plants
to take other kinds of jobs would alleviate fears about
the future. Nelson, who thought that the Army was "out to
protect war production by the simple means of creating pools
of unemployment," predicted that unemployed workers were
more likely to leave the job market than criss-cross the country in search of employment. Nor did he envision many
workers forsaking defense jobs for those with better peacetime prospects. "What gives workers and others 'cutback
jitters' is the fear that they will find themselves thrust into
a planless and chaotic economic state of affairs as soon as
war orders fall off on a large scale, becoming worse when
peace comes."[25]

Military leaders seemed to be peering into an entirely different crystal ball. To resume civilian production, they insisted, would destroy any remaining sense of urgency, drive
workers from war jobs, induce manufacturers to turn down
war contracts, and "open the way for dangerous leakages of
materials and manpower." While Nelson accused the military
of callously tolerating unemployment, it charged him with
coddling civilians; while Nelson argued that labor was not a
commodity easily controlled, the Army was urging Congress
to enact national service legislation. Military spokesmen
opposed expanding civilian output until every last military
need had been satisfied. "If we permit other programs to
compete with the war program," Patterson argued, "there
will be continuing deficits in war production." Somervell
complained to General Marshall that the high wartime
standard of living, by breeding complacency, had made it
difficult to convince the American people that further sacrifices would be necessary: "They have never been bombed,
they have little appreciation of the horrors of war and only in

a small percentage of instances do they have enough hate, for that alone to act as a driving force."[26]

The rivalry between Nelson and his military counterparts formed the outer shell of the reconversion controversy; what gave it substance were the conflicting social interests involved. Nelson drew most of his support from small businessmen, from organized labor, and from Democratic congressmen—such as Senators James E. Murray and Harry S. Truman—who spoke for these groups. They believed that reconversion, by freeing material for the fabrication of experimental peacetime models and by permitting civilian production to begin, would give a competitive headstart to small firms which were not essential cogs in the war machine. This could make partial amends for the wartime practice of awarding contracts to the largest corporations. For obvious reasons organized labor feared the consequences of allowing war production to proceed full blast and then halting it abruptly. Union leaders resented the Army's tendency to cancel orders without advance warning and to lay workers off in areas where there was a surplus rather than a shortage of labor. In May 1944, when the Navy announced a cutback at a Brewster aircraft plant on Long Island, the employees, in a widely-publicized incident, refused to leave the plant until new work was provided. Soon labor periodicals were running articles entitled "The Next Depression?"[27]

Many civilians nevertheless stood shoulder to shoulder with the military in the battle over reconversion. These included: Paul McNutt of the War Manpower Commission, who feared that too many workers were leaving critical war jobs or refusing to move into them; most WPB officials who sided with Wilson rather than Nelson and favored giving control of reconversion to the PEC; and some large war contractors who stood to lose if their smaller competitors got a jump on them. Automobile manufacturers, for example, opposed allowing some firms to resume passenger car production while others were still making airplanes; they suggested instead "that quotas be assigned to each company on an equitable basis." As *Business Week* noted, "Industry men see the threat of a resumption of competitive business wholly outside the normal framework of competition, regulated only by such factors as: who . . . can be spared from war production first; what material happens first to be released from the monopoly of war; and where a labor surplus results soonest."[28]

Significantly, each side justified its stand by reference to the ideal of competition. If a manufacturer was prevented from producing civilian goods when his factory was no longer needed for munitions, Nelson asserted, artificial barriers to competition would be erected. The public interest demanded that the WPB "maintain a competitive economy. I do not believe you can have a democracy and at the same time forbid new competition." Nelson's critics, however, held it a very strange idea of competition that would permit one manufacturer to reenter the civilian market when another could not. Again, *Business Week* noted that piecemeal reconversion could "snarl up the orderly processes of military supply now and . . . of business competition later."[29] Just as both sides agreed that "essential" military needs had to be met but disagreed as to what those needs were, just as they agreed that workers' "morale" had to be maintained but disagreed as to how to go about maintaining it, so they agreed that "competition" was desirable but stood light years apart.

Given these conflicting interests a showdown was perhaps unavoidable. On June 6 Allied troops opened the long-awaited second front in France, and just a week later Nelson presented a four-part reconversion program to the WPB. It permitted manufacturers to use aluminum and magnesium, to make and test a single experimental model of a peacetime product (but not to create consumer demand by exhibiting it), and to order the machine tools necessary for returning to a peacetime basis. Last and most important, Nelson proposed a system of "spot authorizations" under which WPB regional directors could allow manufacturers to resume civilian production as long as adequate raw materials, manpower and facilities existed and were not needed to fill war orders. Predictably, the armed forces pounced on Nelson's plan and especially on the spot authorization. On June 29 the Joint Chiefs warned that "a dangerous state of mind which cuts war production by causing people to throw up their war jobs is just as harmful as desertions on the fighting front."[30] The battle thus joined was to be the last of Nelson's public career.

On July 4 the War Production Board met to consider Nelson's proposals. Nelson, hospitalized with pneumonia, did not attend but was represented by Charles Wilson who found himself in an awkward position. Wilson favored a more cautious approach than did Nelson, but he felt obligated to defend his chief's policies. Also, he deeply resented the insinuation that, as a member of the corporate elite, he was biased toward big business. Representatives of the Army and Navy argued that a "serious slippage" was occurring in war production; if it continued, "the ability of our soldiers to pour it on in full measure to the Germans and the Japs is sure to be impaired." The Board ultimately agreed, ostensibly "out of courtesy to the chairman," not to issue any orders until his return. Wilson said he would transmit this message, but noted that Nelson could promulgate reconversion orders on his own authority. The services reacted in a flash: if orders were sent out "over the dead bodies of the War and Navy Departments," they would appeal over Nelson's head to OWM director James Byrnes.[31]

Clearly a new and decisive element had been introduced into the equation, and during the summer of 1944 Nelson and the military vied with each other to win over Byrnes. On July 11 Byrnes effected a compromise: he accepted Nelson's four proposals but staggered the orders over a month's time so that spot authorizations would not begin until mid-August. The services then used the period of grace to press their claim. They appealed to the OWM, tried to block reconversion in WPB committees, and undertook a campaign to convince the public that American fighting men would be left unarmed and defenseless if Nelson had his way. Finally Byrnes met with the contesting groups and on August 4 announced yet another formula: the spot authorization program could start on schedule, but only if approved by local committees of the War Manpower Commission. Since McNutt, and the WMC itself, favored using economic pressure to steer workers into war jobs, this decision cut the heart out of reconversion. Only 18,000 workers would ever be employed under the spot authorization plan.

In part Nelson lost the argument because Roosevelt, fearing that Germany could hold out on her own soil for quite some time, was unwilling to take any chance on short-changing the military.[32] Sometime in July the President decided that Nelson had outlived his usefulness. In classic Rooseveltian style he did not fire Nelson but asked him to serve temporarily as a special emissary to Chiang Kai-shek. On August 18 Nelson agreed, with the understanding that Wilson would assume control until his return. Nelson's "exile to Siberia," however, was widely interpreted as a repudiation of his reconversion policies and protests poured into the White House. Wilson, learning that his chance of inheriting the top job had vanished, also resigned. On August 24 Julius A. Krug, a 36-year-old former WPB official who had been serving as a lieutenant-commander in the Navy for several months, was recalled from Europe. When Nelson returned from China late in September he resigned and Krug formally replaced him.

With Krug in the driver's seat the conflict over reconversion lost much of its personal, bitter quality. Yet the dispute dragged on, for Krug, like Nelson, believed that the WPB should plan ahead for a smooth transition to peace. In September Krug claimed that production was holding up well and added that victory in Europe "would surely come in the not too distant future." The new WPB director also objected to statements given out by the military hinting that production lags caused battlefield shortages. Patterson, he complained,

"has been going a little too far" in making such assertions:
"The difficulty with Patterson's statement was that many an
American mother will feel and the American public [will be]
under the impression that Eisenhower planned the invasion
date and Marshall approved it before they had enough
ammunition to fight and for that reason are losing our boys."
Early in November Krug agreed not to expand the modest
spot authorization program, but did his best to resist military
pressure for total suspension.[33]

Krug's best, however, was not good enough. In the fall, as
the Allied advance bogged down and the prospect of an early
victory grew dim, the Army's case against reconversion became irresistible. Patterson informed Byrnes "that the thinking down the line in the War Production Board was for civilian
production and that it is up to the top side to reverse the
present trend." Week by week the services chipped away at
the remains of Nelson's program. On November 16 Byrnes
announced that he would halt reconversion if manpower
shortages persisted. On November 23 the WPB and the services agreed not to lift additional restrictions on civilian production for the time being. On December 1, asserting that
"it is just as urgent to maintain and, in certain areas, to build
up war production today as it was on the day after Pearl
Harbor," Krug, Patterson, Forrestal and McNutt agreed to a
virtual suspension of the spot authorization program.[34] When,
early in December, Byrnes asked Major General Lucius D.
Clay to leave Somervell's staff and join his own as Deputy
Director of OWM it appeared that the military held all
the trump cards.

Even before the Germans launched their counteroffensive
in the Ardennes on December 16 reconversion had become a
dead letter; for some time afterward it became a source of
embarrassment. In January Byrnes confessed that a premature start on reconversion had hampered war production,
and the output of munitions and supplies was set for the year
at $64.6 billion, $8 billion more than had been planned in

October. The first three months of 1945 saw a sharp upsurge in war production. Reconversion had become an issue when civilians attempted to protect workers and businessmen hurt by military cutbacks; with war orders again on the rise, with manpower and facilities again in full use, the problem was brushed aside. Nelson had expected a gradual winding-down of military demands, but events upset his calculations. Most civilians eventually accepted the view that "there must not be any feeling that the war is over until the military says you can cut back."[35] Not until March 1945, two months before V-E Day, did the WPB again openly discuss reconversion.

Then, within a period of four months, the government largely dismantled the elaborate structure of economic controls. On April 27 the WPB reinstated spot authorizations without a murmur from the military, and in the two weeks after Germany surrendered on May 8 the Board lifted 130 orders prohibiting the use of materials for civilian production. At the same time the armed services cancelled war contracts right and left. By August aircraft plants, munition factories and shipyards employed only half as many people as in May; in another month, 2.5 million more workers left war jobs. Almost immediately after V-J Day on August 16 the War Manpower Commission dropped all labor controls, the Office of Defense Transportation revoked bans on commercial traffic, and the War Production Board removed most remaining controls on industry. Similarly, the Office of Price Administration freed gasoline, fuel oil and processed foods from rationing. By the end of 1945 only a skeleton system of controls remained.

The decision to lift controls as rapidly as possible was a deliberate one. It reflected the belief that the public was tired of regimentation, that pent-up consumer buying power would insure the reemployment of war workers and veterans, and that left to their own devices businessmen could quickly get back on a peacetime footing. The New Deal economist Isador Lubin expressed the prevailing view succinctly: "The quickest way to get reconversion would be to remove all controls. Businessmen are ingenious. They can be relied upon to find ways and means of reconverting their plants and going ahead with the production of the innumerable items required by the civilian economy." Some favored a different approach. Many of the same groups which had formerly backed Nelson now called for a selective use of controls to guarantee small businessmen access to raw materials, insure full employment and prevent inflation. But they were too weak to prevent the headlong rush to remove controls.[36]

The imposition of wartime controls, and the conflict over administering them, had long-lasting consequences. That conflict did not result in military domination of the economy. But it did transfer power from men like Nelson who fundamentally distrusted the military to men like Byrnes who viewed military claims with considerably more sympathy. Moreover, it brought big businessmen and the military closer together than ever before. Although the two groups continued to disagree over many matters including, for example, national service, their cooperation in procurement and their opposition to early reconversion underscored their mutual interests.

No one more clearly expressed this mutuality of interest than Charles E. Wilson. In a speech to the Army Ordnance Association in January 1944, Wilson asserted that "our approach as a people to war" had in the past been unrealistic. Americans had refused to admit that "the tendency to war is inevitable," and so had refused to plan ahead. This had resulted in production delays that would be intolerable in a future war. "Instead of looking to disarmament and unpreparedness as a safeguard against war—a thoroughly discredited doctrine—let us try the opposite: full preparedness according to a continuing plan." Wilson envisaged a partnership between government, industry and the military: not only should civilian scientists and the military cooperate in developing new weapons, but businessmen and the military should make contingency plans for war production. Each large military supplier should designate a "permanent liaison man" to "keep ready at all times a broad plan for converting and re-equipping his company;" by commissioning him a reserve colonel, the services could "bind him closer to them and give him added stature within his company in peacetime." Such a device, Wilson imagined, would prepare America for war without creating another layer of bureaucracy, requiring a huge standing army, or causing militarism. "The peaceful temperament of the American people is well known. We can possess the mightiest and deadliest armament in the world without becoming aggressors in our hearts, because we do not have that intoxicating lust for blood and power which periodically transforms the German military caste. "[37]

Wilson's plan, which in all likelihood represented the views of a minority of businessmen, was never adopted. But in the following decade the wartime movement of businessmen into military procurement agencies was reversed as generals and admirals took executive positions with firms holding defense contracts. If the military-industrial complex reached maturity in the era of the Cold War, it just as surely was born and nurtured in World War II.

Epilogue

THE EXPERIENCE OF MOST Americans during World War II was unlike that of most other people around the world. For millions of English, French, German, Russian, Chinese and Japanese people the war meant air raids, armies of invasion and occupation, devastation and terror, fields turned into battlefields. The war also remade the maps of Europe and Asia: some countries disappeared, others gobbled up their neighbors, and still others were eventually split in two. Empires were lost, great powers became second-rate powers, and whole systems of government were overturned. None of this happened in the United States: there was no physical destruction, no redrawing of territorial lines, no change in the outward structure of government. Yet in more subtle ways the war exerted a profound impact upon the American people and their political, social and economic institutions.

During World War II the federal government employed

more people, spent more money, and exerted wider control over citizens' lives than ever before. From 1940 to 1945 the number of civilian employees of the government climbed from 1 million to 3.8 million, and expenditures soared from $9 billion to $98.4 billion. In addition, war multiplied the points of contact between the government and the individual, and in some instances, such as in the creation of a broadly-based system of taxation, did so in an enduring way. With the return of peace in 1945 the government reduced its operations but they remained well above prewar levels. Nondefense spending, for example, which had risen during the war from $7.2 billion to $17 billion would climb to $25 billion in 1947. The war taught people to look to Washington for solutions to problems, and the lesson was not easily forgotten.

Although the power of the federal government increased, all branches of government did not share equally in the exercise of that power. Instead, the war speeded up the erosion of legislative and the growth of executive authority that had marked Roosevelt's years in office. Congress delegated sweeping powers to the President who in turn delegated them to administrators in war agencies. The big decisions during the war were usually made by men responsible to the President— Harry Hopkins, James F. Byrnes, Henry L. Stimson, Leon Henderson, Donald Nelson—and not by congressional leaders. The Supreme Court, which had in the past struck down laws that in its judgment constituted improper delegations of legislative authority, refused even to review such cases during the war.

Big government, however, did not mean despotic government. The men at the top always preferred voluntary compliance to compulsion, and knew that the political process placed restraints on what they could do. Also, the imposition of many day-to-day controls—from deciding who would be drafted to distributing ration stamps—was left to local committees composed of people sensitive to their neighbors' opinions. What is striking is how often the government failed to get its way, even when it wanted to: coal miners defied War Labor Board edicts, advocates of national service were thrown on the defensive, farmers kept their draft exemptions. Although personal liberties were restricted to a degree that would have been unthinkable in peacetime, and groups such as the Japanese-Americans lost nearly everything, the fear that war would create a full-fledged totalitarian regime proved without foundation.

As the government expanded, however, it established a web of institutional relationships in fields that it had not dared enter before. Nowhere was this more evident than in scientific research and development. As late as 1935 a proposal to award research grants to universities was rejected as improper, but in the 1940s all such inhibitions vanished. Under contracts granted by the Office of Scientific Research and Development, universities and corporations put their facilities at the government's disposal. Massachusetts Institute of Technology (which in June 1945 held $117 million in contracts) specialized in radar development, California Institute of Technology in rockets, Princeton in ballistics and Penn State in hydraulic fluids. To develop the atom bomb, the "Manhattan District" employed 150,000 people, spent $2 billion, and erected new cities at Oak Ridge, Tennessee, Hanford, Washington and Los Alamos, New Mexico. Virtually every major university in the country released scientists to the project, and Du Pont, General Electric and other firms built the plants necessary to produce fissionable materials.

War transformed the economic arrangements under which Americans lived. The huge outlay of funds for military purposes (which at the height of the war reached $250 million a day) enormously inflated industrial capacity: manufacturing output doubled during the war, and gross national product rose from $88.6 billion in 1939 to $198.7 billion five years later. Brand new industries, based originally on the need to find substitutes for critically-short materials, came into being. To take only one example, synthetic rubber production was nearly one hundred times greater in 1944 than in 1941. Finally, the desire to obtain the most war production in the least time resulted in awarding a predominant share of military contracts to large corporations and fostering the tendency toward business consolidation. At the same time, new channels were opened between business executives and armed forces procurement officers, and they remained open after the war ended.

The same process of modernization and consolidation that affected industry was also at work in agriculture. Farmers did not bring much additional acreage under cultivation during the war; nevertheless, output increased by approximately 15 percent as a result of good weather, longer hours of work, and more widespread use of tractors and fertilizer. Because so many people who left the countryside for jobs in factories or shipyards did not return, there were fewer farmers at the end of the war than at the start. Those who remained on the land were less likely to be tenants and more likely to be landowners, less likely to be heavily in debt and more likely to have some money in the bank, less likely to have a few acres and more likely to have expanded their holdings. The war brought the era of large-scale, mechanized, corporate farming a good deal closer.

For the first time in American history more people belonged to labor unions than worked on farms. But labor, as it gave up its orphan's status and extended its economic and political influence, found that government was no longer the dependable ally it had been during the late 1930s. The postwar restraints on unions written into the Taft-Hartley Act were, in fact, patterned after legislation first adopted in 1943. Nevertheless, industrial relationships ultimately conformed to the new realities. Before 1941 large numbers of businessmen had refused to concede that industrial unions were here to stay; by 1945 many more were reconciled to the inevitability if not the desirability of collective bargaining.

In the United States, unlike most other nations, the same

political party held power on the day the war ended as on
the day it began. Yet this continuity should not obscure the
changes in political life that occurred. Before 1941 the issues
of American involvement in world affairs and government
intervention in the economy were undetermined; four years
later both were decided. The question was no longer whether
to pursue an isolationist policy or scrap the New Deal, but
how extensive intervention abroad and the welfare state at
home would be. With the injection of new issues into politics,
the parties' bases of electoral support shifted. As economic
fears related to the depression were replaced by a concern
with inflation, foreign policy and civil rights, the Democrats
learned that they could not count as confidently as before on
the support of blue-collar workers, southern and midwestern
farmers, and certain immigrant groups.

The war years were not marked by racial or religious tolerance. Wartime tensions triggered outbursts of violence aimed
at blacks and Mexican-Americans, a virulent form of anti-
Semitism festered in some places, and racial slurs comprised
an essential ingredient in the propaganda war against Japan.
Yet it is clear in retrospect that the war did much to undermine racial injustice. The federal government, through the
Fair Employment Practices Committee and the Supreme
Court decision banning white primaries, took the first hesitant
steps on the road to protecting the political and economic
rights of racial minorities. Even more important, when motion
pictures and photographs of German concentration camps
were made public in 1945 more Americans than ever before
realized that the doctrine of racial supremacy, carried to its
logical conclusion, led to the gas chamber. Racial and religious
discrimination surely did not vanish from American life after
the war, but the ideology upon which they rested was discredited.

Everywhere the war acted as a catalyst for social change.
Millions of Americans moved to new homes, particularly in
cities and in the West; millions of others, particularly women,

took jobs that otherwise would not have existed. The GI Bill of Rights enabled a whole generation of young men to obtain a college education or technical training. Wartime advances in medicine, particularly in the production of penicillin (which first became generally available for civilian use in the spring of 1944) saved countless lives. Many of these changes would have occurred even if the United States had not gone to war, but they would not have occurred as quickly. One observer noted at the time, "the whole pattern of our economic and social life is undergoing kaleidoscopic changes, without so much as a bomb being dropped on our shores." At the end of the war the United States was a more urban, technological and industrial society than when it had entered.

"To win this war," Margaret Mead wrote in *And Keep Your Powder Dry*, a study of American national character that appeared in 1942, "we must feel we are on the side of the Right." Throughout the war years most Americans felt precisely that way. One congressman even suggested naming the conflict the "War of Armageddon." Ultimately this absolute conviction of the righteousness of one's own cause was as much an intellectual prerequisite for the use of atomic bombs as was the production of a controlled nuclear chain reaction a technological prerequisite. But in the long run the legacy of World War II would not be confidence but uncertainty. If after Pearl Harbor few Americans doubted that they were on the side of the right, after Hiroshima and Nagasaki few would ever again be quite so sure.

Notes

NOTE: Locations of cited manuscript collections are given on pages 281-282.

Chapter 1

[1] Albert A. Blum, "Birth and Death of the M-Day Plan," in Harold Stein, ed., *American Civil-Military Decisions* (Birmingham, 1962), pp. 63-87.

[2] Louis Brownlow, *A Passion for Anonymity* (Chicago, 1958), p. 425; Blum, *loc. cit.;* Press conference, May 30, 1940, Roosevelt Papers.

[3] Press conference, May 30, 1940; Baruch to George Creel, December 8, 1941, Bernard Baruch Papers.

[4] Donald Nelson, *Arsenal of Democracy* (New York, 1946), pp. 20-21.

[5] Harold D. Smith Diary, January 13, 1942, Smith Papers.

[6] Baruch to Nelson, July 6, 1942, Baruch Papers; Nelson, *Arsenal*, pp. 208-9.

[7] Jesse Jones, *Fifty Billion Dollars* (New York, 1951), p. 320.

[8] Civilian Production Administration, *Industrial Mobilization for War* (Washington, 1947), p. 308.

[9] Marx Leva to John L. O'Brian,

245

April 28, 1942; Leva memorandum, April 10, 1942, Herbert Marks Papers.

[10] Nelson, *Arsenal*, p. 283; Isador Lubin to Hopkins, February 11, 1942, Harry Hopkins Papers.

[11] Henry L. Stimson Diary, August 26, 1940, Stimson Papers.

[12] Eliot Janeway, *Struggle for Survival*, (New Haven, 1951), p. 165.

[13] *Minutes of the Planning Committee of the War Production Board* (Washington, 1946), June 26, 1942, p. 67.

[14] Stimson Diary, January 9, 1943.

[15] Robert Nathan to Nelson, September 1, 1942, Donald Nelson Papers.

[16] Edward R. Stettinius to Roosevelt, October 23, 1940, Roosevelt Papers, OF 813-A.

[17] Ickes to Baruch, July 14, 1942, Baruch Papers; J. Folger to Roosevelt, July 25, 1942, Roosevelt Papers, OF 510.

[18] Samuel I. Rosenman ed., *The Public Papers and Addresses of Franklin D. Roosevelt* (New York, 1950), XI, pp. 272-73; Petroleum Industry War Council Bulletin, June 25, 1942, Roosevelt Papers, OF 4435-B.

[19] Homer M. Adkins to Donald Nelson, June 26, 1942, Roosevelt Papers, OF 4920; Edwin Pauley to Frank Walker, May 25, 1942, *ibid.*, OF 56-B; Charles Michelson to Roosevelt [May] 1942, *ibid.*, OF 56-B.

[20] Bruce Catton, *The War Lords of Washington* (New York, 1948), pp. 172-75; Roosevelt to Baruch, August 6, 1942, Roosevelt Papers, OF 510; Karl Compton, *My Several Lives* (New York, 1970), p. 314.

[21] Nelson to Jeffers, December 8, 1942, Baruch Papers; Baruch to Karl T. Compton, March 17, 1943, *ibid.*

[22] Ickes to Roosevelt, April 21, 1942, Roosevelt Papers, OF 4435; Arthur M. Johnson, *Petroleum Pipelines and Public Policy* (Cambridge, 1967), p. 318; Nelson memorandum, May 1, 1942, Roosevelt Papers, OF 4435.

[23] Ernest Kanzler to Nelson, May 28, 1942, Nelson Papers; Hillman to Roosevelt, March 22, 1942, Sidney Hillman Papers; Roosevelt to Baruch, Byrnes and Rosenman, November 11, 1942, Roosevelt Papers, OF 4905.

[24] Oscar Cox to Harry Hopkins, October 5, 1942, Roosevelt Papers, OF 1413-F; Frederic A. Delano to Roosevelt, December 7, 1942, *ibid.*, OF 1092.

[25] Stimson Diary, November 4, 1942.

[26] Roland Young, *Congressional Politics in the Second World War* (New York, 1956), pp. 70-72.

[27] Smith Diary, October 20, 1943; National War Labor Board minutes, February 6, 1942, Roosevelt Papers, OF 4710.

[28] Baruch to Claude Pepper, November 20, 1944, Baruch Papers.

[29] Smith, "A War Program to Prevent Inflation," March 26, 1942; Smith, Henderson, Eccles, Wallace and Wickard, "Memorandum for the President Urging an Anti-Inflation Program," April 20, 1942, Roosevelt Papers, OF 327.

[30] Morgenthau, "A Program to Control the Cost of Living," Roosevelt Papers, OF 327; John M. Blum, *From the Morgenthau Diaries: Years of War* (Boston, 1967), pp. 38-39.

[31] Paul A. C. Koistinen, "The Hammer and the Sword" (unpub. Ph.D. diss., University of California, 1964), pp. 165-66; Murray to Coy, March 6, 1942, Wayne Coy Papers.

[32] William Davis Memoir, p. 128; Fred M. Vinson to Roosevelt, July 10, 1943, Roosevelt Papers, OF 5530; Wagner to Rosenman, August 7, 1942, Samuel I. Rosenman Papers.

[33] Roosevelt to Homer Green, December 23, 1942, Roosevelt Papers, PPF 3196.

[34] Henry L. Morgenthau Diary, May 25, 1942, Morgenthau Papers.

[35] James W. Gerard to Roosevelt, January 11, 1943, Roosevelt Papers, OF 977; Randolph Paul, *Taxation for Prosperity* (Indianapolis, 1947) pp. 117-18, 131-33.

[36] Smith, Henderson, Eccles, Wallace and Wickard to Roosevelt, April 20, 1942, Roosevelt Papers OF 327.

[37] Blum, *Morgenthau Diaries*, pp. 17, 19-20; War Savings Staff report, July 11, 1942, Lowell Mellett Papers.

[38] Roosevelt to Bankhead, August 31, 1942, Roosevelt Papers, OF 258; Ickes to Roosevelt, September 2, 1942, *ibid.*, OF 327.

[39] Chester Bowles to Wallace, February 15, 1944, Wallace Papers.

[40] La Guardia to Prentiss M. Brown, April 21, 1943, Roosevelt Papers, OF 4403.

[41] Eugene Casey to Roosevelt, May 22, 1942; Thomas L. Bailey to Roosevelt, September 21, 1944; Jim Mathews to Marvin McIntyre May 5, 1942, Roosevelt Papers, OF 4403.

[42] Henderson to Roosevelt, April 24, 1942, December 15, 1942, Roosevelt Papers, PSF 53.

[43] Lucius Clay telephone conversation with Krug, December 7, 1944, Julius Krug Papers; Byrnes to Roosevelt, May 14, 1943, Roosevelt Papers, PSF 46.

Chapter 2

[1] Basil Manly to Roosevelt, May 1, 1941, Roosevelt Papers, PPF 1820; Archibald MacLeish to Grace Tully, *ibid.*, Coy to Roosevelt, May 6, 1942, Wayne Coy Papers.

[2] Frank Cestare, "A National YCL Conference," *Weekly Review* (January 12, 1943), p. 7; Irving Howe and Lewis Coser, *The American Communist Party* (Boston, 1957), pp. 387-436; Earl Browder, "The Study of Lenin's Teachings," *Political Affairs*, XXIV (January, 1945), 3-10; Citizens' Committee to Free Earl Browder, *Mr. President—Free Earl Browder* (New York, 1942).

[3] Howe and Coser, *Communist Party; Life*, March 29, 1943.

[4] Frankfurter to Frank Murphy, May 31, 1943, Felix Frankfurter Papers.

[5] *New York Times*, June 14, 1942; James M. Landis to Roosevelt, April 27, 1942, Roosevelt Papers, OF 4422.

[6] *National Defense Migration*, Hearings before the Select Committee Investigating National Defense Migration, House of Representatives, (Washington, 1942), p. 11128.

[7] Michael Sayers and Albert Kahn, *Sabotage! The Secret War Against America* (New York, 1942); John Roy Carlson, *Under Cover* (New York, 1943).

[8] Francis Biddle to Roosevelt, October 29, 1942 (quoting Roosevelt's memorandum of June 30), Roosevelt Papers, OF 3603; Biddle to Roosevelt, June 30, 1942, *ibid.*, OF 5036; Francis Biddle, *In Brief Authority* (New York, 1962), p. 339; Daily Calendar, June 30, 1942, Oscar Cox Papers.

[9] Biddle to Roosevelt, October 29, 1942, Roosevelt Papers, OF 3603; see also "Notes on The Schneiderman Case," December, 1942, June, 1943, Frankfurter Papers.

[10] Roosevelt to Biddle, May 7, 1942, Roosevelt Papers, OF 4866; Roosevelt to Morris Ernst, October 6, 1942, in Elliott Roosevelt ed., *F.D.R.: His Personal Letters* (New York, 1950), II, 1351.

[11] Freda Kirchwey, "Curb the Fascist Press!" *The Nation*, CLIV (March 28, 1942), 357-58; Arthur Garfield Hays, "Civil Liberties in War Time," *Bill of Rights Review*, II (Spring, 1942), 170-82; Letter to Roosevelt, February 17, 1942, Aubrey Williams Papers.

[12] Reinhold Niebuhr, "The Limits of Liberty," *The Nation*, CLIV (January 24, 1942), 86-88: Niebuhr, *The Children of Light and the Children of Darkness* (New York, 1944), p. 78.

[13] Charles Tull, *Father Coughlin and the New Deal* (Syracuse, 1965), p. 229.

[14] Maximilian St. George and Lawrence Dennis, *A Trial on Trial* (National Civil Rights Committee, 1945), pp. 250, 347; Lawrence Dennis to Villard, Feb. 4, 1944, Oswald G. Villard Papers.

[15] Alpheus T. Mason, *Harlan Fiske Stone: Pillar of the Law* (New York, 1957). p. 691.

[16] Gladys M. Kammerer, *Impact of War on Federal Personnel Administration* (Lexington, 1951), p. 125; Roosevelt to Biddle, August 31, 1943, Roosevelt Papers, OF 10-L; Interdepartmental Committee on Employee Investigations, "Outline of Policy and Procedure," September 1, 1943, William McReynolds Papers; Harold Ickes to Wallace, June 30, 1943, Wallace Papers.

[17] Lowell Mellett to Roosevelt, December 29, 1941, Mellett Papers; Theodore F. Koop, *Weapon of Silence* (Chicago, 1946), pp. 164-69.

[18] Davis, "Diary-First Day in Office," June 16, 1942, Elmer Davis Papers.

[19] A. H. Feller, "OWI on the Home Front," *Public Opinion Quarterly*, VII (Spring, 1943), 57; Archibald MacLeish to Roosevelt, September 29, 1941, Roosevelt Papers, OF 4619.

[20] Letter to Elmer Davis, August 25, 1943, Davis Papers.

[21] Ulric Bell and William B. Lewis to Archibald MacLeish, February 3, 1942, Henry F. Pringle Papers.

[22] Sidney Weinberg, "What to Tell America: The Writers' Quarrel in the Office of War Information," *Journal of American History*, LV (June, 1968), 87.

[23] "Roosevelt of America," *Victory*, I (1942), 17-19.

[24] Oscar Ewing to Roosevelt, March 16, 1943, Roosevelt Papers, OF 5015; Fred Busbey to Taber, October 15, 1943, John Taber Papers.

[25] Mulford Q. Sibley and Philip E. Jacob, *Conscription of Conscience* (Ithaca, 1952), pp. 112-21, 424-27.

[26] Socialist *Call*, May 15, 1942; Norman Thomas to Roosevelt, May 5, 1943, Roosevelt Papers, OF 111.

[27] "The Christian and the War," *The Christian Century*, LIX (January 28, 1942), 102-04; Lawrence S. Wittner, *Rebels Against War* (New York, 1969), pp. 72-76.

[28] Colonel Kosch to General Hershey, June 7, 1943, Roosevelt Papers, OF 111; Sibley and Jacob, *Conscription of Conscience*, pp. 315-19.

[29] Steve Early to Wayne Coy, June 15, 1942, Roosevelt Papers, OF 111.

[30] Sumner Welles to Roosevelt, December 5, 1941, Roosevelt Papers, OF 111.

[31] Osmond K. Fraenkel, "War, Civil Liberties and the Supreme Court," *Yale Law Journal*, LV (June, 1946), 719; Irving Dilliard ed., *One Man's Stand for Freedom* (New York, 1963), pp. 104-06.

[32] Biddle to Roosevelt, March 3, 1944, Roosevelt Papers, OF 111.

[33] Roosevelt to Stimson, May 5, 1942, Roosevelt Papers, OF 4849.

[34] Stetson Conn, *et al.*, *Guarding the United States and its Outposts* (Washington, 1964), pp. 117-18.

[35] Stimson Diary, February 3, 1942; Jacobus ten Broek *et al.*, *Prejudice, War and the Constitution* (Berkeley, 1954), pp. 109-10.

[36] War Department, Chief of Staff, *Final Report: Japanese Evacuation from the West Coast, 1942* (Washington, 1943), p. 34.

[37] *National Defense Migration*, Hearings, pp. 11010-19; Stimson Diary, February 10, 1942.

[38] Conn, *Guarding the United States*, pp. 123-25.

[39] Morton Grodzins, *Americans Betrayed: Politics and the Japanese Evacuation* (Chicago, 1949), p. 20; "Exploratory Study of West Coast Reactions to Japanese," February 2, 1942, Pringle Papers.

[40] Conn, *Guarding the United States*, p. 128.

[41] War Department, *Final Report*, vii-x.

[42] Conn, *Guarding the United States*, p. 122.

[43] Stimson Diary, February 11, 1942.

[44] ten Broek, *Prejudice, War and the Constitution*, p. 84.

[45] Stimson Diary, February 27, 1942.

[46] U.S. Department of the Interior, *WRA: A Story of Human Conservation* (Washington, 1946), p. 7; Milton Eisenhower to Roosevelt, June 18, 1942, Roosevelt Papers, OF 4849.

[47] War Department, *Final Report*, pp. 77-78.

[48] ten Broek, *Prejudice, War and the Constitution*, pp. 122-24.

[49] *War Relocation Centers*, Hearings before a Subcommittee of the Committee on Military Affairs, U.S. Senate, (Washington, 1943-44), p. 158.

[50] Staff report on WRA budget, Taber Papers.

[51] *War Relocation Centers*, Hearings, pp. 41-43.

[52] Department of the Interior, *WRA*, pp. 59-61; Stimson to Myer, May 10, 1943, Dillon Myer Papers.

[53] Stimson Diary, May 17, 1944, May 26, 1944, November 10, 1944; Roosevelt to Ickes, June 12, 1944, *Personal Letters*, II, 1517-18.

[54] Department of the Interior, *WRA*, p. 153.

[55] Eugene V. Rostow, "The Japanese-American Cases—a Disaster," *Yale Law Journal*, LIV (June, 1945), 505; Sidney Fine,

"Mr. Justice Murphy and the Hirabayashi Case," *Pacific Historical Review*, XXXIII (May, 1964), 204-09; J. Woodford Howard, *Mr. Justice Murphy* (Princeton, 1968), pp. 303-07.
⁵⁶ Mason, *Stone*, pp. 676-81; Howard, *Murphy*, p. 333.

Chapter 3

¹ "Defeatist Liberals," *New Republic*, CX (March 6, 1944), 302.
² Rexford Tugwell, "After the New Deal," *New Republic*, CI (July 26, 1939), 324; Harold Laski to Roosevelt, December 17, 1942, Roosevelt Papers, PPF 3014.
³ David K. Niles to Grace Tully, December 10, 1941, Roosevelt Papers, PPF 1792; Herbert Hoover, *Addresses upon the American Road: World War II* (New York, 1946), pp. 160-71.
⁴ David Lilienthal, *The Journals of David E. Lilienthal*, (New York, 1964), I, 43, Delia Kuhn to Archibald MacLeish, January 15, 1942, Pringle Papers.
⁵ Roosevelt to Louis Brownlow, December 29, 1943, Roosevelt Papers, PPF 1820; Bruce Bliven, "Liberals Today and Tomorrow," *New Republic*, CVIII (May 17, 1943), 658-61.
⁶ Robert F. Wagner, "Post War Security for All the People," *Progressive*, September 27, 1943; Wallace to Roosevelt, February 4, 1943, Roosevelt Papers, OF 4351.
⁷ *Minutes of the Advisory Commission to the Council of National Defense* (Washington, 1946), pp. 40-47.
⁸ Stimson Diary, January 16, 1942; March 2, 1942; March 4, 1942.
⁹ "Anti-Trust Procedure Memorandum," March, 1942, Rosenman Papers; Richard Lee Strout, "The Folklore of Thurman Arnold," *New Republic*, CVI (April 27, 1942), 570-71.
¹⁰ "New York State Campaign Against Child Labor in Bowling Alleys," *The Child*, IX (May 1945) 173-74; "A 16-Year Minimum Age for Employment," *ibid.*, (January, 1945), 107-09.
¹¹ John Taber to Ray P. Chase, January 15, 1942, Taber Papers.
¹² Harold D. Smith Diary, December 18, 1941; January 16, 1942; John Salmond, *The Civilian Conservation Corps* (Durham, 1967), pp. 200-17.
¹³ Florence Kerr to Hopkins, June 2, 1942, Harry Hopkins Papers; "Memorandum for Discussion," November 9, 1942, *ibid.*
¹⁴ *Termination of Civilian Conservation Corps and National Youth Administration*, Hearings before the Committee on Education and Labor, U.S. Senate, 77th Congress, 2nd Session (Washington, 1942), pp. 511, 115, 162; Williams to Eleanor Roosevelt, April 14, 1942, Aubrey Williams Papers.
¹⁵ Smith Diary, March 17, 1943; Earl E. Krum to John Taber, January 21, 1943, Taber Papers.
¹⁶ John Taber to Charles A. Cannon, June 1, 1943, Taber Papers; Williams to James Richmond, July 6, 1943, Williams Papers.
¹⁷ Malcolm Cowley, "The End of the New Deal," *New Republic*, CVIII (May 31, 1943), 729-32.
¹⁸ Aubrey Williams telephone conversation with J. S. Samler, May 31, 1943, and with Dillon S. Myer, June 1, 1943, Williams Papers.
¹⁹ T.R.B., "Washington Notes,"

New Republic, CVI (February 23, 1942), 269.

[20] "Charter for America," *New Republic*, CVIII (April 19, 1943), 542; Delano to Roosevelt, October 14, 1942, Roosevelt Papers, OF 1092; Roosevelt to Carter Glass, March 24, 1943, *ibid*.

[21] Sterling Cole to Ernest Merritt, February 22, 1943, Sterling Cole Papers.

[22] John Beecher, "Save Farm Security!" *New Republic*, CVIII (April 26, 1943), 561-63; John K. Galbraith to Leon Henderson, October 27, 1942, Leon Henderson Papers.

[23] *Farm Security Administration*, Hearings before the Select Committee of the House Committee on Agriculture (Washington, 1944), IV, 1553, 1557.

[24] James G. Patton to Roosevelt, April 8, 1943, Roosevelt Papers, OF 1568; Baldwin to Roosevelt, September 24, 1943, *ibid*.

[25] Sidney Baldwin, *Poverty and Politics: The Rise and Decline of the FSA* (Chapel Hill, 1968), p. 284; John Taber to Thomas Dewey, February 23, 1943, Taber Papers; *Farm Security Administration*, Hearings, II, 801.

[26] Arthur Altmeyer to Isador Lubin, November 19, 1943, enclosing draft of "An Expanded Social Security System," Isador Lubin Papers.

[27] Grace Tully memorandum, February 18, 1943, Roosevelt Papers, PSF 21; John M. Blum, *From the Morgenthau Diaries: Years of War* (Boston, 1967), p. 72.

[28] *Substandard Wages*, Hearings before a Subcommittee of the Committee on Education and Labor, U.S. Senate (Washington, 1945),

pp. 86-89; *Wartime Health and Education*, Hearings before a Subcommittee of the Committee on Education and Labor, U.S. Senate (Washington, 1945), III, x-xi.

[29] *Substandard Wages*, Hearings, p. 245; *Wartime Health and Education*, Hearings, pp. 1233-43; Seymour E. Harris, *Inflation and the American Economy* (New York, 1945), pp. 360-63.

[30] Randolph Paul to Samuel Rosenman, May 12, 1942, Rosenman Papers.

[31] Richard Rovere, "Warning to the Liberals," *Common Sense*, XI (August, 1942), pp. 266-68.

[32] Frederick C. Crawford, "A Better America Through Freedom of Enterprise," in National Association of Manufacturers, *A Better America* (New York, 1944), p. 3; *Business Week*, November 13, 1943, p. 116; October 9, 1943, p. 108.

[33] James Wechsler, "The Last New Dealer," *Common Sense*, XII (May, 1943), 163-64.

[34] Thomas Amlie to Victor Reuther, May 16, 1942, Union for Democratic Action Papers; "War Thoughts on Labor," *New Republic*, CVIII (January 25, 1943), pp. 103-104.

[35] Max Lerner, *Public Journal* (New York, 1945), p. 382.

[36] Stuart Chase, "New Deal Dead—So What?" *Common Sense*, XI (September, 1943), 385; Thomas Amlie to James Loeb, May 12, 1942, UDA Papers.

[37] Alfred Bingham, *The Practice of Idealism* (New York, 1944), pp. 81-82; Chester Bowles to Wallace, September 15, 1944, Wallace Papers.

[38] David R. B. Ross, *Preparing for Ulysses: Politics and Veterans*

during World War II (New York, 1969), p. 108.

Chapter 4

¹ Collier Anderson to Roosevelt, August 16, 1940, Roosevelt Papers, OF 93.

² "Close Ranks," *The Crisis*, XVI (July, 1918), 111.

³ *Amsterdam News*, June 7, 1941; June 19, 1943; December 20, 1941.

⁴ *New York Times*, September 15, 1942; Roi Ottley, *'New World A-Coming': Inside Black America* (Cleveland, 1943), pp. 334-38; *Amsterdam News*, September 19, 1942.

⁵ Herbert Garfinkel, *When Negroes March* (Glencoe, 1959), pp. 32-33.

⁶ Ottley, *New World*, p. 291.

⁷ A. Philip Randolph, "March on Washington Movement Presents Program for the Negro," in Rayford W. Logan ed., *What the Negro Wants* (Chapel Hill, 1944), pp. 135-62; *Amsterdam News*, August 28, 1943.

⁸ "Proposals of the Negro March on Washington Committee to President Roosevelt," [June, 1941], Roosevelt Papers, OF 391.

⁹ Roosevelt to Knudsen and Hillman, May 26, 1941; Knudsen to Roosevelt, May 28, 1941, Roosevelt Papers, OF 93.

¹⁰ Roosevelt to Knudsen and Hillman, June 12, 1941, Sidney Hillman Papers.

¹¹ Roosevelt to Marvin McIntyre, June 7, 1941, Roosevelt Papers, OF 391; Garfinkel, *When Negroes March*, p. 61.

¹² Steve Early to Wayne Coy, June 6, 1941, Roosevelt Papers, OF 391.

¹³ *Amsterdam News*, July 5, 1941.

¹⁴ Garfinkel, *When Negroes March*, pp. 86-87; Randolph, "March on Washington Movement," in Logan, *What the Negro Wants*, pp. 135-62.

¹⁵ A. Philip Randolph, "Is Civil Disobedience Practical?" *The Negro Digest*, I (March, 1943), 27-29; Lawrence Wittner, *Rebels against War* (New York, 1969), pp. 64-66.

¹⁶ *The Negro Digest*, I (March, 1943), 27-29; Garfinkel, *When Negroes March*, p. 143.

¹⁷ James Farmer to A. J. Muste, March 9, 1942, cited in Francis L. Broderick and August Meier, *Negro Protest Thought in the Twentieth Century* (Indianapolis, 1965), p. 219.

¹⁸ Thurgood Marshall, "The Legal Attack to Secure Civil Rights," July 13, 1944, *ibid.*, p. 235; Minutes, Board of Directors, December, 1945, National Association for the Advancement of Colored People Papers.

¹⁹ Press conference, December 28, 1943, Roosevelt Papers; Roosevelt to Frederick M. Davenport, May 4, 1942, *ibid.*, PPF 5485.

²⁰ *The Negro Digest*, I (October, March, April, 1943).

²¹ *Race Relations*, I (September, 1943), 22; *The Southern Frontier*, January, 1943.

²² Howard W. Odum, *Race and Rumors of Race* (Chapel Hill, 1943), pp. 57, 69, 73.

²³ Frank Boykin to Roosevelt, March 6, 1943, Roosevelt Papers, OF 93; Eugene Connor to Roosevelt, August 7, 1942, *ibid.*, OF 4245-G.

²⁴ Alpheus T. Mason, *Harlan Fiske Stone: Pillar of the Law* (New York, 1957), pp. 614-17.

25 *Time*, XLIII (April 17, 1944).

26 Donald B. Strong, "The Rise of Negro Voting in Texas," *American Political Science Review*, XLII (June, 1948), pp. 510-22; John H. McCray, "The Progressive Democratic Party in South Carolina," *The Southern Frontier*, August, 1944.

27 Jonathan Daniels to Roosevelt, September 28, 1944, Roosevelt Papers, OF 93. See also Francis Biddle to Roosevelt. October 30, 1943, *ibid.*; PSF 24.

28 "Survey of Employment Prospects for Negroes in Armament Industries," [1941], Hillman Papers; Louis Kesselman, *The Social Politics of FEPC* (Chapel Hill, 1948), p. 7.

29 Louis Ruchames, *Race, Jobs, and Politics* (New York, 1953), p. 30.

30 Robert Weaver, *Negro Labor: A National Problem* (New York, 1946), pp. 143-44; Oscar Cox to Francis Biddle, May 18, 1943, Francis J. Haas Papers.

31 Welles to Roosevelt June 20, 1942; Welles to Marvin McIntyre, July 24, 1942; Lawrence Cramer to Roosevelt, July 10, 1942; Malcolm Ross to Jonathan Daniels, November 4, 1943, Roosevelt Papers, OF 4245-G.

32 Minutes, Board of Directors, September 14, 1942, NAACP Papers; Memorandum on FEPC [December, 1943], Taber Papers.

33 Ottley, *New World*, p. 302; George Tindall, *Emergence of the New South* (Louisiana, 1967), pp. 715-16; Ruchames, *Race, Jobs, and Politics*, pp. 87-99.

34 Ethridge to Steve Early, August 20, 1941, Roosevelt Papers, OF 93; MacLean to Marvin McIntyre, February 24, 1942, *ibid.*

35 Haas to Jonathan Daniels, September 10, 1943, Roosevelt Papers, OF 4245-G; Malcolm Ross, *All Manner of Men* (New York, 1948).

36 Ruchames, *Race, Jobs, and Politics*, p. 197.

37 "Hate Strike," *Race Relations*, II (August-September, 1944) 6-7.

38 "War Department Policy in Regard to Negroes," October, 1940, Roosevelt Papers, OF 93.

39 Ulysses Lee, *The Employment of Negro Troops* (Washington, 1966), p. 137.

40 Henry L. Stimson Diary, October 25, 1940; Richard M. Dalfiume, *Desegregation of the United States Armed Forces* (Columbia, 1969), p. 57.

41 Lee, *Negro Troops*, pp. 140, 158-59; Stimson Diary, January 24, 1942.

42 Memorandum for the Attorney General prepared by Malcolm Ross (based on Francis J. Haas' notes), July 5, 1943, Haas Papers.

43 Michigan *Chronicle* cited in Alfred McClung Lee and Norman D. Humphrey, *Race Riot* (New York, 1943), pp. 40-41; Henry S. Aurand to Allen W. Guilion, July 3, 1943, cited in Robert Shogan and Tom Craig, *The Detroit Race Riot: A Study in Violence* (Philadelphia, 1964), p. 81.

44 Shogan, *Detroit Race Riot*, pp. 106-07; Lee, *Race Riot,* pp. 60-66; Police Commissioner Witherspoon to the Detroit Common Council, June 28, 1943, Roosevelt Papers, OF 93-C.

45 Kenneth B. Clark, "Group Violence: A Study of the 1943

Harlem Riot," *Journal of Social Psychology*, XIX (May, 1944), pp. 319, 337; *Amsterdam News*, August 14, 1943, August 28, 1943.

⁴⁶ Selden Menefee, *Assignment: U.S.A.* (New York, 1943), pp. 186-91; Carey McWilliams, *North From Mexico* (Philadelphia, 1949).

Chapter 5

¹ Malcolm Logan, *The Home Front Digest* (New York, 1942); T. A. Larson, *Wyoming's War Years, 1941-1945* (Laramie, 1954), p. 80; W. Lloyd Warner, "The American Town," in William F. Ogburn ed., *American Society in Wartime* (Chicago, 1943), pp. 45-46.

² Office of Civilian Defense, *What Can I Do?* (Washington, 1942).

³ Elmer Davis to Steve Early, September 4, 1942, Roosevelt Papers, OF 5015; Edgar A. Schuler, "V For Victory: A Study in Symbolic Social Control," *Journal of Social Psychology*, XIX (May, 1944), 283-99.

⁴ John Morton Blum, "The G.I. in the Culture of the Second World War," *Ventures*, VII (Spring, 1968), 51.

⁵ *New York Times*, May 17, 1942; June 13, 1942.

⁶ Rex Stout, "We Shall Hate, or We Shall Fail," *New York Times Magazine*, January 17, 1943; W. Lloyd Warner, *Democracy in Jonesville* (New York, 1949), p. 288; New York *Herald-Tribune*, June 14, 1942.

⁷ *Advertising in a War Economy* [n.d.]; Raymond Rubicam, "Advertising," in Jack Goodman ed., *While You Were Gone* (New York, 1946), pp. 426-39.

⁸ Memorandum on Government War Graphics, June 1, 1942, Pringle Papers; P. Hamburger to Thomas D. Mabry, March 31, 1942, *ibid.*

⁹ See Marshall B. Clinard, *The Black Market: A Study of White Collar Crime* (New York, 1948), *passim.*

¹⁰ Charles H. Stember, *Jews in the Mind of America* (New York, 1966); Eileen H. Posner, "Anti-Jewish Manifestations," *The American Jewish Yearbook*, XLVI (1944), 133-41; *Boston Globe*, November 10, 1943. See also E. L. Horowitz to Leo C. Rosten, December 17, 1942, Philleo Nash Papers.

¹¹ "Willow Run Bomber Plant," *Architectural Record*, XCII (September, 1942), 39-46.

¹² "Housing Muddle," *Business Week*, (March 13, 1943), pp. 75-76.

¹³ Lowell J. Carr and James E. Stermer, *Willow Run: A Study of Industrialization and Cultural Inadequacy* (New York, 1952), p. 238.

¹⁴ Glendon Swarthout, *Willow Run* (New York, 1943).

¹⁵ Agnes E. Meyer, *Journey Through Chaos* (New York, 1944), pp. 193-201; *Wartime Health and Education*, Hearings Before a Subcommittee of the Committee on Education and Labor, U. S. Senate, 78th Congress, 1st Session (Washington, 1944), p. 734.

¹⁶ Robert J. Havighurst and H. G. Morgan, *The Social History of a War-Boom Community* (New York, 1951), pp. 172, 102.

¹⁷ George H. Bach, "Father-Fantasies and Father-Typing in Father-Separated Children," *Child Development*, XVII (March-June, 1946), pp. 63-80.

¹⁸ Dorothy K. Newman, "Employing Women in Shipyards,"

Bulletin of the Women's Bureau, No. 192-6 (Washington, 1944), pp. 1-6.

[19] Ethel Erickson, "Women's Employment in the Making of Steel," *Bulletin of the Women's Bureau*, No. 192-5 (Washington, 1944), pp. 19-20; Ann Pendleton [pseud.], *Hit the Rivet, Sister* (1943); Josephine von Miklos, *I Took a War Job* (New York, 1943), pp. 3, 4, 10.

[20] Josephine D. Abbott, "What of Youth in Wartime?" *Survey Midmonthly*, LXXIX (October, 1943), 265-67; David M. Levy, "The War and Family Life," *American Journal of Orthopsychiatry*, XV (1945), 140-46.

[21] Levy, "The War and Family Life," *loc. cit.*

[22] "The Federal Government and A Child Care Program," November 5, 1943, Coy Papers.

[23] Paul Wiers, "Wartime Increases in Michigan Delinquency," *American Sociological Review*, X (August, 1945), 515; John Slawson, "The Adolescent in a World at War," *Mental Hygiene*, XXVII (October, 1943), 534; *Wartime Health and Education*, pp. 100-115.

[24] *Wartime Health and Education*, pp. 6-7, 84-100, 263.

[25] "The War Against Prostitution Must Go On," *Journal of Social Hygiene*, XXXI (November, 1945), 500-07; Harry P. Cain, "Blitzing the Brothels," *ibid.*, XXIX (December, 1943), 594.

[26] Gene Tunney, "The Bright Shield of Continence," *Readers' Digest*, XLI (August, 1942), 43-46; Gaylord W. Anderson, "Venereal Disease Education in the Army," *Journal of Social Hygiene*, XXX (January, 1944), 20.

[27] Henry L. Stimson Diary, October 20, 1942; Sam Morris, *Booze and the War* (Grand Rapids, 1944), pp. 9, 20.

Chapter 6

[1] William Green to Archie P. Owens, December 15, 1941, William Green Papers.

[2] Forrestal and Patterson to Roosevelt, January 5, 1942, James Forrestal Papers.

[3] Frances Perkins to Roosevelt, January 8, 1942, Roosevelt Papers, OF 4710.

[4] *The Termination Report of the National War Labor Board* (Washington, 1947) I, 87.

[5] Michigan CIO Council, *Proceedings*, 6th Annual Convention, pp. 136-46; Combined Labor War Board to Roosevelt, June 3, 1943, Roosevelt Papers, OF 4735.

[6] Daniel J. Tobin to Roosevelt, March 30, 1942, Roosevelt Papers, PPF 1180.

[7] Michigan CIO Council, *Proceedings*, pp. 136-46.

[8] Wayne Morse to Roosevelt, May 26, 1943, Roosevelt Papers, OF 407-B.

[9] James Wechsler, *Labor Baron* (New York, 1944), pp. 214-24; Saul Alinsky, *John L. Lewis*, (New York, 1949), pp. 286-88; United Mine Workers, *Proceedings of the 38th Convention*, pp. 98-112.

[10] William Davis to Roosevelt, April 28, 1943, Roosevelt Papers, OF 407-B; Wayne Morse to Roosevelt, June 2, 1943, *ibid.*

[11] Cox telephone conversation with Harry Hopkins, June 3, 1943, Oscar Cox Papers.

[12] Ickes to Roosevelt, July 9, 1943, Roosevelt Papers, OF 407-B; Ickes to Roosevelt, July 28, 1943,

ibid., OF 4710; Abe Fortas to Ickes, June 19, 1943, *ibid.*, OF 4735; *Minutes of the War Production Board* (Washington, 1946), p. 287.

13 Roosevelt to Thomas Lamont, November 10, 1941, Roosevelt Papers, PPF 70; Biddle to Roosevelt, September 28, 1943, *ibid.*, PSF 24.

14 Ickes to Roosevelt, June 17, 1943, Roosevelt Papers, OF 407-B; William Davis Memoir, pp. 159-160.

15 Alinsky, *Lewis*, pp. 272, 307-09; Paul A. C. Koistinen, "The Hammer and the Sword" (unpublished Ph.D. dissertation, Berkeley, 1964), p. 270.

16 Boris I. Bittker to Cox, April 27, 1943, Cox Papers.

17 "The Shape of Things," *Nation*, CLVI (May 8, 1943), 650; "The Miners Have a Case," *New Republic*, CVIII (June 14, 1943), 780; E. R. Elliott, " 'Big Jawn' —Hitler's Man," *Weekly Review*, May 18, 1943.

18 UMW *Proceedings*, 13-17; "King Coal," *The Economist*, May 22, 1943, pp. 655-57.

19 Isador Lubin to Harry Hopkins, May 27, 1943, Roosevelt Papers, PSF 45.

20 Byrnes to Roosevelt, May 3, 1943, *ibid.*, PSF 46.

21 Davis to Byrnes, June 18, 1943, *ibid.*, OF 407-B.

22 Cox telephone conversation with Isador Lubin, June 21, 1943, Cox Papers.

23 Samuel I. Rosenman ed., *The Public Papers and Addresses of Franklin Roosevelt* (New York, 1950), XII, 271; Stimson, "Coal," June 25, 1943, Roosevelt Papers, OF 407-B.

24 AFL-CIO to Roosevelt [n.d.],

Roosevelt Papers, OF 407-B; Joel Seidman, *American Labor from Defense to Reconversion* (Chicago, 1953), pp. 188-90.

25 Colston E. Warne ed., *Yearbook of American Labor: War Labor Policies* (New York, 1945), pp. 301-3; *United Mine Workers' Journal*, LIV (April 1, 1943), 10.

26 "The Stewardship of Sewell Avery," *Fortune*, XXXIII (May, 1946), 111-13, 179-84; *Investigation and Seizure of Montgomery Ward & Co.*, Hearings before the Select Committee, House of Representatives, 78th Congress, 2nd Session (Washington, 1944), pp. 315-21, 361.

27 *Seizure of Montgomery Ward*, Hearings, pp. 121, 307-12.

28 Robert Patterson to Byrnes, April 12, 14, 18, 1944, Roosevelt Papers, OF 4451; Henry Stimson Diary, April 14, May 1, 1944.

29 Byrnes to Roosevelt, April 22, May 1, 1944, Roosevelt Papers, OF 4451; Francis Biddle, *In Brief Authority* (New York, 1962), pp. 313-15; *Seizure of Montgomery Ward*, Hearings, p. 331.

30 Biddle, *In Brief Authority*, pp. 318-20; John Taber to LeRoy Wright, May 16, 1944, Taber Papers.

31 Clark to Robert Patterson, November 10, 1942, Patterson Papers.

32 Knox to Roosevelt, June 8, 1943, Roosevelt Papers, OF 4735.

33 Stimson Diary, June 29, December 31, 1943; Stimson to Clark, January 1, 1944, James Wadsworth Papers.

34 *Public Papers and Addresses*, XIII, 37-39.

35 Harold Smith Diary, January 7, 1944.

36 Wadsworth to J. M. Wain-

wright, February 14, 1944, Wadsworth Papers; Rosenman to Roosevelt, April, 1944, Roosevelt Papers, OF 1413-F.

[37] Seidman, *American Labor*, pp. 162-64; *National War Service Bill*, Hearings before the Committee on Military Affairs, United States Senate, 78th Congress, 2nd Session (Washington, 1944), pp. 177-232; Byron Fairchild and Jonathan Grossman, *The Army and Industrial Manpower* (Washington, 1959), pp. 226-237.

[38] Paul McNutt to Roosevelt, October 28, 1942, Roosevelt Papers, OF 4905; Wadsworth to Clark, March 29, 1944, Wadsworth Papers.

[39] Wadsworth to Clark, July 13, 1942, Wadsworth Papers.

[40] Baruch to Roosevelt, September 8, 1943, Roosevelt Papers, OF 1413-F; Stimson Diary, April 4, 1944.

[41] Clark to Robert Patterson, April 21, 1944, Patterson Papers.

[42] Dwight Macdonald, "Comment," *Politics* I (February, 1944), p. 2; Robert M. La Follette, Jr., "This is the Road to Slavery," *Progressive*, January 24, 1944.

[43] *Congressional Digest*, XXIII (April, 1944), 125.

[44] *National War Service Bill*, Hearings, pp. 101-25.

[45] Stimson to Roosevelt, July 1, 1943, Roosevelt Papers, OF 1413-F; Eugene Duffield to Forrestal January 2, 1945, Forrestal Papers.

[46] Albert A. Blum, *Drafted or Deferred: Practices Past and Present* (Michigan, 1967), p. 197; Wadsworth to George S. Patton, March 13, 1945, Wadsworth Papers.

Chapter 7

[1] Joseph C. Latham to Sterling Cole, March 15, 1942, Sterling Cole Papers.

[2] Robert Taft to Richard Scandrett, January 26, 1942, Richard Scandrett Papers; Daniel Reed to Roy Woodruff, August 25, 1942, Daniel Reed Papers.

[3] Oscar Ewing Minneapolis address, February 23, 1942, Roosevelt Papers, PPF 1820; *Congressional Record*, 77th Cong., 2nd Sess., App. 352-53.

[4] Harold Ickes to Roosevelt, March 24, 1942, Roosevelt Papers, PSF 21.

[5] John Taber to Pennington Sefton, February 10, 1942, Taber Papers.

[6] Lewis B. Schwellenbach to Joseph Guffey, January 14, 1943, Roosevelt Papers, PPF 1820.

[7] Edwin Pauley to Roosevelt, December 14, 1942, Roosevelt Papers, PPF 1820; Kent Keller to Henry A. Wallace, December 21, 1942, *ibid.*

[8] Frederick E. Butcher questionnaire, [December] 1942, Union for Democratic Action Papers.

[9] Hadley Cantril to Roosevelt, December 14, 1942, Roosevelt Papers, PPF 8229.

[10] Roosevelt to Henry Epstein, November 12, 1942, Roosevelt Papers, PPF 500.

[11] Augustus Bennet to Richard Scandrett, June 13, 1942, Scandrett Papers; Grace Tully to James Kiernan, August 12, 1942, Roosevelt Papers, PSF 53.

[12] James Townsend to Roosevelt, November 18, 1942, Roosevelt Papers, PSF 53.

[13] David Hughes, "Politics in Wartime: The Elections of 1942,"

(Unpub. M.A. thesis, Cornell University, 1969).

[14] Charles Johnson, *To Stem this Tide* (Boston, 1943), pp. 63-65; George B. Tindall, *The Emergence of the New South* (Louisiana, 1967), pp. 722-23.

[15] John Robert Moore, "The Conservative Coalition in the United States Senate, 1942-1945," *Journal of Southern History*, XXX-III (August, 1967), 368-76.

[16] James Wadsworth to Frank S. Hayden, July 6, 1943, Wadsworth Papers.

[17] *Congressional Record*, 78th Cong., 1st Sess., pp. 474-86.

[18] *Goodwin B. Watson, William E. Dodd, Jr., and Robert Morss Lovett*, Hearings before the Special Subcommittee of the Committee on Appropriations, House of Representatives, 78th Congress, 1st Session (Washington, 1943), p. 157; Press conference, March 31, 1942.

[19] Ed Flynn memorandum [May] 1944, Roosevelt Papers, OF 1113.

[20] Roosevelt to Byrnes, September 8, 1943, Roosevelt Papers, OF 1113; Samuel Rosenman to Roosevelt, March 15, 1944, *ibid.*

[21] "Should Absentee Soldier Voting Be Federally Controlled?" *Congressional Digest*, XXIII (January, 1944).

[22] Richard Hartshorne to Ostertag, March 24, 1944, Herman C. Ostertag Papers.

[23] Roosevelt to Byrnes, April 8, 1944, Roosevelt Papers, OF 1113.

[24] Rosenman to Roosevelt, February 14, 1944, Rosenman Papers.

[25] Alben W. Barkley, *That Reminds Me* (New York, 1954), pp. 170-82.

[26] Harold D. Smith Diary, February 16, 1944.

[27] Roosevelt to Patrick H. Drewry, March 7, 1944, Roosevelt Papers, PSF 47.

[28] Ellsworth Barnard, *Wendell Willkie* (Marquette, Mich., 1966), pp. 336-41, 424-25, 433-35.

[29] *Ibid.*, pp. 458-69.

[30] Barry Keith Beyer, "Thomas E. Dewey, 1937-1947: A Study in Political Leadership," (Unpublished Ph.D. dissertation, University of Rochester, 1962), pp. 438, 426.

[31] Ickes to Roosevelt, July 24, 1944, Roosevelt Papers, PSF 21.

[32] Hillman to Roosevelt, July 27, 1943, Hillman Papers.

[33] Philip Murray and Sidney Hillman to union leaders, April 3, 1944, Philip Murray Papers.

[34] William H. Riker, "The CIO in Politics, 1936-1948," (Unpublished Ph.D. dissertation, Harvard University, 1948), p. 163.

[35] PAC Draft Program, June 16, 1944, Hillman Papers.

[36] Joseph Gaer, *The First Round: The Story of the Political Action Committee* (New York, 1944), pp. 17-48, 469.

[37] Hillman "CIO-PAC: Seattle and California Conferences," September, 1943, Philip Murray Papers; Matthew Josephson, *Sidney Hillman*, (New York, 1952), p. 598.

[38] Francis Biddle to Roosevelt, August 30, 1944, Roosevelt Papers, OF 670; Robert F. Carter, "Pressure from the Left: The American Labor Party, 1936-1954," (Unpublished Ph.D. dissertation, Syracuse University, 1965), pp. 152-213.

[39] Scrapbooks, X-XI, Hillman Papers; Josephson, *Hillman*, pp. 630-31.

[40] Beyer, *Dewey*, p. 333; *Time*, November 13, 1944, p. 23.

[41] Biddle to Samuel Rosenman, November 3, 1944, Rosenman Papers.

[42] *Congressional Record*, 78th Cong., 2nd Session, App. 3988-89; James H. Rowe to Roosevelt, November 8, 1944, Roosevelt Papers, PPF 7368.

[43] Richard Scandrett to Oscar Ewing, September 23, 1944, Scandrett Papers.

[44] Beyer, *Dewey*, pp. 429-30.

[45] *Ibid.*, pp. 117-21; "Dewey vs. Roosevelt: An Analysis of the Presidential Campaign," Reed Papers.

[46] Hadley Cantril to Samuel Rosenman, August 3, September 30, October 18, 1944, Rosenman Papers; Hadley Cantril, *The Human Dimension: Experiences in Policy Research* (New Brunswick, 1967).

[47] Robert Taft to Frank Gannett, November 28, 1944, Frank Gannett Papers.

[48] Emil Hurja to Earle D. Wiley, December 12, 1944, Emil Hurja Papers.

[49] Fred Norman, Calvin D. Johnson questionnaires, [December] 1944, Hurja Papers.

[50] Stephen A. Day questionnaire, [December] 1944, Hurja Papers.

Chapter 8

[1] Donald M. Nelson, *Arsenal of Democracy: The Story of American War Production* (New York, 1946), p. 363; Bruce Catton, *The War Lords of Washington* (New York, 1948), p. 177.

[2] Baruch to Lt. General Brehon B. Somervell, December 24, 1942, Baruch Papers.

[3] Samuel P. Huntington, *The Soldier and the State* (Cambridge, 1957), p. 315; Bureau of the Budget, *The United States at War* (Washington, 1946), p. 130.

[4] R. Elberton Smith, *The Army and Economic Mobilization* (Washington, 1959), p. 241.

[5] Press conference, May 30, 1940, Roosevelt Papers.

[6] Robert H. Connery, *The Navy and Industrial Mobilization in World War II* (Princeton, 1951), p. 123; Smith, *Army and Economic Mobilization*, p. 414.

[7] Huntington, *Soldier and the State*, p. 365; "The Future of Our Association," *The Quartermaster Review*, XXIII (January-February, 1944), 93; Levin H. Campbell, Jr., *The Industry-Ordnance Team* (New York, 1946), p. 71.

[8] Elting E. Morison, *Turmoil and Tradition: A Study of the Life and Times of Henry L. Stimson* (Boston, 1960), p. 556; Richard N. Current, *Secretary Stimson: A Study in Statecraft* (New Brunswick, 1954), pp. 10-11.

[9] Donald H. Riddle, The Truman Committee (New Brunswick, 1964), p. 76; John D. Millett, *The Organization and Role of the Army Service Forces* (Washington, 1954), pp. 2-6.

[10] Henry L. Stimson Diary, July 22, 1942, Stimson Papers; R. V. Gilbert to Leon Henderson, October 21, 1942, Henderson Papers.

[11] Millett, *Army Service Forces*, pp. 446-51.

[12] Civilian Production Administration, *Industrial Mobilization for War* (Washington, 1947), p. 278.

13 *Minutes of the Planning Committee of the War Production Board* (Washington, 1946), March 17, 1942, pp. 127-30.

14 Roosevelt to Nelson, February 11, 1942, Roosevelt Papers, OF 4735.

15 Committee on Public Administration Cases, *The Feasibility Dispute* (Washington, 1950), pp. 88-90.

16 *Ibid.*, pp. 76-87.

17 *Ibid.*, pp. 90-96; *Minutes of the War Production Board* (Washington, 1946), October 6, 1942, pp. 140-42.

18 *WPB Minutes*, October 6, 1942, pp. 141-42.

19 Committee on Public Administration Cases, *Feasibility Dispute*, pp. 102-06.

20 Nelson, *Arsenal of Democracy*, pp. 385-90.

21 Somervell to Wilson, November 16, 1942, Baruch Papers; Millett, *Army Service Forces*, pp. 220-26.

22 Bernard M. Baruch, *The Public Years* (New York, 1960), pp. 313-18.

23 Harold D. Smith to Roosevelt, February 8, 1943, Roosevelt Papers, PSF 46.

24 Forrestal to W. M. Kiplinger, March 5, 1945, Forrestal Papers.

25 "An Appraisal of Manpower Problems in War Production," July, 1944, Donald Nelson Papers; Nelson, *Arsenal of Democracy*, pp. 402-08.

26 J. Carlyle Sitterson, *Development of the Reconversion Policies of the War Production Board* (Washington, 1945), pp. 40-43; Patterson to Baruch, November 18, 1944, Baruch Papers; Millett, *Army Service Forces*, pp. 385-86.

27 Philip Murray to J. Raymond Walsh, September 24, 1943, Murray Papers; Boris Shishkin, "The Next Depression?", *The American Federationist*, LI (October, 1944), 3-6, 21-22.

28 Sitterson, *Reconversion Policies*, pp. 56-62; "For Peace on the Home Front," *Business Week*, August 5, 1944, p. 120.

29 Sitterson, *Reconversion Policies*, pp. 32-37; *Business Week*, August 5, 1944.

30 Jack Peltason, "The Reconversion Controversy," Harold Stein ed., *Public Administration and Policy Development* (New York, 1952), pp. 242-43.

31 *WPB Minutes*, July 4, 1944, pp. 341-44; Peltason, *Reconversion Controversy*, pp. 243-45; Millett, *Army Service Forces*, pp. 229-30.

32 Harold D. Smith Diary, August 31, 1944, Smith Papers.

33 Drummond Jones, *The Role of the Office of Civilian Requirements* (Washington, 1946), pp. 305-308; Transcript of Krug-Elmer Davis conversation, November 28, 1944, Julius A. Krug Papers.

34 Patterson to Baruch, November 14, 1944, Baruch Papers; Statement, December 1, 1944, Krug Papers.

35 Baruch to Krug, February 13, 1945, Baruch Papers.

36 *WPB Minutes*, September 5, 1944, p. 353; Barton Bernstein, "The Removal of War Production Board Controls on Business, 1944-1946," *Business History Review*, XXXIX (Summer, 1965), 243-60.

37 Charles E. Wilson, "For the Common Defense: A Plea for a Continuing Program of Industrial Preparedness," *Army Ordnance*, XXVI (March-April, 1944), 285-88.

Bibliography

General Accounts

THERE ARE SEVERAL GENERAL studies of the United States during the war. The Bureau of the Budget, *The United States at War* (Washington, 1946), the first in the series of "historical reports on war administration," is a straightforward economic and administrative history. Both A. Russell Buchanan, *The United States in World War II*, 2 vols. (New York, 1964), and Kenneth F. Davis, *Experience of War* (Garden City, 1965) treat events at home in a cursory fashion. Three social histories, all of which attempt in some degree to evoke a mood of nostalgia, have appeared: William Kenney, *The Crucial Years* (New York, 1962); A. A. Hoehling, *Home Front, U.S.A.* (New York, 1964); and Richard R. Lingeman, *Don't You Know There's A War On?* (New York, 1970). Although he devotes most of his attention to foreign policy and military affairs, James MacGregor Burns's *Roosevelt: The Soldier of Freedom* (New York, 1970) contains valuable insights into political, economic and social developments.

The publication of diaries and correspondence provides a convenient way of assessing what political leaders were saying and doing. For Roosevelt's views see Elliott Roosevelt, ed., *F.D.R. His Personal Letters, II* (New York, 1950), and Max Freedman, ed., *Roosevelt and Frankfurter: Their Correspondence, 1928-1945* (Boston, 1967). Samuel I. Rosenman, ed., *The Public Papers and Addresses of Franklin D. Roosevelt, X-XIII* (New York, 1950) includes excerpts from the President's press conferences as well as his speeches and public statements. The diary kept by Roosevelt's secretary, William D. Hassett, *Off the Record with FDR, 1942-1945* (New Brunswick, 1958), is also useful. See Charles A. Lindbergh, *The Wartime Journals of Charles A. Lindbergh* (New York, 1970) for the fate of the prewar isolationist movement and technical difficulties encountered at Willow Run. John Morton Blum's skillful editing of *From the Morgenthau Diaries, Years of War* (Boston, 1967) sheds considerable light on wartime economic policy. *The War Diary of Breckinridge Long* (Lincoln, 1966), edited by Fred Israel, discusses the interplay of politics and foreign policy. A variety of Republican views are presented in Arthur H. Vandenberg, Jr., *The Private Papers of Senator Vandenberg* (Boston, 1952), Walter Johnson, ed., *Selected Letters of William Allen White* (New York, 1947), and Herbert C. Hoover, *Addresses upon the American Road: World War II* (New York, 1946). Alfred D. Chandler, ed., *The Papers of Dwight David Eisenhower: The War Years* (Baltimore, 1970) is predominantly concerned with military strategy but has some items relating to the Army's racial policies. For developments in public power, see David E. Lilienthal, *The Journals of David E. Lilienthal: The TVA Years* (New York, 1964).

Autobiographies and memoirs, while sometimes self-serving, nevertheless yield considerable insight into past events. Four books that are indispensable for understanding their authors' careers are James F. Byrnes, *All In One Lifetime* (New York, 1958), Bernard Baruch, *The Public Years* (New York, 1960),

Francis Biddle, *In Brief Authority* (New York, 1962), and
Henry L. Stimson and McGeorge Bundy, *On Active Service in
Peace and War* (New York, 1948). The choice of a Democratic
vice-presidential nominee in 1944 is discussed in Edward J.
Flynn, *You're The Boss* (New York, 1947), James A. Farley,
Jim Farley's Story (New York, 1948), and Alben Barkley,
That Reminds Me (New York, 1954). Aspects of economic
policy are treated in Jesse H. Jones, *Fifty Billion Dollars*
(New York, 1951), Marriner S. Eccles, *Beckoning Frontiers*
(New York, 1951), and Thurman Arnold, *Fair Fights and
Foul* (New York, 1965). George Creel's reminiscences, *Rebel at
Large* (New York, 1947) record the disillusionment of one old
Wilsonian with Roosevelt's program, while Louis Brownlow,
A Passion for Anonymity (Chicago, 1958), indicates the en-
thusiasm of another for that same program. The auto-
biographies of NAACP leader Walter White, *A Man Called
White* (New York, 1948), and of FEPC chairman Malcolm
Ross, *All Manner of Men* (New York, 1948), offer insight into
the civil rights movement. Information about science and
education may be found in James B. Conant, *My Several
Lives* (New York, 1970).

The War Economy

The role of the War Production Board is considered in Civilian
Production Administration, *Industrial Mobilization for War*
(Washington, 1947), Bruce Catton, *The War Lords of Wash-
ington* (New York, 1948), and John Lord O'Brian and Manly
Fleischman, "The War Production Board: Administrative
Policies and Procedures," *The George Washington Law Review*,
XIII (December, 1944). For a defense of Donald Nelson see
his *Arsenal of Democracy* (New York, 1946), and for a harsh
critique consult Eliot Janeway, *The Struggle for Survival* (New
Haven, 1951). The Minutes of the War Production Board, and
its Planning Committee, have been published. For a first-rate
analysis of the agency that eventually absorbed many WPB
functions see Herman Miles Somers, *Presidential Agency: The*

Office of War Mobilization and Reconversion (Cambridge, 1950).

Government regulation of the economy is discussed in David Novick, *et al.*, *Wartime Production Controls* (New York, 1949), . Chester W. Wright, ed., *Economic Problems of War and Its Aftermath* (Chicago, 1942), and Lester V. Chandler and Donald H. Wallace, eds., *Economic Mobilization and Stabilization* (New York, 1951). The best studies of taxation and finance are Randolph E. Paul, *Taxation for Prosperity* (Indianapolis, 1947), and Henry C. Murphy, *The National Debt in War and Transition* (New York, 1950). On price control and inflation see Harvey C. Mansfield, *et al.*, *A Short History of the OPA* (Washington, 1947), Lester V. Chandler, *Inflation in the United States, 1940-1948* (New York, 1951), John K. Galbraith, "Reflections on Price Control," *Quarterly Journal of Economics*, LX (August, 1946), and two books by Seymour E. Harris: *Price and Related Controls in the United States* (New York, 1945) and *Inflation and the American Economy* (New York, 1945). There are several useful studies of consumer rationing and the problems to which it gave rise: Martin Kriesberg, "Cancellation of the Ration Stamps," in Harold E. Stein, ed., *Public Administration and Policy Development* (New York, 1952); Paul M. O'Leary, "Wartime Rationing and Governmental Organization," *American Political Science Review*, XXXIX (December, 1945); James A. Maxwell and Margaret N. Balcom, "Gasoline Rationing in the United States, *Quarterly Journal of Economics*, LX (August, 1946); and Judith Russell and Renee Fantin, *Studies in Food Rationing* (Washington, 1947).

The conversion of industry to war production is critically evaluated in Barton J. Bernstein, "The Automobile Industry and the Coming of the Second World War," *Southwestern Social Science Quarterly*, XLVII (June, 1966), and is celebrated in Christy Borth, *Masters of Mass Production* (Indianapolis, 1945), and Francis Walton, *Miracle of World War II* (New York, 1956). The shortage of rubber and how it was overcome are the subjects of Alfred Lief, *The Firestone Story* (New York, 1951), Howard Wolf, *The Story of Scrap Rubber* (Akron, 1943), Frank A. Howard, *Buna Rubber, The Birth of an Industry* (New York, 1947), and J. M. Ball, *Reclaimed Rubber* (New York, 1947). In *Petroleum Pipelines and Public Policy, 1906-1959* (Cambridge, 1967), Arthur M. Johnson discusses the decision to build the "Big Inch." In addition, see John W. Frey and H. Chandler Ide, *A History of the Petroleum Administration for War* (Washington, 1946). The adjustments that war required in transportation are described in Joseph R. Rose, *American Wartime Transportation* (New York, 1953), and S. Kip Farrington, Jr., *Railroads at War* (New York, 1944).

The impact of the war upon agriculture and labor has received careful attention. The farmer's position is analyzed in Walter W. Wilcox, *The Farmer in the Second World War* (Ames, 1947), and farm policies are sharply criticized in Bela Gold, *Wartime Economic Planning in Agriculture* (New York, 1949). Samuel Liss has discussed the stabilization of farm wages in three articles in *Agricultural History* (January, 1950; July, 1953; July, 1956). Labor's response to the war is the subject of Joel Seidman, *American Labor from Defense to Reconversion* (Chicago, 1953), Aaron Levenstein, *Labor Today and Tommorrow* (New York, 1946), Irving Howe and B. J. Widick, *The UAW and Walter Reuther* (New York, 1949), and Hugh M. Ayer, "Hoosier Labor in the Second World War," *Indiana Magazine of History*, LIX (June, 1963). Colston E. Warne, *et al.*, *Yearbook of American Labor: I, War Labor Policies* (New York, 1945), and the National War Labor Board's termination report, *Industrial Disputes and Wage Stabilization in Wartime*, 3 vols. (Washington, 1947) provide a wealth of information about government policy toward unions.

Efforts to bring about industrial harmony are considered in Dorothea De Schweinitz, *Labor and Management in a Common Enterprise* (Cambridge, 1949), International Labor

Office, *Labor-Management Co-operation in United States War Production* (Montreal, 1948), and Allen Richards, *War Labor Boards in the Field* (Chapel Hill, 1953). The causes and consequences of industrial strife are evaluated in U.S. Department of Labor, Bureau of Labor Statistics, *Problems and Policies of Dispute Settlement and Wage Stabilization During World War II* (Washington, 1950), Rosa L. Swafford, *Wartime Record of Strikes and Lockouts, 1940-1945* (Washington, 1946), and Milton Derber, "Labor-Management in World War II," *Current History*, XLVIII (June, 1965). Labor's dissatisfaction with wage control and with its limited role in economic planning is treated in Kathryn S. Arnow, "The Attack on the Cost of Living Index," in Stein, *Public Administration*, and in Bruno Stein, "Labor's Role in Government Agencies During World War II," *Journal of Economic History*, XVII (September, 1957).

For the background of the 1943 coal strike consult: Morton S. Baratz, *The Union and the Coal Industry* (New Haven, 1955); McAlister Coleman, *Men and Coal* (New York, 1943); Saul Alinsky, *John L. Lewis* (New York, 1949); and James Wechsler, *Labor Baron: A Portrait of John L. Lewis* (New York, 1944). The miners' position is set forth in the *United Mine Workers Journal*, and in an appendix to the *Proceedings of the 38th Constitutional Convention* (1944) entitled "Bituminous Wage Negotiations, 1942-1944." Roosevelt's clash with Sewell Avery of Montgomery Ward is placed in its broader context by John L. Blackman, Jr., *Presidential Seizure in Labor Disputes* (Cambridge, 1967).

The most comprehensive analysis of the manpower problem is Albert A. Blum, *Drafted or Deferred* (Ann Arbor, 1967). In *Wartime Manpower Mobilization: A Study of World War II Experience in the Buffalo-Niagara Area* (Ithaca, 1951), Leonard P. Adams takes a microcosmic approach. *Paul V. McNutt* (Indianapolis, 1966) by I. George Blake is an uncritical biography of the chairman of the War Manpower Commission. The best study of national service appears in

Byron Fairchild and Jonathan Grossman, *The Army and Industrial Manpower* (Washington, 1959). A biased, but nevertheless useful account, is Grenville Clark and Arthur L. Williston, *The Effort for a National Service Law in World War II* (1947). The controversy may also be followed in testimony before the House and Senate Military Affairs Committees.

Civil Liberties and Civil Rights

The wartime civil liberties record is surveyed in Edward S. Corwin, *Total War and the Constitution* (New York, 1947), Ernst W. Puttkammer, ed., *War and the Law* (Chicago, 1944), and the reports of the American Civil Liberties Union: *Freedom in Wartime* (New York, 1943) and *Liberty on the Home Front* (New York, 1945). For the role of the Supreme Court see Osmond K. Fraenkel, "War, Civil Liberties and the Supreme Court 1941 to 1946," *Yale Law Journal* LV (June, 1946), and C. Herman Pritchett, *The Roosevelt Court* (New York, 1948). Two important biographies of Supreme Court justices are: J. Woodford Howard, *Mr. Justice Murphy* (Princeton, 1968), and Alpheus T. Mason, *Harlan Fiske Stone* (New York, 1956).

The prowar position of the Communist Party is expounded in Earl Browder, *Wage Policy in War Production* (New York, 1943), William Z. Foster, *American Democracy and the War* (New York, 1944), and articles in the *Daily Worker* and *Political Affairs*. In *The American Communist Party* (Boston, 1957) Irving Howe and Lewis Coser describe the twists and turns in Communist policy. The views of radicals who did criticize the war may be found in Dwight Macdonald's journal *Politics*. Charles J. Tull, *Father Coughlin and the New Deal* (Syracuse, 1965) discusses the fate of one enemy of the administration. An early appraisal of the case of the German saboteurs may be found in Cyrus Bernstein, "The Saboteur Trial," *The George Washington Law Review*, XI (February, 1943); the fullest account is Eugene Rachlis,

They Came to Kill (New York, 1961). For diametrically opposite views of the 1944 sedition trial see O. John Rogge, *The Official German Report* (New York, 1961) and Maximilian St. George and Lawrence Dennis, *A Trial on Trial* (1945). The Office of Censorship is the subject of Theodore Koop, *Weapon of Silence* (Chicago, 1946). For the Office of War Information consult Harold F. Gosnell, "Obstacles to Domestic Pamphleteering by OWI in World War II," *Journalism Quarterly*, XXIII (December, 1946); William M. Leary, Jr., "Books, Soldiers and Censorship during the Second World War," *American Quarterly*, XX (Summer, 1968); and Sidney Weinberg, "What to Tell America: The Writers Quarrel in the Office of War Information," *Journal of American History*, LV (June, 1968).

Two excellent studies of conscientious objectors have appeared: Mulford Q. Sibley and Philip E. Jacob, *Conscription of Conscience: The American State and the Conscientious Objector, 1940-1947* (Ithaca, 1952), and Lawrence S. Wittner, *Rebels Against War: The American Peace Movement, 1941-1960* (New York, 1969). R. R. Russell, "Development of Conscientious Objector Recognition in the United States," *The George Washington Law Review*, XX (March, 1952) puts the World War II experience in perspective. Jim Peck, *We Who Would Not Kill* (New York, 1958) gives the response of a member of the War Resisters League to imprisonment. One should also consult Julien Cornell, *The Conscientious Objector and the Law* (New York, 1943), and such journals as *The Conscientious Objector, Fellowship* and *The Christian Century*.

Perhaps no subject has been studied more intensively than the evacuation and relocation of Japanese-Americans. The books with which to start are: Morton Grodzins, *Americans Betrayed: Politics and the Japanese Evacuation* (Chicago, 1949), Jacobus ten Broek *et al.*, *Prejudice, War and the Constitution* (Berkeley, 1954), Stetson Conn *et al.*, *Guarding the United States and Its Outposts* (Washington, 1964) and Audrie

Girdner and Anne Loftis, *The Great Betrayal* (London, 1969). In *The Salvage*, (Berkeley, 1952), Dorothy Swaine Thomas and her associates studied evacuees who left the relocation centers and settled elsewhere; in *The Spoilage* (Berkeley, 1946), she and R. S. Nishimoto studied those who sacrificed their American citizenship. The social and economic costs of evacuation are considered in Leonard Bloom and Ruth Reimer, *Removal and Return* (Berkeley, 1949). The policies of the War Relocation Authority are examined in Department of the Interior, *WRA: A Story of Human Conservation* (Washington, 1946), Albert B. Turner, "The Origins and Development of the War Relocation Authority," (Ph.D. diss., Duke University, 1967), and Edward N. Barnhart, "The Individual Exclusion of Japanese-Americans in World War II," *Pacific Historical Review*, XXIX (May, 1960). Another study, Allan R. Bosworth, *America's Concentration Camps* (New York, 1967) is of limited use. The Utah relocation center is described in Leonard J. Arrington, *The Price of Prejudice* (Logan, 1962), and the riot at Camp Manzanar in James C. Davis and George Wada, "Riots and Rioters," *Western Political Quarterly*, X (December, 1957). The contrasting experience of Japanese in Hawaii is treated in Gwenfread Allen, *Hawaii's War Years* (Honolulu, 1950). For an appraisal of the constitutional issues involved see: Charles Fairman, "The Law of Martial Rule and the National Emergency," *Harvard Law Review*, LV (June, 1942); Eugene V. Rostow, "The Japanese-American Cases—A Disaster," *The Yale Law Journal*, LIV (June, 1945); Nanette Dembitz, "Racial Discrimination and the Military Judgment: The Supreme Court's Korematsu and Endo Decisions," *Columbia Law Review*, XLV (March, 1945); and Sidney Fine, "Mr. Justice Murphy and the Hirabayashi Case," *Pacific Historical Review*, XXXIII (May, 1964). Virtually every word written about the episode goes to refute the official explanation for evacuation given in War Department, Chief of Staff, *Final Report: Japanese Evacuation from the West Coast, 1942* (Washington, 1943).

The wartime experience of black Americans is discussed in Roi Ottley, *'New World A-Coming:' Inside Black America* (Cleveland, 1943) and, to a lesser extent, Gunnar Myrdal, *An American Dilemma*, 2 vols. (New York, 1944). A variety of black leaders express their views in Rayford W. Logan, ed., *What the Negro Wants* (Chapel Hill, 1944). The appeal of radicalism is assessed in Wilson Record, *The Negro and the Communist Party* (Chapel Hill, 1950), and of fascism in Lunabelle Wedlock, *The Reaction of Negro Publications and Organizations to German Anti-Semitism* (Washington, 1942). A. Philip Randolph's March on Washington Movement, and the Fair Employment Practices Committee it produced, are treated in Herbert Garfinkel, *When Negroes March* (Glencoe, 1959); Louis Ruchames, *Race, Jobs, and Politics: The Story of FEPC* (Chapel Hill, 1948); Louis C. Kesselman, *The Social Politics of FEPC* (Chapel Hill, 1948); and Will Maslow, "FEPC—A Case History in Parliamentary Maneuver," *University of Chicago Law Review*, XIII (June, 1946). Additional information about the civil rights movement may be found in such journals as *Race Relations, The Crisis, Opportunity, The Negro Quarterly, The Southern Frontier*, and *The Negro Digest*.

Robert Weaver, *Negro Labor* (New York, 1946) and Herbert R. Northrup, *Organized Labor and the Negro* (New York, 1944) explore the impact of war on the status of black workers. Two excellent studies of the opportunities—and absence of opportunities—for blacks in military service are Richard M. Dalfiume, *Desegregation of the U.S. Armed Forces, 1939-1953* (Columbia, 1969) and Ulysses Lee, *The Employment of Negro Troops* (Washington, 1966). Wartime racial tensions are examined in Charles S. Johnson, *To Stem This Tide* (Boston, 1943); Howard W. Odum, *Race and Rumors of Race* (Chapel Hill, 1943); and John Temple Graves, *The Fighting South* (New York, 1943). For the effect of an important Supreme Court decision see two articles in the *American Political Science Review*, XLII (June, 1948): O. Douglas Weeks, "The

White Primary: 1944-1948," and Donald B. Strong, "The Rise of Negro Voting in Texas." Constance M. Green, *The Secret City* (Princeton, 1967) describes the effect of war on race relations in Washington, D.C. Neil A. Wynn, "The Impact of the Second World War on the American Negro," *Journal of Contemporary History*, VI (1971), discusses how the manpower shortage improved the Negro's position.

The Detroit race riot, one of the bloodiest in American history, is examined in: Earl Brown, *Why Race Riots? Lessons from Detroit* (New York, 1944); Alfred McClung Lee and Norman D. Humphrey, *Race Riot* (New York, 1943); Robert Shogan and Tom Craig, *The Detroit Race Riot* (Philadelphia, 1964); and Harvard Sitkoff, "The Detroit Race Riot of 1943," *Michigan History*, LIII (Fall, 1969). In "Group Violence: A Preliminary Study of the Attitudinal Pattern of Its Acceptance and Rejection," *Journal of Social Psychology*, XIX (May, 1944), Kenneth B. Clark studied responses to the Harlem riot. Social and economic discrimination against Mexican-Americans, and the zoot-suit riots in Los Angeles, are discussed in: Robert C. Jones, *Mexican War Workers in the United States* (Washington, 1945); Otey M. Scruggs, "Texas: Good Neighbor?" *Southwestern Social Science Quarterly*, XLIII (September, 1962); Beatrice Griffith, *American Me* (Boston, 1948); Carey McWilliams, *North From Mexico* (Philadelphia, 1949); and Fritz Redl, "Zoot Suits: An Interpretation," *Survey Midmonthly*, LXXIX (October, 1943). See, in addition, Otey M. Scruggs, "Evolution of the Mexican Farm Labor Agreement of 1942," *Agricultural History*, XXXIV (July, 1960).

Politics and Reform

The problems besetting social reformers during the war are clearly discussed in the pages of the *Nation*, the *New Republic*, *Common Sense* and the *Progressive*. For contemporary critiques of liberalism see Norman Thomas, "Totalitarian Liberals," *The Commonweal*, XXXVII (January 22, 1943), and Oswald

G. Villard, "The Collapse of the War Liberals," *The Christian Century*, LXI (October 25, 1944). For contemporary evaluations consult J. Donald Kingsley, "Congress and the New Deal," *Current History*, IV (March, 1943), and Louise Overacker, "Should the New Deal Be Dropped," *Current History*, VI (February, 1944). More recent studies are Alonzo L. Hamby, "Sixty Million Jobs and the People's Revolution," *The Historian*, XXX (August, 1968), and Mary Hedge Hinchey, "The Frustration of the New Deal Revival, 1944-1946" (Ph.D. diss., University of Missouri, 1965).

The fate of New Deal agencies in wartime is discussed in John A. Salmond, *The Civilian Conservation Corps, 1933-1942* (Durham, 1967) and Sidney Baldwin, *Poverty and Politics: The Rise and Decline of the Farm Security Administration* (Chapel Hill, 1968). For the lack of progress in social welfare legislation consult Arthur J. Altmeyer, *The Formative Years of Social Security* (Madison, 1966) and J. Joseph Huthmacher, *Senator Robert F. Wagner and the Rise of Urban Liberalism* (New York, 1968). The impact of the war on child labor is spelled out in the Children's Bureau journal, *The Child*, and in the Council of State Governments, *The Book of the States* (Chicago, 1943, 1945). David R. B. Ross, *Preparing for Ulysses, 1940-1946* (New York, 1969) is a fine study of government aid to veterans and the GI Bill of Rights. The contribution of Keynesian thought to the Full Employment Act of 1946 is treated in Robert Lekachman, *The Age of Keynes* (New York, 1966), and Stephen K. Bailey, *Congress Makes A Law* (New York, 1950).

Information about the businessmen who replaced New Dealers in Washington is available in George W. Auxier, *Dollar-a-Year and Without Compensation Personnel Policies of the War Production Board* (Washington, 1947), and I. F. Stone, *Business as Usual* (New York, 1941). The sorry consequences of wartime mobilization for small business are revealed in Report of the Smaller War Plants Corporation, *Economic Concentration and World War II* (Washington, 1946).

The effect of war on patterns of income distribution is measured in Robert J. Lampman, *The Share of Top Wealth-Holders in National Wealth, 1922-1956* (Princeton, 1956); Simon Kuznets, *Shares of Upper Income Groups in Income and Savings* (New York, 1953); and Gabriel Kolko, *Wealth and Power in America* (London, 1962).

There are as yet few studies of Congress during the war. Roland Young, *Congressional Politics in the Second World War* (New York, 1956) is the best starting point, but it rarely goes beyond what can be told from the Congressional Record. In "The Conservative Coalition in the United States Senate, 1942-1945," *Journal of Southern History*, XXXIII (August, 1967), John Robert Moore has, through the application of statistical techniques, identified the origins of the Republican-Dixiecrat alliance. Congressional investigations into national defense programs are described in Harry A. Toulmin, *Diary of Democracy* (New York, 1947), and Donald H. Riddle, *The Truman Committee* (New Brunswick, 1964). Other useful studies are: Hadley Cantril and John Harding, "The 1942 Elections: A Case Study in Political Psychology," *Public Opinion Quarterly*, VII (Summer, 1943); Floyd M. Riddick, "Congress versus the President in 1944," *South Atlantic Quarterly*, XLIV (July, 1945); Ray F. Harvey, *et al.*, *The Politics of This War* (New York, 1943); Rhoda D. Edwards, "The Seventy-Eighth Congress on the Home Front: Domestic Economic Legislation, 1943-1944," (Ph.D. diss., Rutgers University, 1967); and George W. Robinson, "Alben Barkley and the 1944 Tax Veto," *The Register of the Kentucky Historical Society*, LXVII (July, 1969). See, in addition, Allen Drury, *A Senate Journal* (New York, 1963); Arthur Krock, *Memoirs: Sixty Years on the Firing Line* (New York, 1968); Leon Friedman, "Election of 1944," in Arthur M. Schlesinger, Jr., ed., *History of American Presidential Elections* (New York, 1971); and Booth Mooney, *Roosevelt and Rayburn: A Political Partnership* (Philadelphia, 1971).

Many of the books on wartime public administration have

been written by wartime public administrators. The most useful studies are: J. Donald Kingsley, *et al.*, *What We Learned in Public Administration During the War* (Washington, 1949); Luther Gulick, *Administrative Reflections from World War II* (University, 1948); Paul H. Appleby, *Big Democracy* (New York, 1945); and Harold D. Smith, *The Management of Your Government* (New York, 1945). Growth in the size and influence of the executive branch is discussed in Gladys M. Kammerer, *Impact of War on Federal Personnel Administration, 1939-1945* (Lexington, 1951), and Nathan D. Grundstein, *Presidential Delegation of Authority in Wartime* (Pittsburgh, 1961).

Biographical studies offer a certain amount of information about the 1944 election. See Russell Lord, *The Wallaces of Iowa* (Boston, 1947) for a sympathetic portrait, and Dwight Macdonald, *Henry Wallace* (New York, 1947) for a sharp attack. Other studies of Democrats include: Robert E. Sherwood, *Roosevelt and Hopkins* (New York, 1948), Bascom N. Timmons, *Jesse H. Jones* (New York, 1956), and Eugene Francis Schmidtlein, "Truman the Senator" (Ph.D. diss., University of Missouri, 1962). For the Republican side consult Ellsworth Barnard, *Wendell Willkie* (Marquette, 1966); Joseph Barnes, *Willkie* (New York, 1952); and Donald R. McCoy, "Republican Opposition in Wartime, 1941-1945," *Mid-America*, XLIX (July, 1967). Barry Keith Beyer, "Thomas E. Dewey, 1937-1947," (Ph.D. diss., University of Rochester, 1962) may remain the most useful study until Dewey's papers are opened for research in 1975. Robert A. Divine considers the foreign policy issue in the 1944 campaign in *Second Chance* (New York, 1967). Edgar Eugene Robinson's discussion of the campaign in *The Roosevelt Leadership, 1933-1945* (Philadelphia, 1955) is superficial. Two relevant articles appeared in the *American Political Science Review*, XXIX: Boyd A. Martin, "The Service Vote in the Elections of 1944," (August, 1945), and Louise Overacker, "Presidential Campaign Funds," (October, 1945). For developments in public opinion polling consult Daniel Katz, "The Polls and the 1944 Election," *Public Opinion Quarterly*, VIII (Winter, 1944-1945), and two books by Hadley Cantril: *Gauging Public Opinion* (Princeton, 1944), and *The Human Dimension: Experiences in Policy Research* (New Brunswick, 1967).

Matthew Josephson's biography of the leader of the CIO Political Action Committee, *Sidney Hillman* (New York, 1952) is of help in understanding labor's political role. Joseph Gaer, *The First Round: The Story of the CIO Political Action Committee* (New York, 1944) is an account by a PAC partisan that includes several election pamphlets. The Committee has also been the subject of several doctoral dissertations. The best is William Riker, "The CIO in Politics, 1936-1948" (Harvard University, 1948), but see in addition Delbert D. Arnold, "The CIO's Role in American Politics, 1936-1948" (University of Maryland, 1952), and Martha Lee Saenger, "Labor Political Action at Mid-Twentieth Century" (Ohio State University, 1959). For the CIO's relationship with the American Labor Party consult Alan Schaffer, *Vito Marcantonio* (Syracuse, 1966), Robert F. Carter, "Pressure from the Left: The American Labor Party, 1936-1954" (Ph.D. diss., Syracuse University, 1965), and William Spinrad, "New York's Third Party Voters," *Public Opinion Quarterly*, XXI (Winter, 1957-1958).

The Social Impact of War

Several historians and sociologists have discussed the manner in which societies have responded to war. I found the following most useful: Jesse D. Clarkson and Thomas C. Cochran eds., *War as a Social Institution* (New York, 1941); Pitirim A. Sorokin, *Man and Society in Calamity* (New York, 1942); Gaetano Mosca, *The Ruling Class* (New York, 1939); Stanislaw Andrzejewski, *Military Organization and Society* (London, 1954); and a chapter entitled "War and Social Policy," in *Essays on "The Welfare State"* (London, 1958) by Richard Titmuss. A good analysis of the war's impact on the

United States is Francis E. Merrill, *Social Problems on the Home Front* (New York, 1948). Other accounts are William F. Ogburn, ed., *American Society in Wartime* (Chicago, 1943), and David Hinshaw, *The Home Front* (New York, 1943). In *While You Were Gone* (New York, 1946), Jack Goodman compiled essays designed to acquaint returning veterans with the changes that had occurred in American life. Three writers and journalists who travelled across the country left particularly revealing accounts: John Dos Passos, *State of the Nation* (Boston, 1944); Selden Menefee, *Assignment: U.S.A.* (New York, 1943); and Agnes E. Meyer, *Journey Through Chaos* (New York, 1944). Margaret Mead, *And Keep Your Powder Dry* (New York, 1942) reverses the emphasis: rather than examining the war's effect on American society, she investigates how American character might affect the conduct of the war.

One way to study the social impact of war is to examine particular localities or communities in depth. Perhaps the best such study is Robert J. Havighurst and H. Gerthon Morgan, *The Social History of a War-Boom Community* (New York, 1951), which nearly does for Seneca, Illinois what the Lynds did for Muncie, Indiana in their books on Middletown. Lowell J. Carr and James E. Stermer, *Willow Run: A Study of Industrialization and Cultural Inadequacy* (New York, 1952) describes the quality of life in the best known "defense city." W. Lloyd Warner, *Democracy in Jonesville* (New York, 1949) is useful but disappointingly thin on the war experience. The sources of conflict among one group of war workers are analyzed in Katherine Archibald, *Wartime Shipyard: A Study in Social Disunity* (Berkeley, 1947). Of the many studies that have been done of states, three proved most helpful: Mary Watters, *Illinois in the Second World War*, 2 vols. (Springfield, 1951-1952); T. A. Larson, *Wyoming's War Years, 1941-1945* (Laramie, 1954); and Karl D. Hartzell, *The Empire State at War* (New York, 1949). The war's impact on the social, political and economic life of the South is considered in

George B. Tindall, *The Emergence of the New South* (Louisiana, 1967).

Wartime population shifts are discussed in Henry S. Shryock, Jr. and Hope T. Eldridge, "Internal Migration in Peace and War," *American Sociological Review*, XII (February, 1947), and Shryock, "Redistribution of Population, 1940 to 1950," *Journal of the American Statistical Association*, XLVI (December, 1951). For one form of wartime "crime," see Marshall B. Clinard, *The Black Market* (New York, 1952). For anti-Semitism see *The American Jewish Yearbook*, XLVI (Philadelphia, 1944), and Charles H. Stember, ed., *Jews in the Mind of America* (New York, 1966). James D. Scott examines wartime advertising in two articles in the *Harvard Business Review*, XXI (1943): "Advertising When Consumers Cannot Buy," and "Advertising When Buying Is Restricted." Popular symbols and myths are discussed in Edgar A. Schuler, "V for Victory: A Study in Symbolic Social Control," *Journal of Social Psychology*, XIX (May, 1944), and John M. Blum, "The G.I. in the Culture of the Second World War," *Ventures*, VIII (Spring, 1968).

The problems of working women are documented in publications of the Women's Bureau of the Labor Department. See, for example, Ethel Erickson, *Women's Employment in the Making of Steel* (Washington, 1944); Dorothy K. Newman, *Employing Women in Shipyards* (Washington, 1944); and *Women's Wartime Hours of Work* (Washington, 1947). The war's effect on family instability and delinquency is discussed in *Wartime Health and Education*, Hearings before a Subcommittee of the Committee on Education and Labor, U.S. Senate (Washington, 1944), and in such journals as: *Mental Hygiene, American Journal of Orthopsychiatry, The Family, Child Development, The Journal of Social Hygiene,* and *Survey Graphic.*

Civil-Military Relations

The fullest discussion of the historical relationship between civilians and the military appears in Samuel P. Huntington, *The Soldier and the State* (Cambridge, 1957). See, in addition, Jerome G. Kerwin, ed., *Civil-Military Relationships in American Life* (Chicago, 1948); Paul Y. Hammond, *Organizing for Defense: The American Military Establishment in the Twentieth Century* (Princeton, 1961); and Paul A. C. Koistinen, "The 'Industrial-Military Complex' in Historical Perspective: World War I," *Business History Review*, XLI (Winter, 1967). Additional information can be obtained in biographies of Stimson by Elting E. Morison, *Turmoil and Tradition* (Boston, 1960), and Richard N. Current, *Secretary Stimson* (New Brunswick, 1959), and studies of Forrestal by Arnold A. Rogow, *James Forrestal* (New York, 1963) and Robert G. Albion and Robert H. Connery, *Forrestal and the Navy* (New York, 1962).

Early planning for industrial mobilization is discussed in Albert A. Blum, "Birth and Death of the M-Day Plan," in Harold Stein, ed., *American Civil-Military Decisions* (Birmingham, 1962). The military's role in the war economy is critically examined in Paul A.C. Koistinen, "The Hammer and the Sword: Labor, the Military, and Industrial Mobilization, 1920-1945," (Ph.D. diss., University of California, 1964). The role of the Army is described in two volumes prepared under the Office of the Chief of Military History: John D. Millett, *The Organization and Role of the Army Service Forces* (Washington, 1954), and R. Elberton Smith, *The Army and Economic Mobilization* (Washington, 1959). For the Navy's part see Robert H. Connery, *The Navy and Industrial Mobilization in World War II* (Princeton, 1951), and Julius A. Furer, *Administration of the Navy Department in World War II* (Washington, 1959). Levin H. Campbell, Jr., *The Industry-Ordnance Team* (New York, 1946) is an account by a former Army ordnance chief.

The various controversies between the War Production Board and the armed services are considered in: Committee on Public Administration Cases, *The Feasibility Dispute*

(Washington, 1950); Jack Peltason, "The Reconversion Controversy," in Stein, *Public Administration*; J. Carlyle Sitterson, *Development of the Reconversion Policies of the War Production Board* (Washington, 1945); and Drummond Jones, *The Role of the Office of Civilian Requirements* (Washington, 1945). For the lifting of wartime controls see Barton J. Bernstein, "The Removal of War Production Board Controls on Business, 1944-1946," *Business History Review*, XXXIX (Summer, 1965), and A.D.H. Kaplan, *The Liquidation of Wa ' Production* (New York, 1944).

Manuscript
Collections

THE MOST IMPORTANT REPOSI-
TORY of manuscripts relating to American participation in
World War II is the Franklin D. Roosevelt Library at Hyde
Park, New York. The Library not only houses Roosevelt's
own private and official correspondence, but also holds the
papers of persons who served in his administration. The col-
lections I found most rewarding were the papers of Oscar Cox,
Wayne Coy, Leon Henderson, Harry Hopkins, Emil Hurja,
Isador Lubin, Herbert Marks, William McReynolds, Lowell
Mellett, Henry Morgenthau, Samuel I. Rosenman, Harold D.
Smith, Henry A. Wallace and Aubrey Williams.

There are virtually hundreds of other manuscript collections scattered about the country and new ones become available every year. The formulation of economic policy may be
followed in the papers of Bernard Baruch (Princeton University), James Fesler (Yale University), Julius A. Krug (Library
of Congress), and Donald Nelson (Huntington Library). In-

formation about the role of organized labor is available in the William H. Davis oral history interview (Columbia University), and in the papers of John Brophy (Catholic University), William Green (Cornell University), Sidney Hillman (Amalgamated Clothing Workers of America), and Philip Murray (Catholic University). For the relationship between the armed services, the economy and politics I consulted the papers of James Forrestal (Princeton University), Robert Patterson (Library of Congress), Henry L. Stimson (Yale University), and James Wadsworth (Library of Congress).

Some of the difficulties confronting social reformers are made explicit in the papers of George Norris (Library of Congress), the Union for Democratic Action (State Historical Society of Wisconsin), and Oswald Garrison Villard (Harvard University). The papers of Frank E. Gannett, Daniel A. Reed, Richard B. Scandrett and John Taber—all located at Cornell University—afford insights into political opposition in wartime. Information about civil liberties and civil rights may be found in the papers of Francis J. Haas (Catholic University) and in four collections at the Library of Congress: the papers of Felix Frankfurter, the National Association for the Advancement of Colored People; Elmer Davis, and Henry F. Pringle. The papers of Dillon Myer and Philleo Nash, both located at the Harry S. Truman Library, also discuss the problems facing minority groups in wartime.

Acknowledgments

I WISH TO THANK Walter LaFeber, Gilbert Osofsky, Marcia Polenberg and Joel Silbey for valuable suggestions concerning the style and substance of this book. I am grateful to Robert D. Cross for his steady encouragement. Robert P. Pace and Robert Ritchie of J. B. Lippincott also provided excellent advice. Many archivists and librarians have aided me, but my thanks go particularly to Elizabeth Drewry, James E. O'Neill and the staff of the Franklin D. Roosevelt Library. I am indebted to Cornell University for a Humanities Research Grant which helped defray travel expenses.

Index